Theories of Justice

Princeton Theological Monograph Series
K. C. Hanson, Charles M. Collier, D. Christopher Spinks,
and Robin Parry, Series Editors

Recent volumes in the series:

Jennifer Moberly
*The Virtue of Bonhoeffer's Ethics: A Study of Dietrich Bonhoeffer's
Ethics in Relation to Virtue Ethics*

Anette I. Hagan
*Eternal Blessedness for All?: A Historical-Systematic Examination
of Schleiermacher's Understanding of Predestination*

Stephen M. Garrett
God's Beauty-in-Act: Participating in God's Suffering Glory

Sarah Morice-Brubaker
The Place of the Spirit: Toward a Trinitarian Theology of Location

Joas Adiprasetya
*An Imaginative Glimpse:
The Trinity and Multiple Religious Participations*

Anthony G. Siegrist
*Participating Witness: An Anabaptist Theology of Baptism
and the Sacramental Character of the Church*

Kin Yip Louie
*The Beauty of the Triune God:
The Theological Aesthetics of Jonathan Edwards*

Mark R. Lindsay
*Reading Auschwitz with Barth: The Holocaust as Problem
and Promise for Barthian Theology*

Theories of Justice
A Dialogue with Karol Wojtyla/John Paul II and Karl Barth

STEPHANIE MAR BRETTMANN

◆PICKWICK *Publications* · Eugene, Oregon

THEORIES OF JUSTICE
A Dialogue with Karol Wojtyla/John Paul II and Karl Barth

Princeton Theological Monograph Series 212

Copyright © 2014 Stephanie Mar Brettmann. All rights reserved. Except for brief quotations in critical publications or reviews, no part of this book may be reproduced in any manner without prior written permission from the publisher. Write: Permissions, Wipf and Stock Publishers, 199 W. 8th Ave., Suite 3, Eugene, OR 97401.

Pickwick Publications
An Imprint of Wipf and Stock Publishers
199 W. 8th Ave., Suite 3
Eugene, OR 97401

www.wipfandstock.com

ISBN 13: 978-1-55635-881-4

Cataloguing-in-Publication data:

Brettmann, Stephanie Mar.

    Theories of justice : a dialogue with Karol Wojtyla/John Paul II and Karl Barth / Stephanie Mar Brettmann.

    xviii + 224 pp. ; 23 cm. Includes bibliographical references.

    Princeton Theological Monograph Series 212

    ISBN 13: 978-1-55635-881-4

    1. Justice. 2. Barth, Karl, 1886–1968—Ethics. 3. John Paul II, Pope, 1920–2005—Ethics. 4. Christian ethics. 5. Feminist ethics. I. Title.

BX4827 B3 B865 2014

Manufactured in the U.S.A.

*This book is dedicated to family:
my parents, Joe and Jan Smith,
my sister, Angelia Natili,
and my husband, Carl Brettmann.*

*Thank you for your ongoing support and love
throughout this long journey.*

Contents

Acknowledgments ix
Abbreviations xi
Introduction xiii

PART ONE: Karol Wojtyla/John Paul II

1. Wojtyla's Affirmation of Human Dignity in Occupied Poland 3

   Son of Poland
   Laying Theological Basis for Justice
   Early Priesthood: Promoting Human Dignity in the Midst of Dehumanization
   A New Method of Investigating Ethical Personhood in the Phenomenology of Max Scheler
   Promoting Human Dignity as a Moral Theologian
   Conclusion

2. The Dignity of Human Persons in Wojtyla's Philosophical and Anthropological Theology 19

   The Shape of Wojtyla's Work: Thomist? Phenomenological? Or Both?
   Wojtyla's Epistemology: The Philosophical Basis for Knowing Justice
   Wojtyla's Account of Justice
   Just Action in Society
   Conclusion

3. The Theological Basis for the Social Doctrine of Pope John Paul II 44

   Knowing Justice: Faith and Reason
   The Theological Basis for Justice: God, Creation, and Moral Law
   The Theological Basis for Justice: Raised to a Dignity Beyond Compare in Jesus Christ
   Theological Basis: Holy Spirit, Giver of Live and Love
   Theological Basis: Conclusion
   Social Doctrine: Human Dignity as the Criterion for Political and Economic Justice
   Conclusion to Part One

Contents

PART TWO: Karl Barth

4 An Early Passion for Justice   83

Barth's Early Life
Shifting Foundations: The Red Pastor in Safenwil
Reformed Theology and the Justice of God for Humanity
The One Word of God
Conclusion

5 Barth's Epistemology and Ethical Method   114

Barth's Epistemology: The Theological Basis for Knowing Justice
Barth's Ethical Method
Conclusion

6 Barth's Theological Framework for Justice   134

Doctrine of God: God's Justice as Right Relations and Mercy
Doctrine of Creation: Social Justice as Co-Humanity
Doctrine of Reconciliation: Justification, Sanctification, and Witness
Conclusion to Part Two

PART THREE: Critical Dialogue with a Female Interlocutor

7 Sources of Justice   169

How is Justice Known?
Conclusion

8 Theories of Justice   191

What Is Justice?
How Is Justice Cultivated in Society?
Conclusion

Select Bibliography   209

Acknowledgments

THE COMPLETION OF THIS BOOK WOULD NOT HAVE BEEN POSSIBLE without the many mentors and friends who have helped with this process. Thank you to Alan Torrance and the late Ray Anderson, advisers on the doctoral thesis for the University of St. Andrews that was the basis for this work. I will always be deeply grateful for your guidance and inspiration.

My visit with Msgr. Frank Dewane at the Pontifical Institute for Justice and Peace in Rome remains the highlight of my research work. Thank you and the library staff at the Institute for your assistance and for a most memorable lunch. In addition, thank you to Dr. and Mrs. Nathan Hatch and Dan Philpott for your hospitality and for providing access to library resources at the University of Notre Dame. I would also like to thank the following people for taking the time to answer questions, provide advisement, and/or critique: Donald McKim, Mario Aguilar, Alisdair MacIntyre, Stanley Hauerwas, and Fulvio DiBlasi.

Thank you to the many good friends who were so important to this process, including Dave and Tamara Atkins, Eduardo Ismael de Barros, Stephanie Chang, Keith Errickson, Gretchen Gundrum, Kristen (Deede) Johnson, Louise Lawrence, Sherry and Stefan Lukits, Sharon (Jebb) Smith, Wall Wofford, and many others.

Thank you to my patient editor, Chris Spinks, and the wonderful group at Pickwick Publications.

Abbreviations

AP	Karol Wojtyla. *The Acting Person*. Dordrecht: Reidel, 1979.
CA	Pope John Paul II. *Centesimus Annus*. http://www.vatican.va/holy_father/john_paul_ii/encyclicals/index.htm, 1991.
Calvin	Karl Barth. *The Theology of John Calvin*. Translated by G. W. Bromiley. Grand Rapids: Eerdmans, 1995.
CCCC	Karl Barth. "Christian Community and Civil Community." In *Community, Church, and State*. Gloucester, MA: Smith, 1968.
CD	Karl Barth. *Church Dogmatics*. Translated by Geoffrey Bromiley and T. F. Torrance. Edinburgh: T. & T. Clark, 1957–1969.
DM	John Paul II. *Dives in Misericordia*. http://www.vatican.va/holy_father/john_paul_ii/encyclicals/index.htm, 1980.
DV	John Paul II. *Dominum et Vivificantem*. http://www.vatican.va/holy_father/john_paul_ii/encyclicals/documents/hf_jp-ii_enc_18051986_dominum-et-vivificantem_en.html, 1986.
EMT	Karol Wojtyla. "Ethics and Moral Theology." In *Person and Community: Selected Essays*. New York: Lang, 1993.
FR	John Paul II. *Fides et Ratio*. http://www.vatican.va/holy_father/john_paul_ii/encyclicals/index.htm, 1998.
God	John Paul II. *God, Father, and Creator: A Catechesis on the Creed*. Vol. 1. Boston: Pauline, 1996.
GS	Second Vatican Council. *Gaudium et Spes*. London: Catholic Truth Society, 1966.
HSCL	Karl Barth. *The Holy Spirit and the Christian Life*. Translated by R. Birch Hoyle. Louisville: Westminster John Knox, 1993.
Jesus	John Paul II. *Jesus, Son, and Saviour: A Catechesis on the Creed*. Vol. 2. Boston: Pauline, 1996.
John Paul	John Paul II
JPII	John Paul II
LE	John Paul II. *Laborem Exercens*. http://www.vatican.va/holy_father/john_paul_ii/encyclicals/index.htm, 1981.

Abbreviations

LG	Second Vatican Council. *Lumen Gentium*. London: Catholic Truth Society, 1966.
MPB	Karol Wojtyla. "On the Metaphysical and Phenomenological Basis of the Moral Norm." In *Person and Community: Selected Essays*. New York: Lang, 1993.
PSC	Karol Wojtyla. "The Person: Subject and Community." In *Person and Community: Selected Essays*. New York: Lang, 1993.
RH	John Paul II. *Redemptor Hominis*. http://www.vatican.va/holy_father/john_paul_ii/encyclicals/index.htm, 1979.
Romans	Karl Barth. *Epistle to the Romans*. 2nd ed. London: Oxford University Press, 1933.
SC	John Paul II. *Sign of Contradiction*. Translated by Mary Smith. Middlegreen, Slough: St. Paul, 1979.
Sources	Karol Wojtyla. *Sources of Renewal: The Implementation of Vatican II*. San Francisco: Harper and Row, 1980.
Spirit	John Paul II. *The Spirit, Giver of Life and Love: A Catechesis on the Creed*. Vol. 3. Boston: Pauline, 1996.
SRS	*Sollicitudo Rei Socialis*. http://www.vatican.va/holy_father/john_paul_ii/encyclicals/index.htm, 1987.
TP	Karol Wojtyla. "Thomistic Personalism." In *Person and Community: Selected Essays*. New York: Lang, 1993.
VS	John Paul II. *Veritatis Splendor*. http://www.vatican.va/holy_father/john_paul_ii/encyclicals/index.htm, 1993.
WC	Karl Barth. *The Way to Christ: Spiritual Exercises*. Translated by Leslie Wearne. San Francisco: Harper & Row, 1984.
Word	Karl Barth. *The Word of God and the Word of Man*. Translated by D. Horton. London: Hodder and Stoughton, 1936.
WMF	Karol Wojtyla. *The Word Made Flesh*. Translated by Leslie Wearne. San Francisco: Harper & Row, 1985.

Introduction

IN 1990, I TRAVELLED TO THE PHILIPPINES WITH A GROUP LED BY AN Episcopalian priest who managed a sponsor-a-child project for Filipino children. When I met these Filipino teenagers, many of them around my age, I encountered a level of poverty that surpassed my worst imagination. Lying between those beautiful, hopeful, hungry kids and myself, I saw a vast crevasse of social and economic inequity that I felt ill-equipped to traverse.

This inequity forced the question, "What resources do I have to bridge this divide so that these kids can have opportunities like I have?" A child sponsorship program like the one that I had visited the Philippines to promote was a noble effort, yet it seemed woefully inadequate after encountering my Filipino peers. It could help a handful of people but it would never address the systemic and structural inequities that limited their opportunities so severely. In addition, few people in my congregation back home were even paying attention. Issues of social inequity and social justice were given the airtime of a brochure on a table for congregants to pick up on their way out the door.

Over the past twenty years the evangelical context has been changing, thanks in part to global technology, increased mission trips, and prophetic voices. More people, especially the young, are asking the same question, "What resources does the Christian tradition have to bridge this divide?" This book is an exploration into that question from a theological perspective, broken down into three guiding questions that explore theological resources for social justice. We will pose these questions to leading representatives of the Protestant and Catholic traditions in order to assess how well leading theologians of these traditions have equipped the next generation with resources to address the questions that so many of us are asking.

The Guiding Questions

First, we turn to the guiding questions. Our goal is to answer this question: What does theology teach us about how is justice cultivated in society?

Introduction

When all I could see was the vast difference between myself and my Filipino counterparts, how could theology cultivate social justice that might bridge these social and economic divides?

Yet before that question may be answered, we must ask a prior question: What *is* this justice we seek to cultivate? What does justice look like? What are our criteria for judging existing political or economic structures to decide if they are just?

And if someone gives us those criteria or definitions of justice, how do we know if those definitions or criteria for justice are correct? There are wildly different definitions of justice. Hitler sought to create a good society by promoting notions of racial hygiene. Mother Theresa embraced poverty and spent her life serving the poor. How do we know what justice is and what it looks like? What are the sources for justice and what's our method for developing criteria of justice?

In sum, there are three primary of questions we will be asking to explore theological resources for justice. (1) How is justice known? (2) What is justice? (3) How is justice cultivated in society?

The Guides

When I began looking for theological scholarship on social justice within the modern evangelical, Protestant tradition, the list of theologians with substantial writing on justice was short. Karl Barth stood out as a deeply influential evangelical systematic theologian who had forged a thorough theological account of justice while faced with serious forms of inequity and injustice in Nazi Germany.[1] When I expanded my search into the Catholic tradition, a tradition is known for scholarship on social justice and advocacy on behalf of the marginalized, I encountered the writings of Karol Wojyla, who later became John Paul II. Like Barth, Wojtyla forged a thorough account of justice in the context of twentieth century Europe and while reacting to the devastation wrought by two world wars. Like Barth, Wojytla/John Paul II[2] is widely recognized as a representative of

---

1. While Barth was recognized as a leader of evangelical theology in Germany, the varied expressions of evangelicalism may make his influence on evangelicalism outside of Germany more ambigious. McCormack and Anderson's *Karl Barth and American Evangelicalism* traces some lines of Barth's influence upon evangelicalism in the U.S., as does John Lewis' *Karl Barth in North America*.

2. Rather than continuing referring to Wojtyla/John Paul II in this awkward manner, this book will often use the name John Paul to refer to the corpus of his work as Wojtyla and John Paul, especially in the Introduction and in Section Three of this

Introduction

his tradition. In addition, both men made substantive contributions to ecumenical dialogue as representatives of their respected traditions. The lines of dialogue that they themselves drew makes it possible to compare their work.

Perhaps the most compelling reason to choose these two men as guides is that they both approached the question of justice from a decidedly theological perspective and through the lens of theological anthropology. Their theories of justice were grounded in rich descriptions of the moral landscapes in which persons exist and act. They both located ultimate reality in the personal God of Jesus Christ and they held human persons of the highest value over economic systems, technology, political systems, or other depersonalizing forces of modern society. For this reason, this book is able to explore these questions of justice by investigating their theories of human personhood.

Making human personhood the locus of our discussion marks a decided shift away from recent Catholic and Protestant discussions on social justice, which sought commonality in conceptions of natural law and common grace.³ Conceptualizing an alternative starting point in the investigation of human personhood advances ecumenical relations and understanding in several ways. First, Barth's devastating critique of natural law and natural theology continues to haunt ecumenical dialogue and this critique necessitates new avenues for comparative dialogue between theologians influenced by Barth and Catholic theologians.⁴

Second, on the Catholic side, John Paul's appeal to Christological anthropology as basis for social ethics has appealed to Protestants who formerly criticized the Catholic detachment of ethics and theology and it has opened up new alternatives for dialogue. For instance, this turn in Catholic moral theology prompted the Protestant theologian, Carl Braaten, to raise the question about John Paul's encyclicals: "What would Karl

---

book. The context will make it obvious if use of the name, John Paul, refers only to his specific period as Pope or to his wider corpus. For example, when chapter 3 explores his theological works as Pope, the use of the name John Paul obviously refers only to his writings as John Paul II.

3. See for example, Gustafson, *Protestant and Roman Catholic Ethics*; Dieter and Hütter, ed., *Ecumenical Ventures in Ethics: Protestants Engage Pope John Paul II's Moral Encyclicals*; and Cromartie, ed., *A Preserving Grace*.

4. See for instance Schreiner, "Calvin's Use of Natural Law," 53–55; Westberg, "The Reformed Tradition and Natural Law," 114–18. Both attest to the dilemma that Barth's critique raised.

Introduction

Barth have to say about the latest papal encyclicals?"[5] Braaten's inability to answer the question he posed demonstrates the need for such a comparative study.

Third, the critique of natural law raised by the modern philosophical deconstruction of universal categories of justice necessitates new avenues for social dialogue.[6] Given the contemporary distrust of such universal appeals, natural law and common grace seem inadequate starting points for dialogues that seek to engage with persons outside of the Christian faith. To cultivate a just society we must be able to articulate a theory of justice that makes sense beyond the walls of the church. A theory of justice centered on personhood or human dignity is still translate-able in the contemporary philosophical context.[7]

Method of Dialogue

Having established the feasibility of comparing these two theologians, we now turn to the question of method. How should we proceed? In his two books, *After Virtue* and *Whose Justice? Which Rationality?* Alasdair MacIntyre made key arguments that continue to shape the methods of moral philosophy. Specific to our topic, MacIntyre's argued that theories of justice are constructed within historical contexts and traditions of rationality.[8] Because Barth and Wojtyla/John Paul II represent different Christian traditions of faith, a simple comparison of definitions of justice

---

5. Braaten answered his own question, "I don't know." Braaten, *A Preserving Grace*, 34.

6. For instance, Nietzsche argued that there was nothing to natural law but expressions of the will, a projection of one's selfishness. His passage in *The Gay Science* raised questions which deconstructed notions of universal law, "What? You admire the categorical imperative within you? . . . Rather, admire your *selfishness* at this point. And the blindness, pettiness, and frugality of your selfishness. For it is selfish to experience one's own judgment as a universal law; and this selfishness is blind, petty, and frugal because it betrays that you have not yet discovered yourself nor created for yourself an ideal of your own . . ." [trans. Walter Kaufmann, Section 335, page 265.] Cf. "Nietzsche's Theory of Law as a Critique of Natural Law Theory" in Douglas Litowitz's *Postmodern Philosophy and Law*. Alasdair MacIntyre traces the contemporary loss of notions of universal law and moral judgments in *After Virtue*. He likewise appeals to an ontology of personhood but focuses his discussion primarily upon Aristotelian teleology. [*After Virtue*, 49–75, 103–13, 241].

7. See for example, Chris Brown's critique of natural law as a basis for human rights in "Universal Human Rights: A Critique," 106–10.

8. MacIntyre, *Whose Justice?*, 1–11.

Introduction

or an exploration into the language surrounding issues of justice proves an inadequate basis for understanding the real content of their concepts that are "tradition-constituted." Rather, a thorough understanding of each man's theological theory of justice demands a broader inquiry into the contexts and traditions that formed the content of their theologies. For this reason, this book will examine their theories not as disembodied or abstracted themes, as is a common method in systematic theology. Rather, this book approaches each man as an individual whose theories of justice issue from particular historical contexts and traditions of rationality. Such an approach seeks to minimize superficial misunderstandings by seeking an in depth understanding of the context of their concepts.

For instance, for Barth, as a son of the reformed tradition, true justice is revealed by God's mercy toward humans. For John Paul II, justice is a requirement of the moral order that is, at times, surpassed by God's mercy. At first reading, such conceptions of justice seem untranslatable. For example, the two men appear to be in absolute conflict on the relation of justice to mercy. Thus, an examination of the tradition-constituted rationales behind these conceptions is necessary for discerning if common ground might be found and where mutual critique might be deemed appropriate.

In order to provide an adequate introduction for readers who may be unfamiliar with one tradition, this work first examines the work of each man separately, with some reference to common themes, areas of contrast, or academic debates that relate to our topic. Part One will examine Wojtyla/John Paul II and Part Two will examine Barth. Part Three is a critical assessment of their theories.

Working from the insights of MacIntyre, the work of each theologian is explored from two perspectives: historical and theoretical. The first chapter on each person examines the early contexts in which his theological ideas of justice were developed (chapter 1 on Wojtyla and chapter 4 on Barth). In the second and third chapters on each theologian, their theoretical frameworks for justice are critically examined within their traditions of rationality. Our three questions will guide the exposition of their frameworks: (1) How is justice known? (2) What is justice? (3) How is justice cultivated in society?

Those familiar with one author or the other may find that chapters in earlier sections are more introductory in nature. They have been written in that manner in order to translate these theories across traditions. Because Wojtyla/John Paul II appealed to philosophical and theological foundations for justice, chapter 2 examines his earlier theories of justice as a

Introduction

philosopher and chapter 3 expounds his theological theories as Pope John Paul II. These three questions will be examined in each chapter or phase of his career. Because Barth remained a theologian throughout his career, his work is examined according to the theological framework provided in the *Church Dogmatics*, which reflects the historical development of his thought. Chapter Five examines *Church Dogmatics* I–III and Chapter Six expounds his theory of justice as developed further in CD IV and extant relevant works.

Part Three critically engages their theories from the perspective of the author, a female interlocutor. It argues that the theories of these men make substantial contributions to our understanding of human personhood and our quest for theories of justice yet their thought is also undermined by serious biases and shortcomings, which must be addressed when creating theological theories of justice that will yield justice for all persons.

PART ONE

Karol Wojtyla/John Paul II

1

Wojtyla's Affirmation of Human Dignity in Occupied Poland

AS A YOUNG MAN, WOJTYLA EXPERIENCED SUFFERING THAT BROUGHT shape to his mature theories of justice. He encountered both the suffering of his people in occupied Poland as well as his own personal anguish as he lost all of his immediate family members during his early years. Yet despite this suffering, Wojtyla claimed that he witnessed the transcendence of the human spirit, a spirit that refused to bend under oppression and continued to rise above immediate forms of suffering. He credited these early experiences with his insight into the nature of human dignity. This theme of dignity remained the cornerstone for his theory of justice.

Each chapter in Part One of this book will seek to explore dimensions of Wojtyla's theory of justice as shaped by his anthropology. Chapter 1 will trace the early events and the influences on Wojtyla's humanistic impulses and the themes that continued to be developed and reinforced in his mature ideas of justice: the dignity of human persons, the transcendence of God as the being who is "other" yet who graciously gives himself for humanity, and the epistemological basis for knowledge of this God, of the human person, and of the moral law. Chapter 2 will examine Wojtyla's theory of justice as developed in his philosophical works and chapter 3 will examine his theory as developed in his theological works as John Paul II. Early in his life he developed the key theme that underlies his philosophical and theological accounts of justice: the dignity of human persons.

Son of Poland

When Karol Wojtyla was born in Wadowice, Poland on May 18, 1920, his nation experienced the pains of rebirth following World War I. While his fellow Poles worked to build the Second Polish Republic as a free and

PART ONE—Karol Wojtyla/John Paul II

united nation, Wojtyla grew into a promising student and a talented actor despite two family tragedies: the death of his mother and of his only sibling. Though this suffering pressed hard upon Karol and his father, the elder Wojtyla encouraged his son in his studies and in his burgeoning Catholic faith.[1]

Upon graduation from his secondary schooling in 1938, Karol Wojtyla and his father moved to Kraków so that he could attend Jagiellonian University, where he studied language and literature.[2] However, the following September of 1939, when German armies invaded Poland, the Polish army was unable to resist Hitler's forces. Poland became divided as the eastern lands were absorbed into the Soviet Union while central and western Poland were divided, some incorporated into the Third Reich and the remainder placed under the control of Hans Frank. Frank ruled with great cruelty, seeking to destroy Poland by depriving the Poles of their rights and by seeking to eliminate Polish culture.[3]

In one of the many efforts to achieve this goal, the Germans sought to destroy Jagiellonian University by arresting over 180 academics, destroying laboratories, and wrecking libraries. In a defiant act of self-preservation, the University began to hold classes underground. These secret lectures

---

1. Weigel, *Witness to Hope*, 27–30.

2. JPII, *Crossing the Threshold of Hope*, 199. John Paul wrote, "I must say that my concern for 'the acting person' did not arise from the disputes with Marxism or, at least, not as a direct response to those disputes. I had long been interested in *man as person*. Perhaps my interest was due to the fact that I had never had a particular predilection for the natural sciences. I was always more fascinated by man. While studying in the Faculty of Literature, man interested me inasmuch as he was a creator of language and a subject of literature; then, when I discovered my priestly vocation, man became *the central theme of my work.*"

3. Hans Frank was reported to give the following commands to his subordinates: "The Pole has no rights whatsoever. His only obligation is to obey what we tell him. He must be constantly reminded that his duty is to obey. A major goal of our plan is to finish off as speedily as possible all troublemaking politicians, priests, and leaders who fall into our hands. I openly admit that some thousands of so-called important Poles will have to pay with their lives, but you must not allow sympathy for individual cases to deter you in your duty, which is to ensure that the goals of National Socialism triumph and that the Polish nation is never again able to offer resistance. Every vestige of Polish culture is to be eliminated. Those Poles who seem to have Nordic appearances will be taken to Germany to work in our factories. Children of Nordic appearance will be taken from their parents and raised as German workers. The rest? They will work. They will eat little. And in the end they will die out. There will never again be a Poland." Quoted in Michener, *Poland*, 451. Michener claims that this quotation is factual account but provides no references to his source.

enabled Wojtyla to continue his studies in the evenings after working as a manual laborer during the day.[4]

Through this difficult period, Wojtyla was involved in an underground theater and he began writing and directing plays. Most of these plays reflected his struggle to come to terms with the harsh reality of occupation.[5] They explored the experience of human suffering and the potential of humans to transcend their circumstances through faith and action. They also documented the development of the theme that would later characterize Wojtyla's account of justice: the dignity of personhood. In fact, Wojtyla later credited these years under occupation with his insight into human dignity. During this period he witnessed acts of courage in the face of tyranny, expressions of hope in the midst of oppression, and the transcendence of human persons in a context of suffering. He credited this courage, hope, and transcendence to the fundamental dignity of human personhood.

In the midst of his manual work, his studies, and his involvement in theater, Wojtyla returned home one day in February 1941 to find that his father had died in bed. According to Wojtyla, his grief marked a decided turn in his life; abandoning his earlier vocational plans, he decided to seek ordination to the priesthood.[6] This personal suffering initiated his journey into training for the Catholic priesthood, a training which laid the theoretical foundation for his later account of justice.

Laying Theological Basis for Justice

In 1942, Wojtyla began attending the underground seminary in Kraków where he became intimately acquainted with Archbishop Adam Stefan Sapieha. After Wojtyla completed his seminary degree in July 1946 and was ordained in November, Sapieha decided that the young priest should begin doctoral studies in theology at Rome's Pontifical Athenaeum of St. Thomas Aquinas (or "the Angelicum").[7] Wojtyla soon moved to Rome and lived for two years in the Belgian College of the Angelicum. During

---

4. Weigel, *Witness to Hope*, 53–55.

5. See, for example, *Job* and *Jeremiah*. Boleslaw Taborski, introduction to *The Collected Plays* by Karol Wojtyla, 4. Unfortunately the play has been lost. For more on transcendence and suffering in Wojtyla during this stage, see Saward, *Christ is the Answer*, 83–89.

6. JPII, *Gift and Mystery*, 34. Weigel, *Witness to Hope*, 68–69.

7. Weigel, *Witness to Hope*, 78–79.

his studies, he encountered the three forms of Thomism that predominated contemporary Catholic thought: Aristotelian, Existential, and Transcendental Thomism.[8] This encounter marked an important stage in the construction of Wojtyla's theological framework, especially with regard to moral epistemology and anthropology.

Traditional and Existentialist Thomism: The Certainty of Moral Knowledge

The papal encyclical of 1879, *Aeterni Patris*, in which Leo XIII called for the establishment of Christian philosophy in the tradition of Thomas Aquinas, soon gave rise to the reorientation of the philosophical development of the Catholic Church.[9] Theologians of the Aristotelian Thomist strain of thought sought to counter the humanism of modern philosophy by restoring God, not man, to the measure of all things. They argued for a classical view beginning with the certainty of knowledge about the world over against the Cartesian model of investigation, which began with systemic doubt.[10] The classical framework presupposed that that which is real is given to humans in sensation. In other words, through the senses, human reason provides persons with access to that which is real, though humans struggle to describe the truth. In this sense, the epistemology of this school was *a posteriori*: the mind draws its conceptual content from that which is real and which is known through the senses.[11] This view clearly affirmed that humans possess truth about the world and themselves through natural reason. Though some truths exceed the ability of human reason (such as the truth that God is triune), Aquinas argued that natural reason is able to reach certain truths (such as the existence of God).[12]

The Existentialist Thomists agreed with the *a posteriori* epistemology of the Aristotelian Thomists. However, they differed on the precise definition of being, or that which is the real.[13] The Aristotelian Thomists argued that being is a substance that possesses formal act. The Existential Thomists conceived of being in terms of action. They appealed to Aquinas'

---

8. Beabout et al., *Beyond Self-Interest*, 44–46.

9. Nichols, *The Shape of Catholic Theology*, 331.

10. McInerny, *A First Glance at St. Thomas Aquinas*, 33.

11. Knasas, "*Fides et Ratio* and the Twentieth Century Thomistic Revival," paras. 1 and 4.

12. Aquinas, *Contra Gentes* 1.3.2.

13. Knasas, "*Fides et Ratio*," para. 2.

doctrine of *esse* or *actus essendi*, the act of existence. The existence of a thing is its act; the most fundamental act is its act of existing. In God, the act of existing is subsistent. Humans are contingent; their being is a participation in God's act of existence.[14]

The influence of both of the schools of thought is evident in Wojtyla/John Paul II's account of justice. First, he affirmed *a posteriori* epistemology, arguing that the real, and the moral order that issues from it, is accessible through natural reason and through revelation (in cases in which truths transcend human reason.)[15] By implication, moral knowledge is accessible to all persons. Ralph McInerny provides a practical example of this approach when he writes, "The moral philosopher can help us get clear about what we already know, but he does not *confer* our primary moral knowledge on us. Again, he presupposes that we have it."[16] Second, the Existential Thomists paved the path for Wojtyla's emphasis upon the dignity of the human act as an affirmation of existence and of participation with the existence of God. This assumption would become influential in his later phenomenological work.

Transcendental Thomism and the Transcendence of Human Persons

During his study in Rome, Wojtyla was also influenced by Transcendental Thomism, or *la nouvelle théologie*.[17] The rise of modernism had brought new questions for the study of philosophy and theology to the fore in this new school of thought labeled Transcendental Thomism. Karl Rahner, Joseph Maréchal, Jean Daniélou, Louis Bouyer, Marie-Dominique Chenu, and Yves Congar all approached these questions, seeking to engage Thomism with modern schools of thought. With regard to epistemology, the Transcendent Thomists took a decidedly different turn than the Aristotelian or Existentialist Thomists by arguing that human knowing involves not a reception from the real (an *a posteriori* knowledge) but a projection of the knower upon the real (*a priori*).

14. Ibid., para. 3.
15. Ibid., paras. 11 and 13.
16. McInerny, *A First Glance*, 34.
17. This movement was a reaction to the perception that traditional Thomists were growing increasingly scholastic in their method and focusing more discussion on debates within Thomism rather than dealing with the pressing concerns of the present period.

PART ONE—Karol Wojtyla/John Paul II

Interpreter John Knasas explains, "The knower's projection is the knower's own intellectual dynamism to the unconceptualizable term of Infinite Being . . . Intellectual dynamism is not only innate, or *a priori*. It is also 'constitutive' of human awareness. Thanks to its immersion in the dynamism, the data of sense can profile itself in consciousness as finite and limited in perfection."[18] Knasas suggested that these interpreters of Aquinas would soon find themselves disappointed with the encyclical of John Paul II, *Fides et Ratio*, because of his close allegiance with Existential Thomism. Later chapters will suggest that this thesis by Knasas is correct. This allegiance to Existential Thomism may be due in large part to the influence of Wojtyla's thesis advisor, Reginald Garrigou-Lagrange,[19] an avid traditionalist in his reading of Aquinas and an open opponent of Transcendental Thomism.

Yet the manner in which Wojtyla critiqued Marxism upon his return to Poland suggest that he drew some level of intellectual development the Transcendental Thomists, especially the work of Henri de Lubac, who was at the centre of the discussion surrounding *la nouvelle théologie* and who later became an influential friend to Wojtyla.

Based upon his work in the patristic and medieval theology, de Lubac sought to argue that there is only one history of grace, which embraces every individual in this world. In opposition to the neo-scholastic divide between nature and grace, de Lubac contended that in both Augustinian and Thomist thought, the supernatural embraces the natural world and all of reality is infused with God's grace.[20] With regard to humanity, de Lubac believed that all humans contained an eternal element, a "germ of eternity," which already 'breathes the upper air,' which always, *hic et nunc*, evades temporal society. The truth of his being transcends his being itself. For he is made in the image of God, and in the mirror of his being the Trinity is ever reflected."[21] If a man inverts this relationship and declares

18. Knasas, "*Fides et Ratio*," paras. 5–6.

19. Garrigou-Lagrange likely grounded Wojtyla in the basic concepts and origins of Thomist thought, and he taught Wojtyla a methodology to bring other thinkers in dialogue with Aquinas, namely reconciling with Aquinas the mystical writings of St. John of the Cross.

20. Nichols, *Catholic Theology*, 340. Lubac, *Le Mystére du Surnaturel*. Buttiglione claims that Lubac and Balthasar appropriated the work of Barth to develop a similar theme of the nature-grace relation and *analogia fidei*. Buttiglione, *Karol Wojtyla*, 198.

21. Lubac, *Catholicism*, 202. This concept of "infused grace," and the "germ of eternity" likely helped to form Wojtyla's doctrine of the *analogia entis*, the continuity of man with God. Barth critiqued such terms because they depersonalize God and they call into question the purpose of Christ's incarnation. If such "infused grace"

that God is made in man's image, he becomes estranged from himself and remains incomplete.

De Lubac believed the estrangement of this relationship had dangerous consequences for society as well. He critiqued the atheistic humanism prevalent in contemporary social philosophy, arguing that a society that is non-transcendent or that reduces humans to the sum of their material existence or social relationships alone (as Marxism) will beget tyranny.[22] The echo of de Lubac critique can be seen throughout Wojyla's later philosophical and theological critiques of Marxism. Yet while Wojytla later drew from Transcendental Thomists to engage the political situation of Poland through the framework of personhood, the following chapter will suggest that Wojtyla's epistemic assumptions for moral reality were formed by the Aristotelian and Existential schools of Thomism that he encountered during this period.

The Personalist Movement

A final influence during this phase, which deserves mention, was the personalism of Emmanuel Mounier and Jacques Maritain.[23] Though Wojtyla may have encountered personalism before his stay in Rome,[24] he began to interact with the philosophy more directly through the influence of his dissertation advisor, Garrigou-Lagrange[25] and through extended travels in France. Personalism, which grew out of the phenomenology of Husserl and the existentialism of Heidegger, spread through France in the early nineteen-thirties. As a philosophical movement, it sought to offer a new vision of human persons, based upon a belief in the primacy of the person as a spiritual, free, and rational being.[26] Because it conceived

---

characterizes the human person, then what does the grace of Christ have meaning? Does his incarnation indeed need to recreate humanity if persons are infused with grace? I will address these questions in the thesis and in comparison with Barth in chapter 7.

22. Ibid., 203.

23. Hellman, "John Paul II and the Personalist Movement," 409–19; Lescoe, "Pope John Paul II and Existential Personalism," 80–91.

24. Mounier visited Poland in May 1946 and gave a widely publicized talk at Jagiellonian University in Warsaw. His writings had been circulated illegally under the Nazi government. Hellman, "John Paul II and the Personalist Movement," 414.

25. Garrigou-Lagrange's interest in Christian spirituality created ties with the group.

26. Amato summarizes Mounier's anthropology, "Committed to the primacy of

PART ONE—Karol Wojtyla/John Paul II

of human persons as both spiritual and communal, Mounier described the philosophy both in opposition to individualism and collectivism, as well as idealism and materialism. Wojtyla is credited with drawing out the political implications of this new concern for the person upon his return to Poland.[27]

Early Priesthood: Promoting Human Dignity in the Midst of Dehumanization

While Wojtyla was in Rome, his country underwent a tremendous upheaval as the Germans were expelled and replaced by the Stalinist politics of the new Soviet order. In 1948, he returned to become a priest in a country "where the dawn knock on the door was still expected, where prisons were full and beatings many, where the secret policeman was still his brother's keeper, and where the Great Teacher was neither Christ nor Buddha but the megalomaniac son of a Georgian shoemaker through whom millions had died."[28] In this context, Wojtyla utilized the insights of Transcendental Thomism and personalism because it enabled him to criticize Marxist ideology from a Christian perspective. While general Catholic opinion held Communism to be utterly false, the personalists sought dialogue with communist ideology and maintained that there were some truths represented by the movement. Yet, they argued that both Communism and Marxism fail inasmuch as they hold an incomplete and one-sided account of personhood.[29]

This engagement with Marxism is reflected in a play that Wojtyla began writing during seminary and completed during his early years as

---

the person as a free and spiritual being, Personalism denies all attempts to reduce the human person to any immanent order of society, politics, and history. Committed to the person as an embodied and communal being, Personalism equally denies all doctrines that deny man's temporal and historicity in the name of a transcendent order. In its metaphysical impulse, Personalism thus aspires to a new realism by recognizing equally man's spiritual and material nature. In its spiritual inspiration, Personalism affirms that man's freedom is fundamental, but that it is realized only amidst other men in their social and historical conditions. In its ethical and political aspirations, Personalism seeks to affirm the existing unities between thought and action, person and community, community and historical situation." Amato, *Mounier and Maritan*, 1-3.

27. Two books that have outlined the influence of personalism in the thought of John Paul II are *Beyond Self-Interest* by Beabout et al.; and *Human Nature and the Discipline of Economics* by Donohue-White et al.

28. Blazynski, *Pope John Paul II: A Man from Kraków*, 59.

29. Hellman, "John Paul II and the Personalist Movement," 416.

a priest, *Our God's Brother*. The play deals with the vocational struggle to make oneself a gift, as illustrated in the life of artist Adam Chmielowski (1845–1916). After becoming dissatisfied with his life as an artist and angered at social injustice towards the poor in Krakow, Adam devoted the remainder of his life to caring for the poor and the homeless. The play tells the story of Adam in the setting of the protagonist's conscience, as Adam was in the process of "becoming" Brother Albert through a merciful giving of himself exhibited by embracing a life of radical poverty and service. By becoming a servant rather than a revolutionary, Adam did not deny the injustice of society or the anger that injustice spawns. Yet he came to believe that the only social transformation truly worthy of the human person comes through the cross, which "transforms a man's fall into good and his slavery into freedom."[30] The resolution of the drama was found in Brother Albert's dying words, spoken as a worker's insurrection has broken out:

> Ah well. You know that anger has to erupt, especially if it is great.
>
> [*He stops.*]
>
> And it will last, because it is just.
>
> [*He becomes even more deeply lost in thought. Then he adds one sentence, as if to himself, though everyone listens attentively.*]
>
> I know for certain, though, that I have chosen a greater freedom.[31]

Two aspects of this play are especially important for Wojtyla's later account of justice. First, Wojtyla sought to counter political ideology with his belief in the transcendent dignity of human persons that is demonstrated in human action.[32] He believed that, like Brother Albert, all humans are faced with moral struggle and they have the potential to "become" new by giving themselves to others, and thus to God. This third way between Marxism and capitalism through the gift of personhood that is intimated in his play will be a noted theme in the social encyclicals of John Paul II.

Second, this play points to a tension, which I suggest will become a weakness of his account of justice: the tension between justice and mercy. In this play, Brother Albert suggested that the insurrection was an act of justice. Yet he believed that his choice for freedom came through the cross:

---

30. Wojtyla, *Our God's Brother*, in *Collected Plays*, 263.
31. Wojtyla, *Collected Plays*, 266.
32. The Polish communist authorities recognized this threat when they tried to cut this last line about the "greater freedom" from the script when *Our God's Brother* was finally performed in Kraków in 1980.

through the act of mercifully giving of himself to others in accordance with Christ. These two acts—the revolt for justice and the gift of mercy—were both affirmed as good, with the latter act portrayed as superior. In his later works as John Paul, a similarly ambiguous relation with mercy lies at the heart of his account of justice. This relation will be examined critically in chapter three. At this stage, we continue to trace the development of Wojtyla's anthropology, which provided the framework for his mature account of justice.

A New Method of Investigating Ethical Personhood in the Phenomenology of Max Scheler

After working for priest for three years, Wojtyla's archbishop asked him to pursue a second doctoral degree by writing a habilitation thesis, which would qualify him to teach at the university level. Wojtyla began his study of ethics in September 1951, while continuing his work as a priest.

Probably due to the influence of personalism, Wojtyla chose to study the phenomenological approach to ethics in the works of Max Scheler.[33] For Wojtyla, the study of phenomenology opened up a new approach to reality. He later reflected, "St. Thomas gave me answers to many problems, and Scheler taught me a lot about personality and the methods of investigation."[34]

Like Edmund Husserl, who was the founder of phenomenology, Scheler was reacting against the narrowness of scientific naturalism and sought a new way of thinking that would be capable of attaining universal, or general essences, on the basis of intuitive givenness.[35] In Scheler's primary work on phenomenology, *Formalismus in der Ethik und die materiale Wertethik*, he argued that the mind apprehends essence in two stages.[36] First, phenomenology provides a way of viewing whereby the viewer can enter directly into an immediate, intuitive relationship with the essence

---

33. Mounier considered the philosophy of Max Scheler to be of vital importance for personalist philosophy. Hellman, "John Paul II and the Personalist Movement," 413.

34. Malinski, *Pope John Paul*, 159.

35. Kobler, *Vatican II and Phenomenology*, ix.

36. Scheler, *Formalismus* [*Formalism in Ethics and Non-Formal Ethics of Values*] was first published in German in two parts in 1913 and 1916. For a brief introduction to Phenomenology, see Scheler's "Phenomenology and the Theory of Cognition," in *Selected Essays*, 136–85.

of things through experience.[37] In the second stage, the phenomenologist penetrates into what is given as "lived through," discovering the values given through *intentional* feeling.[38] In other words, knowledge is given through experience. Then by abstraction may one distinguish the affective (in which realm values are discovered) from the cognitive.[39] Thus, the phenomenologist seeks to penetrate behind all phenomena to their essential structures (*Wesenheiten*) and to describe these structures in such a way that the modern person is awakened to the poetic dimension of reality that is incomprehensible to modern science.[40]

The significance of Scheler's work for the development of the young priest's anthropology can be seen in the two concluding arguments of Wojtyla's habilitation thesis. First, Wojtyla expressed appreciation for Scheler's phenomenological approach to the study of persons, for his insight into the place of values in ethical decisions, and for the importance of following or of imitation. Scheler believed that human persons could be known and values could be determined through seeing and experience. In other words, he recognized the importance of human action for an ethical system. Wojtyla wrote the following, which is key to his philosophical approach to Christian ethics:

> When . . . with the help of phenomenological experience, we select a value and examine it, we are making an experimental study of moral experience. It is possible to apply this method of experimental examination to Christian ethics. Given that our choice of moral experience as an object of examination derives from the belief in the ethical principles supplied by Christian revelation, then the examination allows us to penetrate into Christian ethical values, to uncover the essence of the experience and to verify its uniqueness and specificity in comparison with non-Christian ethical values, and also the borders at which they touch one another.[41]

In pursuit of the ethical in society, Scheler emphasized both this ascertaining of values and the imitation of primary models of the community.[42] "It is by appropriating another man's ethos that one can identify with

---

37. Staude, *Max Scheler*, 22.
38. Williams, *The Mind of John Paul*, 126.
39. Buttiglione, *Karol Wojtyla*, 68.
40. Staude, *Max Scheler*, 23.
41. Wojtyla, *Max Scheler*, 241. Cf. Buttiglione, *Karol Wojtyla*, 62.
42. Williams, *The Mind of John Paul*, 130.

the values and qualities to which his life testifies."[43] Wojtyla agreed with this personalist approach, which recognized the importance of experience, values, and imitation in contrast to a purely objectivist or metaphysical system of ethics, because it penetrated into the dynamism of human action in ethical life.

His second argument was more critical in nature. He concluded that "the ethical system constructed by Max Scheler is not at all suitable as a means of formulating a scientific Christian ethics."[44] Due to inadequate use of his own method, Scheler failed to substantiate a normative ethical order. For example, Scheler believed that good and evil are bound to emotion and revealed only in moral experience. Wojtyla argued that this failure to recognize ethical norms results from Scheler's inadequate perception of human persons. For Scheler, the human person is the place in which values are made manifest through feeling.[45] Persons are not substance but the unity of lived-through emotional experiences.[46]

The influence of Thomism, particularly Existential Thomism, is evident in Wojtyla's critique. His assumptions were fundamentally Thomistic in orientation, for instance, when he argued for a normative moral order that transcends humanity, rather than an ethic that is bound to the human person. Yet he appreciated phenomenology because it provided a way to include intuition and intentional feeling, or the affective realm, within the realm of the senses. Thus while appropriating the phenomenological method, he continued to believe that persons obtain natural knowledge of the real through the senses, and the real includes the normative moral order. In this manner, Wojtyla's appropriation of Scheler's method continues to demonstrate his thorough optimism regarding the human capacity for knowledge of the moral order.

Promoting Human Dignity as a Moral Theologian

After receiving his doctorate in 1954, Wojtyla was invited to join the Catholic University of Lublin [KUL] Philosophy Faculty. The faculty had been established eight years earlier in reaction against the Nazi's attempted to decapitate Polish intellectual culture and in hope of reflecting upon the questions that arose in the wake of the occupation and imposition of

---

43. Buttiglione, *Karol Wojtyla*, 56.
44. Wojtyla, *Max Scheler*, 232; Buttiglione, *Karol Wojtyla*, 60.
45. Buttiglione, *Karol Wojtyla*, 59.
46. Wojtyla, "Act and Lived Experience," in *Person and Community*, 44.

communism.⁴⁷ Polish people were confronted with new questions about persons and the meaning of humanity:

Why had some men and women acted like beasts while others had shown remarkable heroism? What accounted for the fact that, while some people were grotesquely self-serving, to the point of betraying their friends, others were nobly self-sacrificing, laying down their lives for others they may have known only slightly?⁴⁸

The KUL philosophers sought to address these questions through philosophical anthropology, affirming four theses:

1. "Human beings can only be free in the truth, and the measure of truth is reality."⁴⁹ They agreed that they must be realistic about the world and about the human capacity to know the world. Truth must be an expression of things-as-they-are rather than a function of power.⁵⁰

2. The starting point for philosophical inquiry must begin with disciplined reflection on human experience rather than a cosmology. They sought to get at the truth of things-as-they-are through an analysis of human experience, asking questions like, "What is human vocation?" and "Is the redemption of history to be understood in material and political terms, or does history have a transcendent dimension?"⁵¹

3. They shared a commitment to reason (as opposed to the irrationalism of Nazi propaganda) with the goal to illuminate what good men and women *ought* to do.⁵²

4. They finally agreed to mine both the past and the present in pursuit of the truth so that they would not be slaves to contemporaneity.⁵³

Like Wojtyla, the KUL philosophers located the crisis of modernity and the inadequacies of communism in a misunderstanding of the human person. These four theses share many similarities with Wojtyla's

---

47. Weigel, *Witness to Hope*, 132.
48. Ibid.
49. Ibid., 133.
50. Ibid.
51. Ibid., 134.
52. This use of "ought" echoes the Kant's ethical obligation. We will return to this theme of John Paul in the final section of chapter 7.
53. Four points adapted from Swiezawki, Introduction to *Person and Community* by Wojtyla, xii–xiii.

assumptions about human ethics: the truth of the moral order is founded in the real (which, for Wojtyla, transcends humans) and ethical truth is known through experience, reason, and tradition. Influenced by these philosophers, Wojtyla continued to affirm the dignity of persons evidenced in their capacity to transcend their political context in order to know and affirm the truth of the moral order.

In 1956, at the beginning of his third year on staff, Wojtyla accepted the Chair of Ethics, a position he would hold for twenty-two years.[54] As Wojtyla worked as a philosophical lecturer and a theologian, his theories of the human person solidified, as demonstrated in his writings during this period. The following chapter will examine his theoretical approach to justice, which developed during his years teaching philosophy at KUL.

The Years Leading to His Papacy

In 1958, Wojtyla was named auxiliary bishop of Krakow. He continued teaching in KUL while fulfilling his responsibilities as bishop. The following year, Pope John XXIII announced his intention to call an ecumenical council with a pastoral and ecumenical vision. A few months before the council opened on October 11, 1962, Bishop Wojtyla was elected temporary administrator to the Archdiocese of Krakow to replace Archbishop Baziak.

The three sessions of the Second Vatican Council taking place from 1962-1965 sought to address the problems and issues that had been raised in the modern period. As Bishop of Kraków and later as Archbishop, Wojtyla took part in all three sessions of the council. He addressed the council several times, and he worked on a sub-commission re-drafting of *Gaudium et Spes* [*The Church in the Modern World*], a document that he referred to numerous times in his later work.[55] Wojtyla believed that the

---

54. Unfortunately, the lecture notes that remain offer little insight into the shape of Wojtyla's mature work. The lectures were primarily based upon the work of Wojtyla's predecessor, Jan Piwowarczyk (1889–1959) and displayed little emphasis upon the anthropology that undergirds his later writings. For a brief summary of these social ethics lectures, see Grondelski, "Social Ethics in the Young Karol Wojtyla: A Study-in-Progress," 31–43.

55. Other statements of Vatican II that were of special importance to him were *Lumen Gentium* [*Dogmatic Constitution on the Church*], *Dei Verbum* [*Dogmatic Constitution on Revelation*], *Dignitatis Humanae* [*Declaration on Religious Freedom*], *Nostra Aetate* [*Declaration on the Relation of the Church to Non-Christian Religions*], and *Unitatis Redintegratio* [*Decree on Ecumenism*]. When asked near the end of the council which documents were most important, Wojtyla listed these, in addition to *Gaudium*

root of the issue with which the council was grappling was the topic of the human person.⁵⁶

In 1967, Wojtyla was created Cardinal by Pope Paul VI. He worked to build up the Polish church, and he began to travel more extensively. In 1976, Wojtyla was invited to preach the Lenten retreat to Pope Paul VI and the Roman Curia. After two more years of lecturing and pastoral work in Poland, Wojtyla was elected Pope on October 16, 1978. Chapter Three will examine John Paul's mature, theological theory of justice.

Conclusion

This first chapter began to establish a framework for the theoretical analysis of justice by examining Wojtyla's personal context and the sources of his thought. This chapter suggested that Wotjyla's experiences of personal suffering and of political oppression influenced him in two important ways. First, it enabled him to witness unparalleled acts of courage and self-giving that he attributed to the fundamental dignity of human persons: the capacity for humans to transcend their contexts and affirm their dignity through just and merciful action. Second, these experiences shifted Wojtyla's vocational goals so that he sought ordination for the priesthood. Through his vocational education, in theological and philosophical studies, Wojtyla began to gain a framework for justice that was influenced by Thomism and personalism. Thomism established for Wojtyla a moral epistemology that was fundamentally optimistic about the human capacity for access to a normative order. Personalism enabled him to articulate this normative order in a manner that was oriented around the value and dignity of human persons, over against systems that dehumanize them. His encounter with phenomenology gave him the tools to further analyze humans in ethical situations and the values that their actions reveal.

In sum, Wojtyla emerged from his oppressed homeland with a message of hope and optimism that he attributed to his faith. He found in the Catholic tradition the resources to fight against the dehumanizing forces of Marxism and Communism that dominated his historical context. In addition, he drew from his tradition a hope that God's transcendence and

---

et Spes. Malinski, *Pope John Paul II*, 188. They are consistently referred to throughout his papal encyclicals.

56. Wojtyla, "On the Dignity of the Human Person," in *Person and Community*, 177–80. This essay contains a talk broadcast in Polish over Vatican Radio, 19 October 1964. He made this comment to Malinski before the radio talk, 173.

the transcendent normative order protects and defends human dignity by critiquing injustice and by encouraging humans transcend their oppressive contexts through self-giving action that accords with Christ.

2

The Dignity of Human Persons in Wojtyla's
Philosophical and Theological Anthropology

THIS CHAPTER WILL EXAMINE THE THEORETICAL BASIS OF WOJTYLA'S account of human justice. In investigating Wojtyla's theoretical account of justice, three primary questions will guide this work. First, the question of *epistemology*: How is knowledge about justice acquired? In other words, what is the basis (or what are the bases) for the way that Wojtyla defined justice?

Second, the question of *theory*: How does Wojtyla define justice? Of the numerous ways to define justice as that which gives the greatest utility, as fairness, as liberation, which does Wojtyla choose? This question is important because in defining justice, Wojtyla also defines the critical criterion for determining what just action is and what it is not.

Third, the question of *praxis*: How is justice cultivated in society? This question puts feet on Wojtyla's theory by exploring the nature and the impact of just social action. It also raises the question of psychology: what may impel persons to act with justice evening the midst of unjust circumstances? These three questions of epistemology, theory, and praxis will provide key points for development in the work of John Paul II and for comparison with Karl Barth. Yet before these questions can even be raised, one must discern the assumptions that drove Wojtyla's ethical theory.

The Shape of Wojtyla's Work:
Thomist? Phenomenological? Or Both?

In numerous essays and books written during his years as a University professor, Wojtyla sought to bring various schools of philosophy into dialogue on the subject of ethics and the human person. The manner in which he did so is an important topic for this work because it illuminates

PART ONE—Karol Wojtyla/John Paul II

Wojtyla's epistemic basis for justice, a point on which we will compare his account with Barth's.

Current scholarship is divided on the shape of Wojtyla's work. Was Wojtyla's anthropology fundamentally phenomenological, borrowing elements from Thomism as Anna Tymieniecka and Robert Harvanek propose?[1] Or should his work be interpreted as primarily metaphysical, expanding Thomism with insights from phenomenology as Gerald McCool and John McNerny argue?[2] Other interpreters such as Gerard Beigel and John Saward claim that the later writings have a christocentric structure for anthropology.[3] Do Wojtyla's theological aims provide structure for his philosophical anthropology or *vice versa*? Or perhaps John Kavanaugh's argument hits the mark when he argues:

> Wojtyla's life and work, is a "dialectical" totality. Any approach [to his work] which is one-sided, dualistic or reductionistic will lead one astray. Each aspect of his life and thought cuts through and across the other aspects. The meaning of each part rests upon its relation to the other parts and the living totality itself. His phenomenology is Thomist, socialist, poetic, evangelical, dramatic, political and traditionalist. His Thomism is radical, phenomenological, contemporary, personalistic, and transcendental.[4]

Like McCool and McNerny, I suggest that Wojtyla's epistemological basis for moral theology was Thomist and that phenomenology provided a set of tools to explore and to confirm Thomist presuppositions. In other words, although he employed phenomenological tools for ethical purposes, he rejected Scheler's and other modern epistemologies as a starting point for ethics.

This position was demonstrated most clearly in his essay, "In Search of the Basis of Perfectionism in Ethics." In this essay, he argued that the philosophy of being (illustrated by Aristotle and Aquinas) and philosophy of consciousness (illustrated by Kant and Scheler) are two bases for ethics that stand in "clear opposition."[5] The philosophy of being assumes that

---

1. Tymieniecka, "The Origins of the Philosophy of John Paul the Second," 16–27. Harvanek, "The Philosophical Foundations of the Thought of John Paul II," 1–22.

2. McCool, "The Theology of John Paul II," 29–54. McNerny, *John Paul II*, 14.

3. Beigel, *Faith and Social Justice in the Teaching of Pope John Paul II*; Saward, *Christ is the Answer*.

4. Kavanaugh, "John Paul II and Philosophy," 17.

5. Wojtya, "In Search of the Bases of Perfectionism in Ethics," in *Person and*

metaphysics is a science, a way of accurately describing a transcendent reality in which human beings participate through reason. In contrast, Kant limited human reason to consciousness, which "has no access to objective transcendent being."[6] Wojtyla argued that the phenomenologist, Max Scheler, held this assumption as well. Although Scheler believed that the good stands beyond consciousness, he refused to concern himself with it and dealt only with human consciousness.[7]

In the essay, Wojtyla argued that the philosophy of consciousness is an inadequate basis for moral good. He wrote:

> One could easily succumb to the illusion that for the construction of ethics it is best to proceed from an analysis of consciousness: if whatever is moral is also conscious, an examination of consciousness alone should allows us to discover all that it moral, all that informs the content of ethics . . . This turn out not to be the case. An analysis of consciousness alone allows us to discover only the contents of consciousness. Moral good, however, is not just a content of consciousness; it is also a perfection of the conscious being—and it is this first and foremost. The perfection of being can be apprehended only through an analysis of that being.[8]

This quote demonstrates Wojtyla's belief that the philosophy of being provides the only viable basis for morality because moral good transcends human consciousness.

While he utilized Scheler's phenomenology as a tool for exploring ethics, he continued to assume that the *"basis"* for morality transcended consciousness and must be conceptualized through the Thomistic metaphysics of being.[9] For, he concluded in this essay, "the Kantian norm and the Schelerian value ended up being suspended in a vacuum, so to speak because the complete human being is a being and not just consciousness."[10]

Community, 54. His argument centered around the concept perfectionism in ethics, the idea that "a person is perfected morally by good actions and devalued by bad ones," (46).

6. Wojtyla, "In Search of the Bases," 49.

7. Ibid., 52.

8. Ibid., 54–55.

9. See ibid., 48–49, on his appeal to Thomas as providing a superior Christian philosophy of being. See also "Thomistic Personalism," in *Person and Community*, 175, in which he argued that an examination of the consciousness and values would point toward the eternal or transcendent reality of personhood.

10. Wojtyla, "In Search of the Bases," 55.

Interestingly, as John Paul II, he utilized the same metaphor to make a similar argument in 2005:

> If we want to speak rationally about good and evil, we have to return to Saint Thomas Aquinas, that is, to the philosophy of being. With the phenomenological method, for example, we can study experiences of morality, religion, or simply what it is to be human, and draw from them a significant enrichment of our knowledge. Yet we must not forget that all these analyses implicitly presuppose the reality of the Absolute Being and also the reality of being human, that is being a creature. If we do not set out from such "realist" presuppositions, we end up in a vacuum.[11]

Thus, we may conclude that Wojtyla's epistemological presuppositions were grounded in Thomistic metaphysics.

Yet in his ethical methodology Wojtyla employed phenomenological tools and modern philosophical insights, in order to "supplement" metaphysical reflection.[12] For example, Wojtyla critiqued the Aristotelian and Thomist teleological approaches to ethics in light of the modern turn to the subject. He described the "naturalistic" concept of the human being that both Aquinas and Aristotle employed as "rather inadequate," and as exerting a levelling effect on the concept of human personhood.[13] He argued that the emergence of the philosophy of consciousness and the phenomenological method enriched the study of persons and of morality. For this reason, he moved away from the teleological orientation of ethics toward a normative orientation in which morality is justified on the basis of values and norms. He explained, "'Virtues' and 'norms' themselves are not changing, but the way they are presented in the subject is."[14]

Thus in his ethics, Wojtyla utilized the phenomenological method to explore human consciousness in order to build a more comprehensive description of ethical values and norms. Yet he always assumed that such norms were not limited to human consciousness alone but found some correspondence in an objective order, the order established by the existence of God and the law of God.[15] We may conclude that while Wojtya/

---

11. JPII, *Memory and Identity*, 12.
12. Wojtyla, *Person and Community*, xiv.
13. Wojtyla, EMT, 104.
14. Ibid., 105.
15. Wojtyla, "The Human Person and Natural Law," in *Person and Community*, 184.

John Paul II utilized the phenomenological method, he continued to do so with the presuppositions of the philosophy of being.

Wojtyla's Epistemology: The Philosophical Basis for Knowing Justice

Having establishing that Wojtyla's epistemic basis for morality (and thus for his account of justice) was the metaphysics of Aquinas, a second question immediately poses itself: *How did Wojtyla interpret Aquinas' metaphysics?* This question is important for our examination of his work because it addresses one of the key points of comparison with Barth: the epistemological basis for accounts of justice. Karl Barth's early critique of metaphysics as a basis for ethics is well-known. Barth's particular focus for this argument centered around the Catholic concept of the *analogia entis*, or the analogy of being, which presupposed an analogous relation between the being of God and the being of humanity. Although many interpreters believe that Barth later relinquished this critique, I will argue in chapters four and five that the concerns underlying his initial rejection of the *analogia entis* remained relevant for Barth's ethical methodology. Thus, as we explore the Thomist epistemological starting points for Wojtyla's moral theology, I will examine his use of the *analogia entis*. Although Wojtyla does not use the term "*analogia entis*" in the essays we will examine, I will make the case that his appeal to it is intrinsic to his Existential Thomism.

In 1959, Wojtyla wrote an essay entitled, "On the Metaphysical and Phenomenological Basis of the Moral Norm," in which he interprets Thomist metaphysics.[16] According to Wojtyla, Aquinas reconstructed the Aristotelian concept of the good by giving priority to the aspect of existence. Existence is a good and the good is identical with being. Assuming that every being has existence, every being is a good, for what determines good is sheer being. All beings have their own respective fullness of existence and, thus, of good. Because God has an unconditional fullness of existence, God is the highest good.[17]

Beings have different degrees of perfection and differing types of good. The good that exists in humans is the good of their rational nature,

---

16. In this essay, he argued that the metaphysical framework of Aquinas reveals the weaknesses of Scheler's phenomenology. This argument further substantiates my prior contention that Wojtyla's epistemology was fundamentally Thomist.

17. Wojtyla, "On the Metaphysical and Phenomenological Basis of the Moral Norm," in *Person and Community*, 74.

a good that is not diminished by sin.[18] Another type of good is moral good. Moral good is destroyed by sin. Wojtyla explained, "The good connected with the very substance of our nature is not even diminished by sin, but the good connected with our natural inclination is reduced by sin, although not wholly destroyed, unlike the goods of virtue (moral good) and grace (supernatural good)."[19]

To varying degrees, creatures participate in God's fullness of existence and his unconditional perfection because they owe their existence to God. This belief has two implications. First, participation in existence entails resemblance; so greater participation in God, the fullness of existence, expresses itself in the greater degree of perfection of a given being.[20] Because humans are rational in a manner than animals are not, humans have a greater degree of perfection. Second, God is the supreme and transcendent measure of all beings. Wojtyla named this exemplariness of God, "the heart of the normative order," for the exemplar "is the transcendent measure for what is modelled after it."[21] The human measure of transcendence "results from the being's exemplification of the supreme perfection of Divine Being."[22] Thus, when Wojtyla spoke of the normative order, his basis for this order was God, who is the exemplary measure of all things. This normative order is key to Wojtyla's moral theology.[23]

Although Wojtyla did not use the term, the *analogia entis*, in his interpretation and affirmation of Aquinas' metaphysics, the essay clearly described the manner in which all being is analogous to the being of God. For both Aquinas and Wotjyla, being is only analogous, however. For God's being is perfect and necessary being; human existence is contingent, lived by participation in the existence of God.

18. Cf. Wojtyla, "Human Nature as the Basis for Ethical Formation," in *Person and Community*, 96-97.

19. Wojtyla, MPB, 76.

20. Ibid., 77.

21. Ibid., 78.

22. Ibid.

23. In a subsequent essay, Wojtyla wrote, "From this follows the resemblance to God of all creatures in being; this resemblance has its own gradation. Both the resemblance as such and its gradations are gathered together and known in the mind of God as exemplars: the Creator sees in Himself the highest exemplar out of which beings are created and knows them in His image, that is to say, inasmuch as they imitate his essence, which is the first object of his knowledge. It is here that we find the nucleus of the normative order" (*Il fondamento metafisico e fenomenological dell norma morale sulla base delle concezioni di Tommaso d'Aquino e di Max Scheler*), 111–12. Translated by Buttiglione, *Karol Wojtyla*, 76.

The implications of the *analogia entis* for epistemology were spelled out at the end of his description of Aquinas when he wrote,

> Reason is able to conceive the very essence of the good. This, in turn, occurs without some sort of vision of "the good in itself," without a contemplation of the "Idea of the Good" conceived in a Platonic way. Reason abstracts the general concept of the good from the concrete particular goods we encounter in our actions.[24]

This quote is important for three reasons. First, it clarifies the significance of the *analogia entis* for moral epistemology. Wojtyla suggested that humans are able to posit norms because of "our ability to apprehend by means of reason the very essence of the good in a general way."[25] Why are humans able to do so? Because the goods that humans observe in this world and in their own actions are somehow reflective of, or analogous to, the good of God.[26] When we see a beautiful sunset, we can surmise something about the beauty of God. Likewise, when we see someone performing good action, we know something about the good of God. In this manner, the analogy of being provides the possibility of ethical knowledge when utilizing *a posteriori* reasoning.

Second, this quotation confirms what we suggested in Chapter One: Wojtyla's interpretation of Aquinas' epistemology is not of the Transcendental school of thought, for it appeals to *a posteriori* reasoning, a reasoning dependent upon the *analogia entis*. Third, this quote and this entire essay provides insight into Wojtyla's fundamental optimism in his account of justice. Wojtyla believed that all humans have epistemic access to norms of justice: all humans can posit norms that are good and true (to some extent) because of the *analogia entis* and because human nature (which includes reason)[27] has not been undermined by sin. In the cases when humans do *not* know justice, it seems to be due to the fact that their moral will, which has been weakened by sin, does not make the good its object, thus obscuring the truth about justice. He wrote:

---

24. Wojtyla, MPB, 81.

25. Ibid., 80.

26. Wojtyla, "The Problem of Separation of Experience from Acts in Ethics," in *Person and Community*, 33; and "The Person: Subject and Community," *Person and Community*, 236. See also Buttiglione, 79.

27. Cf. Wojtyla, "Human Nature as the Basis for Ethical Formation," in *Person and Community*, 96–97, in which he explains that the nature of humans is rational.

> The good is the object of the will, whereas the cognitive apprehension of the good—its objectification—is, according to St. Thomas, an object of reason. Both of these faculties work closely together with one another (*utraque ad actum alterius operatur*): the will wills so that reason may know; reason, in turn, knows that the will wills and what the will wills. A result of this cooperation of reason and the will is that the good and the true somehow mutually include one another.[28]

Thus, the will, which has corrupted but not totally destroyed the moral good that belongs to humans, may impair this epistemic capacity by rejecting the good. But humans who desire to know what is right, and desire to do what is good, have access to the objective order of God.

In this manner, by assuming the concept of the *analogia entis*, Wojtyla could universalize his ethic. In other words, he could argue that all persons have epistemic access to the good through reason and so all are held accountable to the good. Yet, in an interesting turn, he argued that reason alone is not enough. For example, while the precept of love is "in principle" accessible to reason, humans are unable to interpret it adequately without knowledge of God's intervention in human history through Jesus Christ.[29] In addition to the norms of natural law, there also exist norms that are revealed. Wojtyla wrote:

> When we shift from teleological ethics to normative ethics and attempt to reconstruct moral theology along the lines of the latter, we are faced with the question: what is the relation between norms contained in revelation and the norms of natural law, between "revealed virtues" and "natural virtues"? Are any of these norms exclusively "revealed," such that they could not be known without revelation? The possibility seems to exist of arriving at a purely philosophical understanding and acceptance of the entire moral content of the evangelical message, especially the precept that persons are to be loved by reason of the dignity vested in them. After all, according to revelation, particularly the teachings of St. Paul, the content of revealed precepts can also be known and is in fact known without revelation, in a natural way. This is also confirmed by general experience, which, in turn, stands at the basis of the current widespread call for dialogue. Obviously, such a purely rational interpretation of revealed norms involves a certain "compression" and "abbreviation" of

---

28. Buttiglione, *Karol Wojtyla*, 76.

29. Wojtyla, "Ethics and Moral Theology," in *Person and Community*, 105. Essay published in 1967.

them. A purely philosophical interpretation is not adequate. In order to arrive at a wholly adequate interpretation, we must turn to theology and draw upon the full content of revelation.[30]

He followed this passage with an argument that moral theology and dogmatic theology must be intimately connected.

Upon first reading, it may appear that Wojtyla was asking the question, "Are there both norms which are revealed and norms which are known to the human without revelation, through natural law?" However, the argument that he proceeded to make does not answer this question and appears self-contradictory when his question is interpreted in this manner. Upon closer reading, I interpret Wojtyla's question to be, not one regarding the impact of revealed norms upon natural norms, but the question of the feasibility of justifying revealed norms apart from revelation. He was asking, "*Can revealed norms be justified by natural law?*" Beginning with this question, the passage can be interpreted more coherently. First, he answered that the possibility exists and he cited the teachings of St. Paul and general experience, to show how revealed precepts can be known in a natural way. Then he argued that purely philosophical interpretation of revealed norms is not adequate because without revelation we would know nothing of God's plan for salvation or of the intervention of the Incarnate God in human affairs. Thus, "not knowing this, we would also not be able to interpret adequately the moral contents of revelation (e.g., the precept of love) that are 'in principle' accessible to reason."[31] Thus, he answered the question, "*Can revealed norms be justified by natural law?*" in the negative. Theology provides the context for fully interpreting revealed norms.

This essay is key to interpreting Wojtyla's philosophical method for social ethics for two reasons. First, Wojtyla was not rethinking the foundation for moral norms in light of God's revelation in Jesus Christ. From a protestant perspective, the question of the relation between revealed norms vs. natural norms, would call into question the feasibility of natural law or knowledge about moral norms apart from scripture. However, Wojtyla so readily accepted the Thomist assumption that the *analogia entis* gives the human the capacity to know natural norms that he, seemingly, did not even notice this tension, which has been such a source of debate in modern theology. Rather, he embraced the conception that natural law does have access to a certain degree of truth.

---

30. Wojtyla, EMT, 105.
31. Ibid.

In a different essay, he explained why natural law is viable. First, he asserted the Thomist definition of the human person as "an individual substance of rational nature." Second, he defined natural law as "the participation of the eternal law in the rational creature."[32] From this he concluded that natural law intimately corresponds to the human being as a person, for "a rational ordinance corresponds to a rational being."[33] In other words, there is an objective rational order, toward which human reason is oriented (because of its correspondence to that order) and through which human reason encounters and participates in the eternal law of God.[34] Thus, the epistemological basis for natural law, for human norms, and specifically for norms of justice is, on the one hand, the correspondence of human reason to the eternal objective order.

On the other hand, the extended quotation above also points to a second aspect of Wojtyla's epistemology. Namely, he believed that Thomas' speculative theology was limited, indicating a limitation on the *analogia entis* as the sole means of knowledge about ethics. He said that philosophy and reason only go so far because they cannot adequately interpret the moral norms revealed by God.[35] Though the precept of love can be known through reason, philosophy is a good tool for "getting to the bottom" of this precept. While the moral contents of revelation are "in principle"

32. Wojtyla, "Human Person and Natural Law," 183.

33. Ibid., 184.

34. Wojtyla wrote: "From these elementary tenets, we see that law does not imply some sort of arbitrary interference of subjective reason in the objective world, but rather implies a basic orientation toward this objective order. This order is the order of values. Reason's orientation toward this objective order is expressed in its discovery and definition of that order. Consequently, this is not a subjective interference of reason in objective reality, in the sense that reason would impose its own categories on reality, as was ultimately the case in Kant's anthropological view, but a completely different orientation and attitude: the attitude of reason discerning, grasping, defining, and affirming, in relation to an order that is Objective and prior to human reason itself. I emphasize *to human reason,* since it should be noted at once that through the orientation of human reason toward the Objective order, which is itself an actual component of this orientation or 'ordinance of reason,' a singular encounter with the divine source of law takes place. This is brought out very strongly in the Thomistic definition of natural law. The encounter of human reason in its orientation toward the objective order is an encounter with the divine source of law. This encounter is very profound, for it involves participation in the eternal law, which is in some sense identical with God, with divine reason." "The Human Person and Natural Law," 184.

35. This presupposition is illustrated in the architectonic of Aquinas's *Summa Contra Gentes*. In books 1–3, Aquinas "dealt with divine things according as the natural reason can arrive at the knowledge of divine things through creatures." *Summa Contra Gentes* 4.1.4.

accessible to reason, "without theology, there is no way to give a fully adequate interpretation of moral norms or of the so-called theological virtues."[36] Which virtues are "theological"? For Wojtyla, they are those virtues that "express in a special way the relation—revealed through 'facts and words'—of human beings to God."[37] By "relation," Wojtyla is referring to the salvation and sanctification of humankind in Jesus Christ.[38] For this reason, virtues like charity, hope, and faith are "theological," because they are only fully known through revelation.

In conclusion, for Wojtyla, human knowledge of justice may come through two venues: natural law and/or theology. Both of these venues are grounded in the reality of God but humans have access to them in different ways: one through the *analogia entis*, by which reason corresponds to the eternal reason of God, and the other through the revelation of God's relation to humanity. For Wojtyla, the ethical knowledge that humans gain through these venues is not contradictory. Rather, revelation offers a more adequate account of those virtues that are revealed. Thus, both of these ways to ethical knowledge must be taken into account in examining our second question for Wojtyla: "What his account of justice?"

Wojtyla's Account of Justice

Wojtyla articulated an account of justice that was based upon the personalistic norm: justice means treating people in accordance with their nature. Perhaps this was best illustrated through the contrast with utilitarianism, a theory that defines justice in terms of that which leads to the greatest amount of utility. Utilitarians believe that, because the aim of all rational individuals is to maximize their own happiness, justice entails facilitating the greatest amount of happiness for the greatest number of people, given the possibilities at hand. Wojtyla critiqued this theory because of its tendency to view people as means to an end.[39] If the aim is pleasure, he said, persons are merely seen as a means to pleasure. By contrast, personalism views the person as an end, as a good in himself or herself.[40] Wojtyla wrote, "the personalist norm says: 'A person is an entity of a sort to which

36. Wojtyla, EMT, 105–6.

37. Ibid., 105.

38. Elsewhere, Wojtyla also includes the work of creation as God's revelation of himself. SC, 46.

39. Wojtyla, *Love and Responsibility*, 37.

40. Ibid., 40–41.

the only proper and adequate way to relate is love."[41] Thus, for utilitarians, the basis for human action is guided by pleasure; for personalists, the basis of action is love.

For Wojtyla, both love and justice interpenetrate the personalistic norm. Justice means "giving others what is rightly due them."[42] Yet what is rightly due to people? They are to be treated in accordance with their nature; justice is treating others with love. How are love and justice different? Wojtyla suggested that justice "concerns itself with things (material goods or moral goods, as for instance of one's good name) in relation to persons" whereas love is concerned with affirming the value of the person more directly and immediately.[43] Justice is one aspect of love; in order to love a person (to affirm their value), one must treat them justly. However, justice is not equated with love, for love does not consist merely in being just.

Wojtyla's Philosophical Account of Human Nature

It is obvious from this brief account of justice that Wojtyla's interpretation of human nature is key to his account of justice. If justice means treating people in accordance with their nature (or essence),[44] then one must also have a clear conception of what that nature is. From a philosophical perspective, Wojtyla appealed to the definition that Aquinas borrowed from Boethius: *persona est rationalis naturae individua substantia.* The human being is an individual substance of a rational nature.[45] One property of rational nature is freedom.[46] Wotyla wrote, "The person, therefore, is always a rational and free concrete being, capable of all those activities that reason and freedom alone make possible."[47] The rational and free nature is Wojtyla's philosophical grounding for human dignity, for the human nature is a good in itself, a good that corresponds to the good of God's existence. The rational and free nature of humans is also Wotjyla's grounding for just action, which will be explored in a subsequent section.

---

41. Ibid., 41.

42. Ibid., 42.

43. Ibid.

44. Wojtyla wrote that "nature is equivalent to a thing's essence," "Human Nature as the Basis of Ethical Formation," in *Person and Community*, 96.

45. Wojtyla, TP, 167.

46. Wojtyla, "Human Nature as the Basis," 98.

47. Wojtyla, TP, 167.

Wojtyla's Theological Account of Human Nature

Yet Wojtyla acknowledged that an account of the dignity of human nature, which is grounded philosophically, may be further investigated in the light of theology. He built a theological basis for the dignity of human nature in his doctrine of God, doctrine of Christ, and his doctrine of the eschaton. We will briefly examine each of these three doctrines.

DOCTRINE OF GOD

First, the doctrine of God reveals human nature because the transcendent God creates humans in his image for covenant with himself. Wojtyla wrote, "Each person is unique and draws his whole greatness from being rooted in his relationship with God, because he was created in the image and likeness of God, and also from the fact that God himself has a special relationship with each individual person."[48] Human nature entails likeness with God, lending humans an incomparable dignity among other beings, and especially over material objects. Second, because of this special relation with God, of creation and of love, the human discloses her own dignity by transcending or going beyond herself. Wojtyla wrote, "Man goes beyond himself by reaching out towards God, and thus progresses beyond the limits imposed on him by created things, by space and time, by his own contingency."[49] This capacity for transcendence critiques systems that define human nature in purely material terms. Third, God's act of creation attributes dignity to the human act. Human activity in creation is both dependent and autonomous: dependent upon the creator yet free for to discover, exploit, and order the laws and values of matter and society.[50] Likewise, action reveals dignity because it forms the human person in the likeness of God. In sum, likeness to God, transcendence, and activity reveal human nature as possessing a dignity beyond compare in the natural world.

---

48. Wojtyla, *WC*, 133.
49. Wojtyla, *SC*, 16.
50. Ibid., 49. He quoted *GS*, 36: "By the very nature of creation, material being is endowed with its own stability, truth, and excellence, its own order and laws. These men must respect as he recognizes the methods proper to every science and technique."

PART ONE—Karol Wojtyla/John Paul II

Doctrine of Christ

The doctrine of Christ also reveals the dignity of human nature. As the Son of God, Jesus Christ reveals the dignity of human nature through his incarnation and through his redemption. First, humans find their dignity in the mystery of the incarnation because it expresses the love of the Father.[51] Wojtyla wrote,

> Contemporary people in this last quarter of the twentieth century, whose human dignity has been ignored and infringed in so many ways, come to Christ's stable in Bethlehem to ask who they are and why they are in the world, bringing with them their existential anxiety. And when they come to Bethlehem, like each of us they find the reply in the manger on the straw: "I have given them power to become children of God."[52]

Human dignity has been so compromised that people no longer understand that they are made in the image of God.[53] Through his incarnation, Jesus brought humans back to this truth. Thus, Jesus "defined and ordained this dignity when he, the Son of God and coexistent with the Father, became one of us—a man."[54] By becoming human, he raised humanity to a dignity "beyond compare."[55]

Second, the covenant, shattered by original sin, is rebuilt by redemption through Jesus Christ, the Son of God.[56] People are divided in themselves because they often refuse to acknowledge God as the source, upsetting the relationship that links them to their final end and breaking the right order that should reign in their relationship to the self and to others.[57] The human is unable to overcome this sin except through the freedom and strength given him in Christ's redemption. Wojtyla wrote, "Redemption is from sin which degrades man, and in this redemption—in its essence and effects—we find the fundamental and inexhaustible means

---

51. Wojtyla, *SC*, 102.
52. Wojtyla, *WC*, 57.
53. Wojtyla, *SC*, 32–33.
54. Wojtyla, *WC*, 58. Wojtyla also wrote, "The incarnation of the Son of God emphasizes the great dignity of human nature; and the mystery of the redemption not only reveals the value of every human being but also indicates the lengths to which the battle to save man's dignity must go." *SC*, 102.
55. Vatican Council, *GS*, 22.
56. Wojtyla, *SC*, 25–26.
57. Vatican Council, *GS*, 13; *SC*, 76–77.

by which man is restored to his proper value."[58] Wojtyla called this redemption universal, in the sense that all people are involved in the paschal mystery of Christ.[59] The human realizes himself and restores dignity to humanity through self-abandonment to God and through the giving of himself to another.[60]

Third, Christ reveals human dignity by calling humans to share in his mission of love. Christ provides the answer to the question, "What is man?" As Wojtyla quoted from *Gaudium et Spes*, "In reality it is only in the mystery of the Word made flesh that the mystery of man truly becomes clear. For Adam, the first man, was a type of him who was to come, Christ the Lord. Christ the new Adam, in the very revelation of the mystery of the Father and of his love, fully reveals man to himself and brings to light his most high calling."[61] When he said this, did Wojtyla mean that no knowledge of the human is possible outside of Christ? Did this mean that he was grounding knowledge of human nature in Jesus Christ? Based upon his method and his definition of the *image of God* above, he was not implying that the mystery of humanity is revealed only in Christ. Rather, the revelation of Christ clarifies that which is already known about humanity. The revelation of grace perfects the revelation of nature. Thus, while the creation reveals that humans have dignity because they are in the image of God, Christ reveals the extent of this dignity through his incarnation, his act of redemption, and his calling for humans to participate in his gift of love.

Eschatology

Finally, humans discover their dignity in the hope of the eschaton. Wojtyla contrasted Christian eschatology with the secular eschatology of temporality and materialism. He questioned positive evaluation of the progress of

---

58. Wojtyla, *SC*, 77.

59. "All this holds true not for Christians only but also for all men of good will in whose hearts grace is active invisibly. For since Christ died for all, and since all men are in fact called to one and the same destiny, which is divine, we must hold that the Holy Spirit offers to all the possibility of being made partners, in a way known to God, in the paschal mystery." *GS*, 22; *SC*, 79–80.

60. Wojtyla, *Sources of Renewal: The Implementation of Vatican II*, 60–61.

61. Wojtyla, *SC*, 75. Vatican Council, *GS*, 22. See also Wojtyla, *SC*, 117. Vatican Council, *GS*, 22, confirms, "It is therefore through Christ, and in Christ, that light is thrown on the riddle of suffering and death which, apart from his Gospel, overwhelms us." *SC*, 80.

humanity as growing material gains have coincided with enormous moral shortcomings. He wrote that our "century of progress" has become the age of totalitarianism's death camps or liberalism's sickening prosperity, which has given rise to drug addictions, murder, and new social problems. Yet the Christian hope affirms that there is "the seed of eternity inherent in man, who cannot be reduced to mere matter, rebels against death."[62]

In sum, Wojtyla argued that the Christian revelation affirms and enhances the philosophical insights of Aquinas because it highlights the dignity of human nature. From a theological perspective, human nature is revealed in the acts and promises of God as well as the human capacity to transcend the material realm and to act freely.

The Justice that Corresponds to Human Nature

This section has raised the question, What was Wojtyla's account of social justice? Thus far we have seen that Wojtyla defined justice by using a personalist norm: justice means treating people in accordance with their nature. Then we explored the meaning of human nature in Wojtyla's philosophical and theological thought. His philosophy affirms that human nature is rational and free. This rationality and freedom affirm the dignity of each person, for it is a rationality and freedom that corresponds to the very nature of God's being. Theology affirms the incomparable dignity of humanity revealed in God's creation, salvation, and eternal preservation of each human life as well as in human transcendence and action. Because every human has such dignity, justice means treating every human in accordance with their nature; therefore treating all human persons with dignity.

This chapter has described Wojtyla's account of justice for individuals, but individuals naturally form into various societies and communities.[63] This reality raises the question of social morality, defined by Wojtyla as the question of "how to create a system of relations between the individual and society that results in the fullest possible correlation between the person's true good and the common good that society naturally seeks."[64] This ideal is a difficult balance between the error of individualism, which places individual good above the common good, and totalism, which attempts to subordinate persons in a way that the true good of persons is excluded. Between these two lies the personalist norm for justice. Wojtyla wrote,

62. Wojtyla, SC, 159.
63. Wojtyla, TP, 173.
64. Ibid., 174.

"Thomistic personalism maintains that the individual good of persons should by nature subordinate to the common good at which the collectivity, or society aims—but this subordination may under no circumstances exclude and devalue the persons themselves."[65]

Throughout his works, Wojtyla utilized this norm of personalism to account for justice. He critiqued those political and economic systems or technological advances or philosophies that did not uphold the dignity of persons, arguing consistently that all human developments must remain at the service of humankind.[66] The particular implications of this ethics of social justice will be examined more fully in his work as John Paul. Important for our purposes is the fact that the account of justice is personalist in nature: justice is treating humans with dignity, in a way that accords with their dignified nature.

Just Action in Society

Our final section explores the question of the cultivation of justice in society. It adds one more layer to the account of justice by drawing the link between theory and praxis. A theory of social justice divorced from an exploration into the question of how just societies are formed provides little benefit. Wojtyla argued that justice begins with individual human actions that shape societies.

The Consciousness and Efficacy of the Person

Wojtyla explored the nature of human ethical action in his book, *The Acting Person*. While continuing to maintain Thomistic assumptions about the rational and free nature of human persons, he used phenomenological tools to shed further light on the person as disclosed in human consciousness. Specifically, in this book, he examined the human's experience of the self in action.[67] He argued that man, himself, is the origin of his acting and the experience of efficacy is the awareness of being the agent and creator of the action being performed.[68] Yet man is not only the agent of action but also the recipient in the sense that "something-happens-in-man" when he acts. Thus, ethical experiences are not only intentional contents

---

65. Ibid.
66. For example, see *Sources*, 301–3; and *SC*, 108.
67. Wojtyla, *AP*, xx.
68. Ibid., 68–69.

of experience but they actually form persons.⁶⁹ For example, beginning with the value of justice and behaving justly in accordance with that value creates a just person.

In phenomenological analysis, this differentiation of human action (between agent and recipient) tends to divide the human. So Wojtyla argued that the metaphysical field of man's ontological structure (as the source of man-person) could synthesize the *efficacy* and the *subjectiveness* of man.⁷⁰ These two aspects of human action prove to be of pivotal importance for Wojtyla's ethics. First, analyzing the experience of *efficacy* provided vital insight into human freedom in action. He identified freedom as the decisive moment of the experience of efficacy. Freedom constitutes the structure of "man-acts."⁷¹ Second, human experience of *subjectiveness* served to explain the formative nature of human action. Wojtyla wrote, "It is man's actions, his conscious acting, that make of him *what* and *who* he actually is. This form of human becoming thus presupposes the efficacy or causation proper to man."⁷² Thus, this phenomenological approach clarifies the structures in which the choice of a good action serves to both create a good and to form the person as good. By implication, to treat another in a manner that is just has a positive impact upon the self because it forms the virtue of justice within one's self.

The Freedom of Human Action

Wojtyla examined the relation between the will and the person in which "the will manifests itself as a feature of the person and the person manifests himself as a reality with regard to his dynamism that is constituted by the will."⁷³ He calls this relation *self-determination*. Yet only through a structure of self-possession in which the person fully possesses and governs himself is self-determination possible.⁷⁴

---

69. Wojtyla, "Act and Lived Experience," in *Person and Community*, 95–96; "The Problem of the Will in Analysis of Ethical Act," in *Person and Community*, 8–17.

70. Wojtyla, *AP,* 74–75.

71. Ibid., 100.

72. Ibid., 98.

73. Ibid., 105. In *The Acting Person*, Wojtyla's argument for the transcendence of the person focuses on the will. In the essay "Act and Lived Experience" he argues that both feelings and cognition also indicate the transcendence of the person. See discussion in Schmitz, *At the Center*, 49.

74. In a side note, Wojtyla explains that the person as creature may also be seen as belonging to God but this relation, which medieval philosophers refer to as *persona est*

Wojtyla showed the connections between the freedom of the will as self-determining and the transcendence of the person in action. In other words, the freedom to choose just action is not determined historically, socially, or materially. It is grounded in the capacity of humans to transcend contexts and boundaries and to act freely. This free action is what determines the self, for "in every 'I will'—the self is the object, indeed the primary and nearest object."[75] Thus, the structure of self-determination in each genuine "I will" reveals the person's transcendence in action.[76] Wojtyla explained this assertion by defining *transcendence* as going over and beyond a threshold or boundary. "In every action, the person transcends his structural boundaries, his nature and its drives, by making himself a somebody through the action."[77] Wojtyla named this indicator of human freedom *vertical transcendence*.[78] Because the person is free and determines himself, he ascends over his own dynamism in vertical transcendence.[79]

Freedom indicated a special self-reliance that goes together with self-determination. Wojtyla wrote, "To say that man 'is free' means *that he depends chiefly on himself for the dynamization of his own subject*."[80] Free will manifests itself in the ability to choose.[81] However, Wojtyla differentiated this freedom from Kant's autonomy by describing the intrinsic relation between human freedom and an objective order of the good and the true. Wojtyla's free will has the freedom *for* objects or values but dependent upon truth.[82] The freedom of the will presupposes a reference to truth for "it is the essential surrender of the will to truth that seems finally to

---

sui iuris, does not overshadow self-possession. AP, 106.

75. Ibid., 108–9.

76. Ibid., 111.

77. Beigel, *Faith and Social Justice in the Teaching of Pope John Paul II*, 16.

78. This contrasts with horizontal experience, which he explains as "transgressing the subject's limits in the direction of an object—and this is intentionality in the 'external' perception or volition of external objects." AP, 119.

79. Ibid., 124.

80. Ibid., 120.

81. Ibid., 132.

82. Ibid.; and Beigel, *Faith and Social Justice in the Teaching of Pope John Paul II*, 17–18. Elsewhere, Wojtyla argued that the will is a potentiality for the good because of the capacity for free will and because it is a specifically rational faction on human nature and in the concrete person. Reason plays a norm-setting role by submitting different goods to the will in light of the objective norms rooted in reality. "The Problem of the Will in Analysis of the Ethical Act," in *Person and Community*, 8–17; and "Act and Lived Experience," in *Person and Community*, 95–96.

account for the person's transcendence in action, ultimately for his ascendancy to his own dynamism."[83] A "moment of truth" is contained in every authentic choice of decision making for "if choice and decision were to be without their inherent moment of truth, if they were to be performed apart from that specific reference to truth, moral conduct most characteristic for the man-person would become incomprehensible."[84] However, despite this moment of truth, humans too often fail to choose the "real good," and this choice of the will leads to the experience of guilt or sin.[85] Thus, the freedom he describes is a freedom in reference to truth and good because truth is the basis for the person's transcendence in action.[86]

The performing of an action not only shapes the human but also brings personal fulfillment. The structure of self-possession, of man's willing and acting, serves as the basis for morality. In other words, ethics cannot be bracketed out or treated as an existential moral reality. Morality is founded in anthropology for it conceives of humans as responsible subjects of their actions that are realized through themselves. The roots of morality grow out of the person while also fulfilling the person. Only in such a cycle can morality be concretized. The truth of moral norms that determine rightness and wrongness are expressed in human experience through the creative role of the conscience, which "shapes the norms into that unique and unparalleled form they acquire within the experience and fulfillment of the person."[87] Through responsible and good action informed by truth, the human fulfils himself.

From this account, Wojtyla's optimism regarding human action is evident. Unlike the Protestant emphasis on the corruption of the will under sin, Wojtyla emphasized the capacity of the will to act justly. For Wojtyla, the will is free to choose just action regardless of the boundaries of nature, history, and society. Such a claim is vital for his theory of justice because gives it a universal appeal; all persons have access to the truth of "what justice is" and all persons have the capacity to behave justly. In as much as Thomistic metaphysics is theological, this claim has theological grounding. However, Wojtyla conceived this capacity as a philosophical claim, a claim dependent upon God's being and the subsequent existence of the normative order. The claim is not by necessity dependent upon

83. Wojtyla, *AP*, 138.
84. Ibid., 139.
85. Ibid..
86. Ibid., 146.
87. Ibid., 165.

God's action. By contrast, Barth had a more pessimistic conception of human capacities to know and to act justly, a pessimism that only took a more optimistic turn because of the action of God.

Wojtyla's emphasis upon the self-determining nature of human action provided insight into his claim that persons make themselves morally good or morally bad. For Wojtyla, the moral act is a free act that is self-determining. What is unclear in his work is the extent to which this moral bad-ness impacts human dignity. Does the person who performs morally bad action somehow reduce his dignity? Or is the dignity of human nature located in the rational nature alone, a good that is not diminished by sin.[88] Certainly Wojtyla would not want to claim that the morally bad person undermines his own dignity and nature through his action, for such a claim would mean that such persons need not be treated with the same dignity as the morally good person. Yet if act is self-determining, then morally bad action may entail a morally bad nature.

Such a concept opens Wojtyla's thought to this potential to treat others justly means to treat them in accordance with their natures. This concept appears to establishe a philosophical basis for retributive justice rather than restorative or transformative justice. Retributive justice maintains that proportionate punishment is a morally acceptable response to a crime. For example, Deuteronomy 19:21 appeals to retributive justice in demanding, "eye for eye, tooth for a tooth, hand for hand, foot for foot." While Wojtyla's *theological* ethic does not lead to this ending point because of his appeal to love and to mercy that surpass justice, his *philosophical* ethic, the ethic by which he made his universal appeals, appears to. This fact suggests some contradiction within his account of Christian justice.

Human Action in Community

After examining the action of the individual person, in his book, *The Acting Person*, Wojtyla then turned to investigate the significance of his findings for the community. Wojtyla aimed to explain the social character of human nature and human action in community using the concept of participation. He introduced the definition of participation: having a share or taking part in something. Then he sought to investigate how a person, when he acts together with other people, retains the value of his own action while sharing in the realization and the results of communal acting. A human's existing and acting together with other persons enables him to

---

88. Wojtyla, MPB, 76.

achieve his own development through participation. Wojtyla contrasted this idea of participation with *individualism*, in which the individual is the supreme and fundamental good and others' interests are seen as limitations, and *totalism*, which subordinates the individual to the community in a coercive fashion. He claimed that the intellectual conception of humanity underlying both systems is impersonal:

> Every human being must have the right to act, which means "freedom in action," so that the person can fulfill himself in performing the action. The total freedom of action, which results from its personalistic value, conditions the ethical order and simultaneously determines it. On the other hand, the moral order instills into human actions—in particular, those within the orbit of acting "together with others"—those determinants, and thus also limitations, which are the consequence of purely ethical values and norms.[89]

Wojtyla argued that the common good is the foundation of authentic human communities. Participation emerges as a property of the human person from the reality constituted by common acting and common being.[90] Because Wojtyla defined human persons in terms individual substance, he did not make the claim that participation in the Other is grounded in human essence.[91] Rather than grounding participation in the material reality of human persons, the human capacity entails potential for participation in the Other, which he may freely choose. In other words, for Wojtya, participation is a potential dependent upon human capacity. In so choosing participation, the human forms himself and contributes to the common good.[92]

Wojtyla named two virtues that promote authentic participation and build up the common good: *solidarity* and *opposition*. *Solidarity* indicates a constant willingness to accept and realize one's share in the community. The attitude of solidarity seeks the benefit of the whole even when the common good requires the sacrifice of one's own share. The attitude of *opposition* means that one will not withdraw his membership in the community but that he will seek the good of the community by contesting that

---

89. Wojtyla, *AP*, 332.

90. Ibid., 339–40.

91. Wojtyla, "Participation or Alienation?," in *Person and Community*, 201.

92. Wojtyla, "Participation or Alienation?," 203. Cf. Gregg, *Challenging the Modern World: Karol Wojtyla/John Paul II and the Development of Catholic Social Teaching*, 201–11.

with which he does not agree. These two attitudes provide the basis for dialogue, a theme constant throughout John Paul's social writings. Dialogue seeks to bring out what is right and true and to eliminate partial, preconceived, or subjective views and attitudes.

In the essay, "The Person: Subject and Community," Wojtyla sought to identify the "special value" of community that corresponds to the person's fulfillment through act.[93] He argued that this special value is the *communio personarum*, or the "communion of persons." This communion takes place in interpersonal relationships as persons face one another in "I-thou" relationships.[94] The *I* and *thou* enable one another to develop by discovering the other and oneself in the other. The fullest experience of interpersonal community occurs when the *I* and *thou* reveal themselves and mutually affirm through word and act the dignity and transcendent value of the person.[95]

In the social dimension of the community, persons stand together in the pursuit of the common good, the good of society. The *I* and *thou* relationships of the interpersonal community become the *we* relationships in the social community as the *I* and the *thou* find their mutual relation in the common good, in accordance with the natural law. The core of the social community is this relation of many *I*'s to a common good.[96]

The implications of Wojtyla's use of the Boethian definition of human nature as "individual substance" is perhaps seen most clearly in his account of participation. Conceiving of humans as individuals means that participation is not a reality but a potential for individuals within society. This point is of vital importance for the later dialogue with Karl Barth, who grounded participation in human nature.

---

93. Wojtyla, "The Person: Subject and Community," in *Person and Community*, 219–63. See also Beigel's summary, *Faith and Social Justice in the Teaching of Pope John Paul II*, 25–28. Wojtyla adopts this language from Martin Buber, *I and Thou*.

94. Wojtyla, *PSC*, 240–44.

95. Ibid., 245–46.

96. Ibid., 247; and Beigel, *Faith and Social Justice in the Teaching of Pope John Paul II*, 27. Because this work is focusing upon the grounding of social ethics in the ontological aspect of personhood as the key point of dialogue, we will not be addressing John Paul's understanding of the common good in fuller detail. Hollenbach deals with such concerns as the notion of the common good impinges on issues of social justice and human rights in *The Common Good and Christian Ethics*. While exploring this notion in comparison with Barth would prove fruitful, it is not within the scope of this work to do so.

PART ONE—Karol Wojtyla/John Paul II

Conclusion

This chapter presented Wojtyla's account of justice in three parts: epistemology, theory, and praxis. It argued that Wojtyla's epistemological basis for justice was two-fold. On the one hand, he appealed to an interpretation of the Thomist metaphysical of being, which assumed the analogy of being in asserting that humans are capable of knowledge of justice through epistemic access to the normative order, or natural law. Through this appeal to natural law, Wojtyla could make knowledge of justice universal, something that all persons had access to through the norms that correspond to their natures. On the other hand, Wojtyla acknowledged that revealed norms also yield important information about justice, such as (a) the connection between justice and love and (b) deeper insight into human nature and dignity.

This chapter secondly described Wojtyla's account of justice. He used the personalist norm to argue that justice means treating persons in accordance with their nature. From a philosophical perspective human nature is rational and free in correspondence to God's being. In addition, revelation demonstrates that humans are dignified "beyond compare" (a) because of the acts of God in creation and salvation (b) and because of the corresponding human capacity for action and for transcendence. To treat another as just is to treat him or her with the dignity according with this nature.

Third, this chapter explored the nature of just human action. Wojtyla argued that persons are both subjects and objections of human action so that human action is self-determining. This self-determination is reaffirmed by Wojtyla's argument that human action is transcendent: it is determined by no one but the one who acts in freedom. This conception proved especially relevant to his context of social and political oppression because it offered persons hope and freedom from the despair that they may be determined by the negative aspects of their context. Wojtya wanted to account for the capacity of humans to free to act justly and courageously even in contexts, such as his own, where systemic dehumanization had reached new heights. Just action depends not upon one's experience of justice or injustice but upon one's capacity to act and to experience one's own just action as self-determining. This capacity is human greatness, Wojtyla believed.

While answering each of these three questions regarding justice, I sought to demonstrate throughout that Wojtyla's epistemology, his theory of justice, and his account of human potential for just action are fundamentally optimistic. As someone who lived within a context of oppression and suffering, Wojtyla appealed to that which he saw as the best in persons and in human potential. He wrote in a manner that sought to lift people up beyond their material contexts and toward discovering the dignity all humans so that they might treat others with dignity and create political and economic systems that maintains the value of the each person.

3

The Theological Basis for the Social Doctrine of Pope John Paul II

IN OCTOBER 1978, WOJTYLA BECAME THE FIRST POLISH BISHOP OF ROME, taking the name John Paul II.[1] He continued to write and to speak on the topic of justice yet with a new focus, a new authority, and an increasingly christocentric appeal. His concern about justice took on a focus that was more global in nature, as he addressed numerous social issues of the late twentieth century including new forms of ethnic violence and genocide, the battling political ideologies of Latin America, and problems of poverty and protectionism that emerged in a globalized market economy. While it is not within the scope of this book to examine his responses to each of these issues in detail, I will illustrate how he addressed justice issues from the same starting point: the personalist norm. Yet as his work became more theological, the criterion of "human dignity" (rather than "human nature") became more dominant in his thought.

Second, Wojtyla took on a new form of authority as John Paul II because he became the leader and key spokesperson of the worldwide Catholic Church. As a result, the assumptions with which one studies his work on justice must shift. On the one hand, his work often reflects a remarkable continuity with his thought as Wojtyla. Alasdair MacIntyre, commenting on *Veritatis Splendor*, wrote that "Any reader of Karol Wojtyla's major philosophical writings, from his doctoral dissertation onward, will recognize, both in the style of arguments and the nuances with which particular arguments are developed, a singular authorial presence in this text."[2] On the other hand, the contributions and influences of Vatican

---

1. This chapter and further chapters will abbreviate Pope John Paul II to John Paul or JPII.

2. MacIntyre, "*Veritatis Splendor* and the Theology of Natural Law," 73. See similar statements or arguments for the continuity of Wojtyla's thought in Conley, "The Philosophical Foundations of the Thought of JPII," 23–24; McNerney, *JPII*, 82–86.

officials and other writers must be taken into account. The influence of anonymous authors varies according to the work under discussion. For instance, the encyclicals *Fides et Ratio* and *Sollicitudo Rei Socialis* are generally acknowledged to have undergone more editorial reviews. One Vatican official reflected on the latter document that, "lots of people wanted to see their particular concerns addressed in the encyclical, and so the Pope tried to accommodate a good number of them at the expense of clarity and logic."[3] This reality inhibits us from knowing which ideas or developments of thought belong uniquely to John Paul II. Thus, this chapter has made two assumptions. First, we have focused on those areas of thought that demonstrate continuity with Wojtyla. These areas provide the strongest indicators for discerning the thought of John Paul II and any development in his own thought. Second, we have assumed that the works signed by and attributed to John Paul II are reflective of his own values and beliefs, even if not penned by him personally.

Third, his role as Pope shifted his emphasis from philosophy to theology. While he did write a few texts that were theological in nature as Wojtyla, he was primarily writing for a philosophical audience. His work as John Paul was predominantly theological in nature. In addition, he made a much more significant and consistent appeal to define human personhood in terms of Christology, he developed the theme of justice theologically, and he spelled out more clearly his beliefs regarding the impact of human sin upon a person's capacity to act justly. For this reason, this chapter will depict and assess John Paul's theological framework for justice in three parts. First, the question of epistemic access to justice will be addressed through a critical evaluation of the encyclical, *Fides et Ratio*. Second, his theological framework for justice and just action will be analyzed. The third section will draw out the implications for justice in the realms of politics and economics. Throughout the chapter, I will seek to demonstrate that John Paul held an optimistic view of the capacities of persons for knowing justice and for acting justly.

Knowing Justice: Faith and Reason

John Paul continued to maintain that the dignity of humans is deeply connected to their capacity to reason and to ascertain truth.[4] As we examined in the previous chapter, the doctrine of the *analogia entis* af-

---

3. Suro, "The Writing of an Encyclical," 159.
4. JPII, *God*, 54.

firms the human person as free and intelligent, with the capacity to know God, truth, and goodness. This doctrine finds its expression in John Paul's affirmation of the capacity for humanity to know God through reason. Although human sin has "impaired" the human capacity "by an aversion to the One who is the source and origin of truth,"[5] the power of human reason can ultimately be trusted to lead humans toward God.[6] He opposed the contemporary abandoning of the search for truth because it obscures this "true dignity of reason."[7]

John Paul explored the relation between faith and reason by examining the relation between theology and philosophy in his encyclical *Fides et Ratio*. He argued that the truth attained through natural reason by philosophy and the truth based upon faith in revelation are neither *identical* nor *mutually exclusive*. On the one hand, they are not *identical*: Philosophical knowledge depends upon sense perception and experience and it advances by the light of the intellect alone. According to John Paul, the human is capable of knowing God by reason alone. He said, "Alongside the 'I believe' [of faith] we find a certain 'I know.' This 'I know' concerns the existence of God and even, to a certain extent, his essence. This intellectual knowledge of God is systematically treated by a science called 'natural theology,' which is a philosophy of nature and springs from metaphysics, that is, the philosophy of being."[8] The quest for this order of knowledge arises from the desire within every human to know the truth and to understand the meaning of life.

Unlike philosophy, faith is based upon God's testimony in his self-revelation of salvation for the world. The Second Vatican Council defined faith as a "particular response on the part of mankind to God's revelation of himself."[9] The Constitution on Divine Revelation stated, "Before this faith can be exercised, man must have the grace of God to move and assist him; he must have the interior helps of the Holy Spirit, who moves the heart and converts it to God. . . . The same Holy Spirit constantly perfects faith by his gifts, so that Revelation may be more and profoundly understood."[10] Whereas reason is the human capacity to discern truth by natural means, faith is initiated by the grace and the self-revelation of God.

5. JPII, *FR*, 22.
6. Ibid., 56.
7. Ibid., 47.
8. JPII, *God,* 40.
9. JPII, *Sources,* 19.
10. JPII, *DV,* 5.

On the other hand, theology and philosophy are not *mutually exclusive*. John Paul wrote:

> The relationship between theology and philosophy is best construed as a circle. Theology's source and starting-point must always be the word of God revealed in history, while its final goal will be an understanding of that word which increates with each passing generation. Yet since God's word is Truth, the human search for truth—philosophy, pursued in keeping with its own rules[11]—can only help to understand God's word better. It is not just a question of theological discourse using this or that concept or element of a philosophical construct; what matters most is that the believer's reason use its powers of reflection in the search for truth which moves from the word of God towards a better understanding of it.[12]

The truth of revelation completes and perfects the truth attained through reason; and philosophy provides the thought-structures for the understanding of faith.[13] For example, moral theology requires a sound philosophical vision of human nature and society.[14]

One problem with John Paul's approach to faith and reason, especially in his encyclical, *Fides et Ratio*, is that, prior to any formal philosophizing, John Paul assumed certain norms that provided a reference point for measuring particular philosophical systems.[15] For example, he condemned fideism and radical traditionalism because they distrust reason's natural capacities. He condemned modern philosophy for a focus on human consciousness that "sundered" humans from the truth.[16] In addition, he condemned rationalism and ontologism for attributing to natural reason a knowledge, which only the light of faith could confer.[17]

---

11. Aquinas would characterize these elements: (1) the principle of contradiction, (2) the principle of finality, (3) the principle of causality, (4) human person as free and intelligent (5) who have the capacity to know God, truth, and goodness, and (6) fundamental moral norms. McInerny, "*Fides et Ratio*," 3.

12. JPII, *FR*, 73. Cf. JPII, *God*, 217: "Therefore, if methodical investigation within every branch of learning is carried out in a genuinely scientific manner and in accord with moral norms, it never truly conflicts with faith. For earthly matters and the concerns of faith derive from the same God."

13. JPII, *FR*, 77.

14. Ibid., 68.

15. Ibid., 4. In McInerny, "*Fides et Ratio*," 4.

16. JPII, *FR*, 5.

17. Ibid., 52.

He critiqued these systems based upon his philosophical commitment to a "core of philosophical insight within the history of thought as a whole."[18] He wrote,

> Consider, for example, the principles of non-contradiction, finality and causality, as well as the concept of the person as a free and intelligent subject, with the capacity to know God, truth and goodness. Consider as well certain fundamental moral norms which are shared by all. These are among the indications that, beyond different schools of thought, there exists a body of knowledge which may be judged a kind of spiritual heritage of humanity. It is as if we had come upon an implicit philosophy, as a result of which all feel that they possess these principles, albeit in a general and unreflective way. Precisely because it is shared in some measure by all, this knowledge should serve as a kind of reference-point for the different philosophical schools.[19]

In this manner, he set up the assumptions of Thomist metaphysics as "the knowledge" that should serve as a kind of "reference point" by which all philosophies might be judged.[20] Yet upon what basis may Thomistic metaphysics claim superiority over other philosophies? How does one know that *that particular* conception of reason may provide a foundation for judging other philosophical assumptions? In the areas where metaphysics and rationalism critique one another, upon what basis can John Paul claim that one is right and one is wrong? Did he make this claim upon the basis of previously assumed norms such as the principle of contradiction? Does this not lead to a circular argument that one may only find her way out of through the light of revelation?

With regard to his theory of justice, he believed that this epistemic basis and these moral norms had a universal appeal. Yet most contemporary theorists and many contemporary persons would critique such a view as naïve at best and hegemonic at worst. Certainly, this view demonstrates his extreme optimism regarding human capacity for knowledge about just norms.

A second critique from the "faith" perspective of Reformed Protestantism addresses the problem of sin. Alvin Plantinga wrote, "What the Catholic view neglects here, according to this Reformed rejoinder, is the fact that non-Christian philosophy is not merely handicapped by

18. Ibid., 4.
19. Ibid.
20. Ibid.

the 'inherent weakness of human reason'; it is rather that philosophers, like humanity in general, are *fallen*, and in need of *conversion*."[21] According to reformed doctrine, the fall both separated humans from God and destroyed their capacity to gain knowledge about God apart from God's revelation. John Paul referred to the effect of sin upon reason as an impairment caused by the human's aversion to God. "All men and women were caught up in this primal disobedience, which so wounded reason that from then on its path to full truth would be strewn with obstacles."[22] The ascent of the creature to God made possible through "the careful and persevering reading of the witness of created things" by human reason has become more difficult.[23] Plantinga critiqued *Faith and Reason* for underestimating the place of sin, apostasy, and the rejection of Christian truth by non-Christian philosophers. He explained,

> It isn't that the result of sin, with respect to our intellectual capacities, is just that we lost a supernatural addition to our natural faculties, those natural faculties themselves functioning more or less as before. It is rather that (a) our natural faculties themselves suffered substantially from the results of sin, so that our ability to know ourselves, others, and God has been damaged, and (b) by virtue of our corruption, we are inclined to set ourselves against God.[24]

Plantinga also critiqued John Paul's optimism regarding the possibilities for philosophical inquiry. He cited for evidence the incompatibility of most of modern philosophy with Christian theism. According to Plantinga, these philosophies are not incomplete approximations to Christian truth; they are antithetical to it.[25]

In his critique Plantinga did not acknowledge that John Paul addressed this incompatibility in his discussion of the warning of Paul to the Colossians: "See to it that no one takes you captive through philosophy and empty deceit, according to human tradition, according to the elemental spirits of the universe and not according to Christ."[26] John Paul argued that these words are appropriate when applied to esoteric superstition that

21. Plantinga, "Philosophers respond to Pope JPII's Encyclical Letter, *Fides et Ratio*," 32.
22. JPII, *FR*, 22.
23. JPII, *God*, 43.
24. Plantinga, "*Fides*," 36.
25. Ibid., 35.
26. JPII, *FR*, 37.

is widespread today. He agreed that one must "sound the alarm when confronted with a cultural perspective that sought to subordinate the truth of Revelation to the interpretation of the philosophers"[27] and he did critique systems of thought, which are opposed to God, such as Nihilism. Where John Paul differed from Plantinga was in his assumption that humans have the capacity to know God and truth and the effect that this assumption has on his approach to anti-Christian philosophies such as Marxism. Yet Plantinga cited an important difference between Protestant and Catholic theology that is based on differing interpretations of the fall and the capacity or incapacity of humanity that resulted. Later chapters will return to this difference in comparing his thought with that of Barth.

In conclusion, although *Fides et Ratio* was heavily edited, it continued to affirm John Paul's theory of rationality that informs his theory of justice. For John Paul, the relation between faith and reason is grounded in a thoroughly Thomist optimism about the capacity of human persons to gain access to transcendent truth and to the normative order. As discussed in chapter two of this work, a basis for this optimism is the notion of the *analogia entis*, in which humans can know truth about God through the correspondence of their rationality, without his act of self-revelation.

Theological Basis for Justice: God, Creation, and Moral Law

As mentioned in the introduction, John Paul's theory of justice developed a decidedly theological orientation during his years in the papacy yet many of the same themes remain: God as the author of moral law, the dignity of the human rationality and being, the relation of justice and love, and the dignity of human action. However, we also see new developments emerge within those themes, especially in his development of the Christological implications for humanity and for justice. This examination of John Paul's theological framework for justice will reflect the three-part structure of his catechesis on the Nicene Creed, given at his general audiences from 1985 to 1991. These talks were published as *God, Father and Creator; Jesus, Son and Savior;* and *The Spirit, Giver of Life and Love*. It will also include relevant material from encyclicals and other writings during his papacy.

---

27. Ibid.

God the Creator

In his catechesis on *God, Father and Creator*, John Paul examined the first article of the creed, "I believe in God the Father almighty, creator . . ." This article affirms belief that God has made himself known to human persons; he is a personal God who has "revealed himself and made known the hidden purpose of his will."[28] This belief in God expresses the conviction that *God exists*, for only one who really exists can reveal himself.[29] Echoing his Thomist affirmations as Wojtyla, John Paul said, "*He who is* expresses the very essence of God, which is self-existence, subsistent Being."[30] Because he is subsisting being (*esse subsistens*), God cannot not be, he is necessary being. The things that receive existence from God are contingent beings.[31] As the absolute fullness of Being, God is completely transcendent in regard to the world; he is the God of infinite majesty before whom humans bend in humility and adoration.[32]

By emphasizing God's transcendence, John Paul sought to build a basis both for the need of God's self-revelation in scripture and for the belief that humans can never fully know God. He said,

> The essence of God—which is the divinity—is found to be outside every category of genus and species which we use in our definitions. So the essence of God cannot be enclosed in any definition. If, in our thought about God, with the category of "being," we use the analogy of being [*analogia entis*], with this we bring out the "non-resemblance" much more than the resemblance. We bring out the incomparability much more than the comparability of God with the creature.[33]

While this quotation may sound like it undermines the argument we have made thus far regarding the *analogia entis* as a basis of moral knowledge, I suggest that it does not. Rather, he still believed that there *is* resemblance and that this resemblance *does* create a means to real moral knowledge, as demonstrated in the section below on the image of God.

---

28. JPII, *God*, 110. *DV*, 2.

29. The existence of God is accessible to human reason because God makes himself visible through his works. The Psalmist writes, "The heavens proclaim the glory of God" (Ps 19:2). In addition, the existence of God through faith has a rational character that reason can investigate. JPII, *God*, 114–16.

30. Ibid., 117.

31. Ibid., 120.

32. Ibid., 121.

33. Ibid., 123.

However, John Paul's emphasis here on the otherness of God and the non-resemblance of the creature sought to create the need for revelation through scripture. In other words, reason works but it is not completely sufficient for knowledge of God. In fact, John Paul would say, God is so transcendence that *nothing* is sufficient for knowing him fully. He wrote, "The human intellect, inasmuch as it possesses a certain idea of God, and although it has been elevated significantly, through the revelation of the Old and New Covenant, to a deeper and more complete knowledge of his mystery, is unable to comprehend God adequately and exhaustively."[34]

Reflecting his affirmations in *Fides et Ratio* and his beliefs as Wojtyla, John Paul asserted two levels of knowledge of which humans are capable: that which is known by the intellect through nature and that which is known through God's revelation in scripture and in Christ. As moral knowledge, these two levels corresponded, respectively, to natural norms and to revealed norms. The third level of knowledge, of which no human is capable, is the full comprehension of God. While John Paul affirmed this belief in absolute transcendence, it did not impact his ethical method as the emphasis on transcendence shaped Barth's method, because John Paul continued to maintain some level of continuity between God and creation that was grounded in creation. In his more philosophically-oriented work, the *analogia entis* served that function. In his theological work, the *imago Dei* served that function, as seen in the following section.

The Imago Dei *and the Moral Law*

God's creation called all things into existence from nothing, including creatures. Among creatures, humans have special dignity because they are created in the image of God. The *imago Dei* is the basis of human morality.[35] John Paul explained,

> Man is created for immortality. He does not cease to be the image of God after sin, even though he is subjected to death. He bears in himself the reflection of God's power, which is manifested especially in the faculty of intelligence and free will. Man is an autonomous subject. He is the source of his own actions,

---

34. Ibid., 123.

35. JPII, *DV*, 36. See also *VS*, 13; and *God*, 224. Essential to the elements of the image of God in humanity are "the capacity for self-knowledge, the experience of man's own being in the world, the need to fill his solitude, his dependence on God." JPII, *God*, 223.

> while maintaining the characteristics of dependence upon God, the Creator (ontological contingency).[36]

Thus, for John Paul, the *imago* is intrinsically significant to his account of justice, both in giving humans the faculty to know justice and in giving humans the capacity to act freely in accordance with justice. Each human has within herself an essential relation to truth that determines her character as a transcendent being. She is capable of discernment between truth and non-truth, between the truth of justice and the non-truth of injustice.

In addition, the human has freedom of her will. John Paul said, "Human acts bear within themselves the sign of self-determination of will and of choice. The whole sphere of morality derives from this. Man is capable of choosing between good and evil, sustained in this by the voice of conscience, which impels him to good and restrains him from evil."[37] Thus the divine image inscribes both freedom and truth in the structure of the human person and from these aspects of humanity, the sphere of morality is derived.

Did John Paul's notion of freedom mean that a human person determines what is morally right or wrong according to "his own counsel?" He rejected such a possibility by grounding the moral law in God's nature.[38] He explained,

> The teaching of the [Second Vatican] Council emphasizes, on the one hand, *the role of human reason* in discovering and applying the moral law: the moral life calls for that creativity and originality typical of the person, the source and cause of his own deliberate acts. On the other hand, reason draws its own truth and authority from the eternal law, which is none other than divine wisdom itself. At the heart of the moral life we thus find the

---

36. JPII, *God*, 223.

37. Ibid., 232–33. In his discussion of truth and freedom in *Veritatis Splendor*, John Paul argued that there could be no morality without freedom. "Genuine freedom is an outstanding manifestation of the divine image in man. For God willed to leave man 'in the power of his counsel' (Sir 15:14) so that he would seek his Creator of his own accord and would freely arrive at full and blessed perfection by cleaving to God." *GS*, 17; *VS*, 34

38. JPII, *DV*, 36. Cf. JPII, *VS*, 35, "Revelation teaches that the power to decide what is good and what is evil does not belong to man, but to God alone. The man is certainly free, inasmuch as he can understand and accept God's commands. And he possesses an extremely far-reaching freedom, since he can eat 'of every tree of the garden.' But his freedom is not unlimited: it must halt before the 'tree of the knowledge of good and evil,' for it is called to accept the moral law given by God. In fact, human freedom finds its authentic and complete fulfillment precisely in the acceptance of that law."

principle of a "rightful autonomy" of man, the personal subject of his actions. *The moral law has its origin in God and always finds its source in him*:[39] at the same time, by virtue of natural reason, which derives from divine wisdom, it is *a properly human law*. Indeed, as we have seen, the natural law "is nothing other than the light of understanding infused in us by God, whereby we understand what must be done and what must be avoided. God gave this light and this law to man at creation."[40]

This passage is important for a few reasons. First, in it John Paul attempted to articulate the "rightful autonomy" of man, who discerns the moral law within his very nature. Elsewhere he explained, "The natural moral law expresses and lays down the purposes, rights, and duties which are based upon the bodily and spiritual nature of the human person. Therefore this law cannot be thought of as simply a set of norms on the biological level, rather it must be defined as the rational order whereby man is called by his Creator to direct and regulate his life and actions and in particular to make use of his own body."[41]

Second, he grounded natural law in terms that are universal, for all persons are created with this light of understanding and can discern the "purposes, rights and duties" that are naturally part of human life. So what does this mean for John Paul's account of justice? It means that all persons have epistemic access to the just norms of God through their creation. In this way, justice is grounded in both the eternal law of God and also in human nature. To act justly means to act in accordance with this nature, as the subject of one's actions. This description here adds one piece to his account, because moral norms not only mean treating others in accordance with their nature but also acting in accordance with one's own nature. Social justice, by implication, means to act in obedience to the natural law, in accordance with human nature as created by God.

In sum, John Paul articulated the doctrine of God and of creation in such a manner that it emphasized the continuity between God and the creature that is grounded God's creation of humans in the *imago Dei*.

---

39. JPII, *God*, 190–91. Cf. Aquinas, *Summa Theologica* I-II, q. 93, a. 1.

40. JPII, *VS*, 40, quoting from Thomas Aquinas, *In Duo Praecepta Caritatis et in Decem Legis Praecepta. Prologus: Opuscula Theologica*, II, No. 1129, 245. John Paul argues that this law does not imply moral heteronomy because (1) the norms are not imposed but infused in his being and (2) each human is held responsible for his own self-determination. The human's genuine moral autonomy means the acceptance of this moral law and obedience to it.

41. JPII, *VS*, 50.

Specifically, that continuity is located in the human reason that reflects God's image. Through human reason, all humans gain access to moral law and to the just norms of God at some level. The fact that all persons have access to these moral norms not only affirms their universal scope but also the universality of human dignity. Dignity arises from the fact that humans are created by God and finds confirmation in this capacity for reason.

The Theological Basis for Justice: Raised to a Dignity Beyond Compare in Jesus Christ

According to John Paul, the *imago Dei* reveals the intrinsic dignity of humanity and the source of natural law. Yet he believed that the full nature of human persons and the ethic to which they are called is revealed more completely in the incarnation, death, and resurrection of Jesus Christ. Jesus Christ, the son of God, became a human person of history. The incarnation of the son of God established human dignity; his mission of salvation affirmed human dignity; and the redemption wrought by him brought humans into a familial relation with God, as daughters and sons, participants in the sonship of Jesus Christ and people who live in the likeness of Christ's human model. This second section will explore these implications of the person and work of Christ for John Paul's anthropology. First, however, we examine the problem that necessitated Christ's life and work and that perpetuates acts of injustice: the problem of human sin.

The Mystery of Sin

According to John Paul, "sin robs man, in various ways, of the decisive element of his true dignity—that of the dignity and likeness of God."[42] In the visible world, each human received his existence as a gift—"as the 'image and likeness of God,' a rational being, endowed with intellect and will."[43] The human person was originally innocent and righteous because he possessed sanctifying grace and supernatural gifts from God.[44] From the beginning, the Creator revealed himself as (1) God of the covenant, of friendship and happiness and (2) the source of good and the source of

---

42. JPII, *Jesus*, 69.
43. Ibid., 23.
44. Ibid., 24.

distinguishing between good and evil.[45] However, the human, by his free choice, rejected the truth of God's command; in pride he rebelled against the truth of his existence, the subordination of creature to Creator; by yielding to the temptation to be "like God," the human became slave and accomplice to rebellious spirits.[46] John Paul explained the concept of sin as the choice of self over God, "*contemptus Dei*, rejection of God, contempt of God, hatred of everything connected with God or that comes from God."[47]

Six points in John Paul's doctrine of sin are especially important to his account of justice:

1. *The Universality of Sin in Human History.* Through the original sin of Adam, sin "invaded" the whole world and infected all of humanity.[48] Injustice arose from the disobedience of humanity. He wrote, "Man first became unjust when he became disobedient to the creator."[49]

2. *The Hereditary Character of Sin.* This sinful situation is repeated from generation to generation in personal and social life. "The sin of Adam, which by origin is unique and transmitted by generation and not by way of imitation is present in all and proper to each."[50] By implication, the sin and the situation of injustice is present in every generation.

3. *The Interiority of Sin.* The root of sin is in the interior of the person, in his conscience and in his heart. "Examining his heart, man finds that he has inclination toward evil too, and is engulfed by manifold ills which cannot come from his good Creator."[51] By implication, injustice is not merely an outward act or a historical situation, but it is rooted in the hearts of humans as an inclination that does not come from God.

---

45. Ibid., 25; Gen 2:16–17. John Paul wrote, "Man in the beginning (in the state of original justice) spoke to the Creator with friendship and confidence in the whole truth of his spiritual—corporeal being, created in God's image. But now he has lost the basis of that friendship and covenant. He has lost the grace of sharing in God's life the good of belonging to him in the holiness of the original relationship of subordination and sonship." Ibid., 40.

46. Ibid., 30–31.

47. Ibid., 31.

48. Ibid., 33.

49. JPII, *SC*, 84.

50. JPII, *Jesus*, 45.

51. Ibid., 36; quoted from Second Vatican Council, *GS*, 13.

4. *The Human Person's Loss of Sanctifying Grace.* According to John Paul, "Original sin in Adam's descendants does not have the character of personal guilt."[52] Rather, through the privation of sanctifying grace, human nature has been diverted from its supernatural end, and the holiness and justice in which they were constituted from the beginning was lost.[53] In other words, the holiness and justice that was originally part of human nature (the end toward which humans were going) has been lost.

5. *Implications of Sin for Human Morality.* The deterioration of the human's physical nature is paralleled by the deterioration of his spiritual faculties, the darkening of the intellect's capacity to know truth and the weakening of free will to choose the good. John Paul explained:

> Even after original sin, man can know by his intellect the fundamental natural and religious truths, and the moral principles. He can also perform good works. One should therefore speak rather of a darkening of the intellect and of a weakening of the will, of "wounds" of the spiritual and sensitive faculties, and not of a loss of their essential capacities, even in relation to the knowledge and love of God.[54]

According to John Paul, this doctrine, affirmed by the Council of Trent, opposes the Lutheran account of sin. "The Council of Trent teaches that as a result of Adam's sin, man has not lost free will. He can therefore perform acts which have an authentic moral value—good or evil."[55] Why, then, was Christ necessary? John Paul explained "Without Christ's help, fallen man is incapable of directing himself to the supernatural goods which constitute his total fulfilment and salvation."[56]

Because of the original sin, human nature bears a "spark of sin," or "concupiscence" that inclines the human person to evil and is the source of the inclination to personal (or actual) sin. John Paul explained that the "spark" of sin "continues in man justified by Christ, therefore even after holy Baptism."[57] The contrast between the moral

---

52. JPII, *Jesus*, 45.
53. Ibid., 41, 45.
54. Ibid., 51–52.
55. Ibid., 52.
56. Ibid.
57. Ibid.

dimension of the Catholic doctrine of sin and Barth's Protestant interpretation will be compared in greater detail in the final chapter. Of most importance for our present purposes is John Paul's emphasis that after the fall, humans retain free will and the capacity to know moral norms, for sin is "a conscious and free act." Characterizing humans as sinful may sound negative. Yet in comparison with the reformed doctrine of total deprativity, John Paul's doctrine of sin is relatively optimistic. He believed that even sinful humans have the capacity to know justice and to act justly.

6. *The Social Dimension of Sin*. Because of the "spark" left by original sin, many personal sins are committed. These form an "environment of sin" that creates conditions for new sins and attracts other humans to sin. Human initiatives, institutions, cultures, and social environments are also "infected" by this sin.[58] For John Paul, this social dimension ofsin is the source of unjust social structures and systems.

The Identity of Christ: True God and True Human

John Paul located the solution to the problem of sin in Jesus Christ, the Son and the Savior. In order to interpret his work of salvation from sin, John Paul said, one must first seek to understand his identity. As the true God and the true human, Christ revealed that human beings have a dignity beyond compare.

According to John Paul, the incarnation reveals the great dignity of humans. In affirmation of the Nicene Creed, John Paul believed that Christ recognized himself as the true God and the true Man. First, he proclaimed himself to be God.[59] John confirmed his full divinity in the prologue to his gospel in which he declared Christ's divine pre-existence.[60] As God the Son who is con-substantial with the Father and the Holy Spirit, Christ claimed divine attributes such as truth, life, redeemer, judge, lawgiver, object of faith, and forgiver of sins.[61]

Second, Jesus is also the true human. Through incarnation, he took flesh and human nature. He grew and became strong, suffered fatigue, torture, and death, and he returned to life in his own human body through

---

58. Ibid., 64.
59. See the "I am" statements of John 8, Matt 28, and Luke 24; JPII, *Jesus*, 212.
60. Ibid.
61. Ibid., 216–43.

the resurrection. As *Gaudium et Spes* confirmed, "By his Incarnation the Son of God has united himself in some fashion with every human person. He worked with human hands, he thought with a human mind, acted by human choice and loved with a human heart. Born of the Virgin Mary, he has truly been made one of us, like us in all things except sin."[62]

The incarnation reveals the great dignity of human persons for two reasons. First, his assumption of humanity (rather than his absorption of humanity) united Christ with each human, raising humans to "a dignity beyond compare."[63] Second, though he was without sin, Jesus sought the company of sinners because of his love for humanity and his mission to bring salvation to the world. He voluntarily emptied himself so that he could restore humans to their original dignity.[64] John Paul expounded this self-giving love further in his discussion of Christ's work of redemption.

The Mystery of Redemption

The redemption wrought by Christ restored dignity to humanity because it freed humans from the destructive nature of sin and restored meaning to human life, as life with God.[65] John Paul named two dimensions of redemption: divine and human. The divine aspect focuses upon the depth of God's love and mercy expressed in the sacrifice of the Son. This dimension is of importance for our study because it reveals the relation between John Paul's theory of redemption for his account of justice. The second dimension, the human dimension, echoes Wojtyla's early personalist interests because it deals with human assimilation of this new reality.[66] The human discovers her dignity by realizing her unity with God in Christ. We now turn to examine these two dimensions.

The Divine Dimension of Redemption and the Norms of Justice

In his encyclical, *Dives in Misericordia* [*Rich in Mercy*], John Paul described the meaning of Christ's redemption in terms of mercy and of justice. In this encyclical, John Paul utilized the term "justice" to describe

---

62. Second Vatican Council, *GS*, 22; JPII, *Jesus*, 300.
63. JPII, *DV*, 8.
64. JPII, *Jesus*, 310–12.
65. JPII, *DV*, 10.
66. Beigel, 40; JPII, *DM*, 7.

three differing forms of justice, only two of which are legitimate: natural justice and revealed justice. In contrast to these two legitimate forms, there is what John Paul called an "alleged justice," in which persons begin with the idea of justice or make claims that their actions are just, when they are actually distorting justice. "In the name of an alleged justice (for example, historical justice or class justice) the neighbor is sometimes destroyed, killed, deprived of justice or stripped of fundamental human rights."[67] He included within this form of justice the retributive justice represented in the attitude of Christ's listeners when Christ critiqued the saying, "An eye for an eye and a tooth for a tooth."[68] When retributive justice is destructive of human persons, John Paul rejected it as an abuse of the idea of justice. Thus, this form of "justice" is no justice at all.

Natural Norm of Justice

The first legitimate type of justice is the *natural norm of justice*, which promotes harmony by establishing equality between persons.[69] This natural norm is accessible to all humans through reason. It appears to correspond to natural law, for John Paul called it "objective justice." The equality it promotes is "limited to the realm of objective and extrinsic goods."[70] This norm of justice provides the basis for claims to rights or the loss of rights claims. For example, in the story of the prodigal son, when the son sinned against his father by leaving and by squandering his inheritance, the son lost his right to sonship: "He realizes that he no longer has any right except to be an employee in his father's house. His decision is taken in full consciousness of what he has deserved and of what he can still have a right to in accordance with the norms of justice."[71] This norm of justice is retributive as well. It is not destructive of the son but it does "demand" just payment (earned as a employee) in order for the son to be restored to sonship.[72]

---

67. JPII, *DM*, 12.
68. Ibid.
69. Ibid.
70. Ibid., 14.
71. Ibid., 5.
72. Ibid.

Revealed Justice

The second legitimate form is *revealed justice*. One discovers this form of justice in the Old Testament as well as in the revelation of Christ. John Paul suggested that the Old Testament taught that, "although justice is an authentic virtue in man, and in God signifies transcendent perfection nevertheless love is 'greater' than justice."[73] Love conditions justice. The superiority of love over justice is revealed throughout the Old Testament in God's acts of mercy. Rather than punishing or abhorring his people, God continued to demonstrate a "fidelity to himself," so that for the psalmists and the prophets, "justice ended up by meaning the salvation accomplished by the Lord and His mercy."[74]

This form of justice took on new significance in the person of Christ. In the cross of Christ, John Paul said, "absolute justice is expressed, for Christ undergoes the passion and cross because of the sins of humanity. This constitutes even a 'superabundance' of justice, for the sins of man are 'compensated for' by the sacrifice of the Man-God." He explained further, "Divine justice revealed in the cross of Christ is 'to God's measure,' because it springs from love and is accomplished in love, producing he fruits of salvation."[75] In other words, Christ revealed that God's justice always involves love. According to this passage, God's justice also required compensation. In other words, this passage employed the satisfaction theory of atonement, in which human sin is seen as a moral injustice that was made right, or satisfied, by the death of Christ.

What does this revealed form of justice that God extended to humans mean for justice within human relations? First, it means that the first and second forms of justice are "not enough" if they are missing love, for love must be the source of justice.[76] Thus, such forms of justice must be "corrected" by love.[77] Social relationship demand not only justice, which brings about equality; mercy must also be a part, for mercy establishes the bond between people. Second, restorative justice means that "the fundamental structure of justice always enters into the sphere of mercy. Mercy, however, has the power to confer on justice a new content, which is expressed most simply and fully in forgiveness."[78] In other words, the

---

73. Ibid., 4.
74. Ibid., and n52.
75. Ibid., 7.
76. Ibid., 12.
77. Ibid., 14.
78. Ibid.

revealed norm of justice finds its sources in love and mercy and it is expressed in forgiveness. In this manner, the revealed norm of justice makes reconciliation between persons a true possibility.

Does this mean that the objective norms of justice are cancelled out? Does revealed justice mean that perpetrators are simply forgiven? John Paul answered in the negative. "Reparation for evil and scandal, compensation for injury, and satisfaction for insult are conditions for forgiveness."[79] I interpret this to mean that in order for forgiveness to take place, reparation is a condition. If reparation does not take place, then there is no forgiveness. In the case God's mercy, the sacrifice of the God-man "compensated for" objective justice. Yet in the case of human relations, John Paul seemed to indicate that compensation must be supplied before the perpetrator can be forgiven. Forgiveness remains dependent upon the perpetrator.

Yet if this is the requirement, then how can solidarity, to which John Paul called persons, ever be a reality? In *Solicitudo Rei Socialis* he wrote the following:

> Solidarity is undoubtedly a Christian virtue. . . . In the light of faith, solidarity seeks to go beyond itself, to take on the specifically Christian dimension of total gratuity, forgiveness and reconciliation. One's neighbor is then not only a human being with his or her own rights and a fundamental equality with everyone else, but becomes the living image of God the Father, redeemed by the blood of Jesus Christ and placed under the permanent action of the Holy Spirit. One's neighbor must therefore be loved, even if an enemy, with the same love with which the Lord loves him or her; and for that person's sake one must be ready for sacrifice, even the ultimate one: to lay down one's life for the brethren (cf. 1 Jn 3:16).[80]

He called for solidarity through forgiveness, yet if forgiveness is dependent upon reparation by the perpetrator and he refuses, then solidarity becomes a mute issue. It simply is not possible. How can one lay down one's life for an unforgiven enemy? How can the value of an unforgiven enemy really be affirmed? The psychological conflict is too great. If one wants to appeal for solidarity, as John Paul did, the choice to forgive must rest in the hands of the victim; it should not be dependent upon the satisfying of objective justice, otherwise the victim remains subject to the decision of the perpetrator. The victim should be able to choose forgiveness and

---

79. Ibid.
80. JPII, *SRS*, 40.

mercy in accordance with her own character, analogous to God's choice to have mercy in accordance with his character.

In a later work, John Paul appeared to have shifted his conceptions of redemption and justice away from the satisfaction theory and toward a theory that would better account for his call to human solidarity. He reinterpreted the cross of Christ:

> What confers on substitution its redemptive value is not the material fact that an innocent person has suffered the chastisement deserved by the guilty and that justice has thus in some way been satisfied (in such a case one should speak rather of a grave injustice). The redemptive value comes instead from the fact that the innocent Jesus, out of pure love, entered into solidarity with the guilty and thus transformed their situation from within.[81]

The satisfaction theory of atonement demands compensation (such as the sacrifice of the God-man or in the human realm, reparation and repentance) in order for forgiveness to be extended and value to be affirmed. This theory was the source of the dilemma of human forgiveness that was just noted. In contrast, this alternate theory of solidarity does not demand reparation. Rather, God's entering into solidarity with the guilty affirms their value and transforms them from within, overcoming in himself "every negation and contrariety linked with human sin in every dimension—interior and historical—in which this sin has weighed on the relationship of man with God."[82] In this manner, love conditions justice and justice serves love.

Interpreting redemption in terms of solidarity rather than the satisfaction of objective norms of justice also demonstrates a better continuity with John Paul's account of the revelation of justice in *Dives in Misericordia*.

---

81. He would have said this sometime in the late 1980s. JPII, *Jesus*, 445. Cf. JPII, *RH*, 9. "He it was, and he alone, who satisfied the Father's eternal love, that fatherhood that from the beginning found expression in creating the world, giving man all the riches of creation, and making him 'little less than God,' in that he was created 'in the image and after the likeness of God.' He and he alone also satisfied that fatherhood of God and that love which man in a way rejected by breaking the first Covenant and the later covenants that God 'again and again offered to man.' The redemption of the world—this tremendous mystery of love in which creation is renewed—is, at its deepest root, the fullness of justice in a human Heart—the Heart of the First-born Son—in order that it may become justice in the hearts of many human beings, predestined from eternity in the Firstborn Son to be children of God and called to grace, called to love."

82. JPII, *Jesus*, 446.

Why he would have described it in terms of satisfaction in that same text is difficult to discern. Perhaps because it was one of his earliest theological encyclicals, he had not yet worked out a theory of atonement that corresponded with his revealed norm of justice. Or perhaps his affirmation of natural norms of justice (his second theory of justice) made the satisfaction theory seem necessary. Or perhaps the insertion of satisfaction theory was the influence of one of his "anonymous" authors. Despite the reason for this problem, his later theory provides a superior basis for his interpretation of the Old and New Testament conceptions of mercy and justice.

As already mentioned, John Paul interpreted the Old Testament justice of God as "fidelity to himself."[83] In other words, when the people of Israel sin, God's juridical obligation to his people ceases. The people cannot lay claim to him because they have broken their side of the covenant. What they can and did hope for was *hesed* ["grace" or "love"] because God's justice was grounded in his love and his personhood. His very acts of mercy in the Old Testament demonstrate that his justice was *not* grounded in objective legal agreements that demanded satisfaction before forgiveness could be extended. John Paul suggested that this means that love overcomes justice.

John Paul interpreted the story of the prodigal son along similar lines. When the son sought to return to the father's house as a slave, he recognized that, in accordance with the norms of justice, he no longer had any right as a son, but that his father would receive him as a servant. According to the norms of justice, he could make no claims upon the father.[84] However, when the son returned home, the father's joy indicated that he had already extended forgiveness before any reparations had been made. John Paul attributed this response to the "father's fidelity to himself—a trait already known by the Old Testament term *hesed*."[85] In other words, the response of the father demonstrated a continuity with God's acts of mercy in the Old Testament. Likewise, that response paralleled the substitutionary theory of redemption in which the human is transformed from within. He wrote:

> Mercy—as Christ presented it in the parable of the prodigal son—has the interior form of the love that in the New Testament is called *agape*. This love is able to reach down to every

83. JPII, *DM*, n52.
84. Ibid., 5.
85. Ibid., 6.

prodigal son, to every human misery, and above all to every form of moral misery, to sin. When this happens, the person who is the object of mercy does not feel humiliated, but rather found again and "restored to value."[86]

In other words, satisfaction is not demanded in order for salvation to take place. Rather, John Paul described salvation, in terms of love. He quoted Aquinas, "In this way [of the cross] man knows how much God loves him, and man on his part is induced to love him in return; in this love consists the perfection of human salvation."[87] In contrast with the satisfaction theory, solidarity creates an inner bond of love that affirms the dignity of the offender. It "restores to value, promotes and draws good from all the forms of evil existing in the world an in man."[88]

When working from this apparently revised theory of atonement, John Paul's call for solidarity makes sense, because it is modeled after the solidarity that Christ revealed in the cross. It does not require that the natural norms of justice be satisfied for a person to act in solidarity, love, and forgiveness. For instance, it makes possible the acts of "Brother Andrew," the character in Wojtyla's play, who—when suffering in an unjust state—chose "the greater freedom" of solidarity with the poor rather than exacting justice from his oppressor through revolt.[89]

Because Christ has given his life in love for humans, humans are called to participate in this divine life by giving of themselves to God.[90] For instance, in the same way that Christ showed mercy and humans obtained the mercy of Christ, humans also give mercy back to Christ in the "wonderful exchange." For Christ said, "As you did it to one of the least of these . . . you did it to me."[91] John Paul challenges, "Could man's dignity be more highly respected and ennobled, for, in obtaining mercy, He is in a sense the one who at the same time 'shows mercy'?"[92]

In sum, the theory of redemption emphasizing solidarity creates a more consistent theological basis for the revealed norm of justice that Wojtyla sought to affirm. God's acts of mercy in the Old Testament and in Christ reveal that (a) justice must be conditioned by love and (b) justice

86. Ibid.
87. JPII, *Jesus*, 442. Quotation from Aquinas, *Summa Theol.* III, q. 46, a. 3.
88. JPII, *DM*, 6.
89. Wojtyla, *Collected Plays*, 266. Cf. chapter 1 of this work.
90. JPII, *DM*, 7.
91. Ibid., 8. From Matt 25:40.
92. Ibid.

is expressed most fully in forgiveness—in the restoration of human relations. Justice re-establishes equality on the material level and mercy makes possible the human bonds of brotherhood that affirm the dignity of all persons. Christian mercy is "the most perfect incarnation of justice."[93]

Natural vs. Revealed Norms of Justice

Yet moving to this theory of redemption does not solve all of apparent inconsistencies in John Paul's thought. In fact, it highlights one of the major issues in his account of justice: the uneasy relation between natural norms (the first type of justice) and revealed norms (the second type of justice). In practice, they articulate two different divine justices: one primarily retributive and one primarily restorative. This fact leaves one wondering how both can be right. In addition, they fail to account for these differences: Why is love only a revealed aspect of justice? If the objective norms are supposed to be based upon God's eternal law and accessible to human reason, then why does John Paul's description of the normative law of justice lack the vital connection with the command to love, which is the most fundamental command of the eternal law? He argued that the Old and New Testaments reveal that love is the source of justice. If reason really can tell us something about God and God's most basic essence and act is love, then how did reason miss it? How did reason not take this aspect of the being of God into account when discerning the norm of justice? Is John Paul's "objective order" merely a projection of human ideals? These are the sorts of challenges posed by his differentiation between the natural norms and revealed norms.

The Human Dimension of Redemption

Having examined what he called the divine dimension of justice, John Paul then expounds the human dimension. In the mystery of redemption, "man finds again the greatness, dignity, and value that belong to his humanity," the human person becomes "newly 'expressed' and in a way, is newly created" because she becomes one with Christ.[94] As the human draws near to Christ, she assimilates the reality of the incarnation and redemption and she becomes amazed in adoration of God and deep wonder

---

93. Ibid., 14.
94. JPII, *RH*, 10.

at his humanity.⁹⁵ This amazement expresses the certainty of faith and it mysteriously gives life to the human as she recognises how precious and valuable she is, that God would give himself for human persons. John Paul explained, "The Redemption that took place through Christ has definitively restored his dignity to man and given back meaning to his life in the world, a meaning that was lost to a considerable extent because of sin."⁹⁶ Therefore, by revealing the dignity of the human in this new way, Christ reveals man to himself.

Through his incarnation and redemption, Christ has united himself with each person. God has chosen humans from eternity and destined all humans for grace. The church is responsible to display the union with Christ by living in unity and to proclaim the mystery of Christ, "in revealing the divine dimension and also the human dimension of the redemption, and in struggling with unweariyingly perseverance for the dignity that each human being has reached and can continually reach in Christ."⁹⁷ The church embraces this struggle by sharing in Christ's triple mission, his triple office of prophet, priest, and king.

As sharers in the mission of the *prophet* Christ, believers serve divine truth in the church and its proclamation in the world. The prophetic role of the church must be carried out in faith with complete fidelity to the truth of God.⁹⁸ Through this truth, persons learn to mature in love and justice as well as their sense of responsibility for this truth.⁹⁹ In his discussion of the *priestly* mission, John Paul emphasised the Eucharist and Penance through which human unite themselves with Christ and grow to spiritual maturity and unity with all Christians.¹⁰⁰

Finally, John Paul located the service aspect of the Christian life in participation in the *kingly* office of Christ. In his kingly office, Christ announced and established the kingdom of God. John Paul explained that with his "'obedience unto death,'"¹⁰¹ Jesus began a new phase of the economy of salvation, whose process will end when God will be 'all in

---

95. The "amazement" regarding incarnation stems from the fact that human nature was assumed by Christ and thus "has been raised to a dignity beyond compare," *RH*, 8.

96. Ibid., 10.

97. Ibid., 11.

98. He describes faith as "a specific supernatural virtue which is infused into the human spirit," which makes us sharers in the knowledge of God. Ibid., 19.

99. Ibid.

100. Ibid., 20.

101. JPII, *Jesus,* 349 and 253. Phil 2:8.

all."¹⁰² Therefore the kingdom of God has truly begun to be realized in the history of humanity and of the world."¹⁰³

This kingdom extends to all people and it is not political, but its growth takes place in the field of human hearts.¹⁰⁴ According to John Paul, liberation in the social and political sense is not the true messianic mission of Christ. However, the work of Christ does liberate the human heart from sin and egoism and that liberation may give rise to socio-political liberation. "Not merely external change of structures brings about a true liberation of society, as long as man is subject to sin and lies, as long as the passions hold sway, and with them exploitation and the various forms of oppression."¹⁰⁵ Thus, Christ's work transforms human hearts through the law of love, which is the constitutional basis for the kingdom of God. All are called and invited into this kingdom but each person is responsible for accepting or refusing the invitation, for his conformity or lack of conformity with this law.¹⁰⁶ The kingdom of God requires this new justice; it requires commitment expressed in the doing of God's will by loving one another.¹⁰⁷

In contrast to what we will see in Barth, John Paul believed that Christ conferred (or conveyed) the kingdom to his disciples. He said that in Jesus' mind, the kingdom of God is connected with the power to conquer sin (and injustice). Therefore, he explained, the kingdom is linked to the paschal mystery and built in the mission of the apostles and their successors. "The purpose of the vocation and mission of the apostles—and therefore the Church—in the world is to establish God's kingdom in human history."¹⁰⁸ Barth, by contrast, argued that only God (and not the church) brings in God's kingdom on earth. Again, we see in this contrast the great optimism of John Paul with regard to human capabilities an intrinsic connection between God's and humanity, that is absent in Barth. For John Paul, the kingdom of God is now present in the world through the followers of Christ, through the church.¹⁰⁹ Through kingship, the

---

102. 1 Cor 15:28.
103. JPII, *Jesus*, 349.
104. Ibid., 350–51.
105. Ibid., 399.
106. Ibid., 353.
107. Ibid., 134.
108. Ibid., 254–55.
109. Ibid., 255, 369.

Christian seeks to build up the Body of Christ by the unreserved giving of one's whole person to Christ and, with Christ, to humankind.[110]

Theological Basis: Holy Spirit, Giver of Life and Love

With regard to the question of the possibility of a just society, John Paul's pneumatology played a large role by sanctifying humans, convicting humans of injustice, and strengthening them for the life of participation in God's gracious justice. In these three manners, the Holy Spirit was primary in the moral formation of personhood.

The Spirit and Sanctification

During his final discourse at the last supper, Christ promised the disciples that he would send "another counselor" (*parákletos*) when he left them. Christ explained, "The Counselor, the Holy Spirit, whom the Father will send in my name, he will teach you all things, and bring to your remembrance all that I have said to you."[111] Jesus taught them that the Spirit would reveal truth, would be a witness in the spreading of the gospel, and would guide the disciples.

According to John Paul, the Spirit is one with the Father and the Son, participating in the work of creation, redemption, and sanctification. First, the Holy Spirit was involved in the original creative work of God's self-giving, in Creation.[112] Second, Holy Spirit was linked with the mystery of redemption, "the new beginning of God's salvific self-communication."[113] Third, when Christ departed, he sent his presence through the Spirit, through whom (a) God communicated with humans in a new way[114] and (b) humans were made participants in the life of God by their sanctification.[115] John Paul called the Spirit the author of sanctification in Christ and in humanity. "By the power of the Holy Spirit, the holiness of the Son of Man constitutes the principal and lasting source of holiness in human and world history."[116] In this manner, the Spirit plays a vital role in the

---

110. JPII, *RH*, 21.
111. John 14:26; *DV*, 3.
112. Ibid., 12.
113. Ibid., 13.
114. John 14:26; Ibid., 3.
115. JPII, *Spirit*, 253.
116. Ibid., 211–13.

salvation and sanctification of God by giving the life of union with the Father in Christ and giving humans participation in this divine life with the Father, through the Son, in the Spirit.

The Spirit and Life

The mystery of the incarnation opened in a new way the source of divine life in the history of humankind: the Holy Spirit. The Word became flesh by the power of the Holy Spirit.[117] According to John Paul, "the filiation of divine adoption is born in man on the basis of the mystery of the Incarnation., therefore through Christ the eternal Son. But the birth, or rebirth, happens when God the Father 'sends the Spirit of the Son into our hearts.'"[118] The divine filiation is planted in the human soul by the Holy Spirit through sanctifying grace. This sanctifying grace is the principle and source of man's new, supernatural life. The Holy Spirit, the uncreated gift, resides in the human heart and initiates the created gift whereby humans become partakers of the divine nature.[119] The Spirit remakes and recreates the human person in the likeness of Christ, giving humanity a dignity beyond compare.[120]

This pneumatology has moral implications for individuals and communities. When "people discover this divine dimension of their being and life," through the influence of the Holy Spirit, they are enabled, by grace, to free themselves from false understandings and domineering pressures of humanity and society. They discover the commandment of love, written on their hearts by the Holy Spirit.[121] Finally, they find freedom and self-fulfilment in relationship with the Triune God and by giving of themselves to God and to others.[122]

The Spirit and Moral Formation

What are the implications of this pneumatology for the moral formation of humans? When Jesus promised to send the Holy Spirit, he explained, "And when he comes, he will convince the world concerning sin and

---

117. JPII, *DV*, 52.
118. Ibid., 52; JPII, *Spirit*, 63–66.
119. JPII, *DV*, 52.
120. JPII, *Spirit*, 64.
121. Ibid., 73.
122. JPII, *DV*, 60; *Spirit*, 407–10.

righteousness and judgment: concerning sin, because they do not believe in me; concerning righteousness, because I go to the Father, and you will see me no more; concerning judgment, because the ruler of this world is judged."[123] This convincing that is attributed to the Spirit serves the salvific purposes of God and the morality of communities.[124] Let us examine how John Paul believed that it did so.

John Paul believed that God created all persons with a conscience. The conscience, he said, does *not* decide good and evil.[125] Good and evil are defined by the law of God. Does this mean that human are not free? No, John Paul explained, for the law is not imposed on the conscience in a hegemonic fashion. Rather, the law teaches and summons the human to love good and avoid evil and the conscience then applies the law to particular cases. The freedom of the human, John Paul explained, "is not only the choice for one or another particular action; it is also, within that choice, a decision about oneself and a setting of one's own life for or against the Good, for or against the Truth, and ultimately for or against God."[126]

The conscience draws the human to cleave to God in freedom. He wrote, "The conscience is the 'voice of God' even when the human recognizes in it nothing more than the principle of the moral order which it is not humanly possible to doubt."[127] In the sanctuary of the conscience, the human "is alone with God, whose voice echoes in his depths."[128] For Christians, God's voice is that of the Spirit, who reveals sin and strengthens the human person to obey her conscience and to wrestle to cling to what is good.[129] In this manner, the Spirit is for humans "the source of the moral order" for it confronts humans with the law and summons them to freely obey it.[130]

123. JPII, *DV*, 27.

124. Ibid., 31.

125. JPII, *VS*, 32 and 57.

126. Ibid., 65. John Paul writes elsewhere, that the question of freedom cannot pressed from the issue of freedom, "for there can be no morality without freedom: 'It is only in freedom that man can turn to what is good.' . . . 'Genuine freedom is an outstanding manifestation of the divine image in man. For God willed to leave man 'in the power of his own counsel' (cf. Sir 15:14), so that he would seek his Creator of his own accord and would freely arrive at full and blessed perfection by cleaving to God.'" JPII, *VS*, 34; quotations from Second Vatican Council, *GS*, 17.

127. JPII, *DV*, 43.

128. Ibid.

129. Ibid., 44.

130. Ibid., 36.

According to John Paul, the relationship between human freedom and God's law, which has its center in the moral conscience, is manifested and realized in human acts. For through his acts, "man attains perfection as man, as one who is called to seek his Creator of his own accord and freely to arrive at full and blessed perfection by cleaving to him."[131] Echoing *The Acting Person*, John Paul explained that human acts are moral acts because "they express and determine the goodness of the individual who performs them."[132] Humans create themselves through their decisions because deliberate choices give moral definition to the person who performs them.

With regard to justice, the implications are obvious. For John Paul, the conscience describes a capacity within each human person to hear God, to relate to God, to know what is just and to respond in obedience. The Holy Spirit serves as the voice of God, convincing persons to freely choose the just act, which accords with the law of God. In addition, the Spirit strengthens persons to act justly. Thus, by the participating Spirit of God, humans are shaped by their own action so that they become just persons.

What is unclear in this discussion is which norm the conscience applies: the natural norm or the revealed norm? John Paul would say that the two do not contradict each other, but as became evident in the above discussion on redemption, at times these two norms do seem to call for two different responses when it comes to just action. Is the voice of God equated with the natural law in the case of non-believers and with revealed norms in the case of believers? Is it related to the *analogia entis* in non-believers and the indwelling of the Spirit in believers? These questions remained unanswered in John Paul's pneumatology.

Theological Basis: Conclusion

This section has examined John Paul's account of justice, as informed by his theological framework. With regard to his epistemological assumptions, John Paul demonstrated continuity with his work as Wojtyla in his description of the two types of moral norms: natural norms and revealed norms. All persons have the capacity to know natural norms because all persons are created by God in his image, specifically with reason. The revealed norm of justice is revealed in the mercy and justice of God in the

131. JPII, *VS*, 71.
132. Ibid.

history of Israel. The revelation reaches its climax in the life, death, and resurrection of Christ. Yet through the Holy Spirit, this revelation is made personal, for the Holy Spirit plays a key role in revealing God to human persons. With regard to moral knowledge, the Holy Spirit acts in cooperation with the human conscience to enable humans to know what is good. According to John Paul, revelation does not contradict the natural norm but it simply adds more information about the moral law of God. We have critiqued this differentiation, by seeking to demonstrate that the two offer differing accounts of justice—one that demands retribution and the other that aims for restoration through mercy. This problem lay latent in the early work of Wojtyla, seen in his play *Our God's Brother*, and became evident in his mature philosophical work. Now we have also seen this confusion in his theological work as well.

With regard to his account of justice, this section has explored his account from a theological perspective. The dignity of human persons revealed both in the *imago Dei* and especially in the incarnation, redemption, and sanctification by Christ and the Holy Spirit provides the primary starting point for his account of justice. In his philosophical account, Wojtyla defined justice as treating another in accordance with their nature. His theological account points toward justice as treating another according to the dignity that is affirmed in God's loving acts of creation, incarnation, and redemption. Just as God loved and extended mercy to humans, so we are to love one another. A theological account of justice must be conditioned by love and expressed most fully in forgiveness and in the restoration of human relations.

Finally, regarding just human action, John Paul believed that sin inclined humans toward evil but did not commit them to do evil. Rather (and in contrast to reformed Protestantism) humans have the capacity for just action, a capacity that is strengthened by the Holy Spirit. With the help of the Holy Spirit, humans freely choose the good. In so choosing, humans are shaped by their own actions: the one who acts justly becomes a just person. On this final account, John Paul again shows a continuity with his thought as Wojtyla, by emphasizing the capacity for just action and the morally formative nature of human action.

PART ONE—Karol Wojtyla/John Paul II

Social Doctrine: Human Dignity as the Criterion for Political and Economic Justice

The final part of this chapter examines the implications of John Paul's theological framework of justice for assessing and promoting justice in political and economic systems. It seeks to illustrate how John Paul's theoretical account of justice applies in a social context. It was in these encyclicals that his personalism became most evident and that his account of social justice most clear. Namely he believed that social justice means treating another in accordance with his or her dignity. In light of this criterion of human dignity, all systems and ideas are critiqued.

His criterion of human dignity was grounded in the theological framework we have described thus far. He wrote, "We can find here [in the gospel of Christ] a new invitation to bear witness together to our common convictions concerning the dignity of man, created by God, redeemed by Christ, made holy by the Spirit and called upon in this world to live a life in conformity with this dignity."[133] Grounded in a theological framework, he utilized the theme of human dignity as the criterion of justice.[134] He wrote, "For the Church does not propose economic and political systems or programs, nor does she show preference for one or the other, provided that human dignity is properly respected and promoted."[135] According to John Paul, the human person must be the highest value of society. The human does not exist for the sake of political or economic advancement. Rather, society exists for the sake of the humans who make up that society; it serves the human person by upholding human rights and advancing human responsibilities.

The Human Person in the Political Sphere

According to John Paul, the state must facilitate the life of the people and "ensure the normal development of man's spiritual and temporal activities."[136] The purpose of the state is this service to the common good

---

133. JPII, *SRS*, 48.

134. JPII, *CA*, 55; and *SRS*, 41. John Paul wrote, "Christian anthropology is really a chapter of theology, and for this reason, the Church's social doctrine, by its concern for man and by its interest in him and in the way he conducts himself in the world, 'belongs to the field . . . of theology and particularly of moral theology.'"

135. JPII, *SRS*, 41.

136. JPII, *CA*, 44. Cf. JPII, *The Person, the Nation, and the State*, 25.

by upholding the rule of law.[137] He opposed the totalitarian state because of its opposition to the rule of law in favor of rule by the power and violence of a few individuals. He argued that totalitarianism arises from a denial of objective truth. Without objective truth, no foundation exists for guaranteeing just relations between people. "If one does not acknowledge transcendent truth, then the force of power takes over, and each person tends to make use of the means at his disposal in order to impose his own interests or his own opinion, with no regard for the rights of others."[138] John Paul located the root of modern totalitarianism in the denial of the transcendent dignity of the human person who is made in the image of God and is the subject of rights that no one may violate. Thus, the atheism of modern totalitarianism led to a denial of the transcendence of the human person, the reality of moral law to which all persons are subject. He believed that this atheism led to an incurable systemic injustice, which brought its eventual demise.

Because of his criterion of human dignity, John Paul favored what he called "authentic democracy," a democratic system that ensures the participation and freedom of citizens while submitting itself to the true and objective law of God.[139] He critiqued the present agnosticism and relativism that adheres to truth and is determined by the majority. He wrote, "If there is no ultimate truth to guide and direct political activity, then ideas and convictions can easily be manipulated for reasons of power. As history demonstrates, a democracy without values easily turns into open or thinly disguised totalitarianism."[140] Thus, the Christian must witness to truth as the foundation for freedom and justice in society.

At both the national and international level, John Paul called for governmental structures to be in place that will uphold the human rights that are intrinsic to the dignity of the human.[141] In an address to the Presidents of European Union Parliaments, John Paul said, "Society acknowledges that it is at the service of its members and their natural aspiration to find fulfillment as individuals and social beings. This aspiration, part of the nature of the person, corresponds to inherent rights of the person, such as

137. JPII, "Protection of Human Rights is Indispensable," 6.
138. JPII, *CA*, 44.
139. Ibid., 46; and JPII, "Democracy must be Based on Moral Norms," 8.
140. JPII, *CA*, 46.
141. Ibid., 48; and *SRS*, 33. Among these rights he includes the right to life, the right to live in a united family conducive to growth, the right to develop one's intelligence and freedom in seeking the truth, the right to work, the right to religious freedom, the right to share in economic development, and the right to own property.

the right to live, to physical and mental integrity, to freedom of conscience, thought, and religion."[142] In sum, John Paul consistently supported those political systems and institutions that upheld dignity, while carefully examining and critiquing these systems in light of the same criterion.

The Human Person in the Economic Sphere

The responsibility of the church in the economic sphere, according to John Paul, is not to propose particular economic systems but to lay down principles and criteria that can guide human action toward the authentic progress of society by safeguarding the dignity and rights of all persons.[143] John Paul employed this norm in his evaluation of economic systems. He critiqued both socialism and capitalism on this basis. He argued that socialism considers the human person as an element, a molecule within a social organism. The system subordinates the human person to the functioning of the socio-economic mechanism, reduces the human to a series of social relationships, and removes the concept of the person as the autonomous subject of moral decisions.[144] While advocates of the free market defend their system for achieving greater satisfaction of material human needs, they encounter a similar danger of reducing the human to the sphere of economics and the satisfaction of material needs.[145]

Utilizing this criterion of human dignity, John Paul argued that economics must recognize, safeguard, and promote the primacy of the person.[146] He warned that the present movement toward a consumer-based society carries great dangers because it ensnares people in a "web of false and superficial gratifications rather than being helped to experience their personhood in an authentic and concrete way."[147] The person concerned solely with possessing or enjoying cannot be free but becomes subject to the consumerist drive of society.[148] He does not recognize the transcen-

---

142. JPII, "Protection of Human Rights," 6.
143. Dulles, *The Splendor of Faith*, 131.
144. JPII, *CA*, 13.
145. Ibid., 19.
146. JPII, "Economy Must Respect Primacy of the Person," 9.
147. JPII, *CA*, 41.
148. Wealthy civilizations find themselves enslaved to an abuse of freedom, "an abuse linked precisely with a consumer attitude uncontrolled by ethics" in which material goods are given greater value than humanity and the accumulation of goods causes great social ills. JPII, *RH*, 16.

dent value of the human person, the grandeur given by God and redeemed by Christ. Rather, by viewing others merely as a means to productive and profitable ends, he cuts himself off from a relationship of solidarity and communion with others. "Indeed," John Paul wrote, "it is through the free gift of self that man truly finds himself. This gift is made possible by the human person's essential 'capacity for transcendence.'"[149]

However, John Paul did not condemn capitalism in total. He recognized the need for business to earn a profit and the value of the free market for allowing humans to participate in the economy. He affirmed the implementation of the capitalist system in the attempt to rebuild developing economies "*If* by 'capitalism' is meant an economic system which recognizes the fundamental and positive role of business, the market, private property and the resulting responsibility for the means of production, as well as free human creativity in the economic sector."[150] He affirmed the positive value of the market and of enterprise as long as it is oriented toward the common good.[151]

With regard to poverty and economic development, John Paul argued that the principle obstacle to development is human sin. In the same way that formation has a moral character, the causes of undevelopment are ultimately moral.[152] Humans create and participate in structures of sin that enable injustice through selfishness, abuse of power, and moral evil. Over against these harmful structures, God's will provides the foundation for the ethic of love and the value for human life. Christ supplies the model for charity and self-giving. Thus, John Paul called for the exercise of solidarity in society by recognizing one another as persons. The strong should feel responsible to care for the weaker and share what they possess. Those who are weaker must also give what the can for the good of all. This solidarity,

---

149. JPII, *CA*, 41.

150. Ibid., 42.

151. JPII, *CA*, 43.

152. JPII, *SRS*, 35. John Paul wrote, "Development which is merely economic is incapable of setting man free, on the contrary, it will end by enslaving him further. Development that does not include the cultural, transcendent and religious dimensions of man and society, to the extent that it does not recognise the existence of such dimensions and does not endeavour to direct its goals and priorities toward the same, is even less conducive to authentic liberation. Human beings are totally free only when they are completely themselves, in the fullness of their rights and duties. The same can be said about society as a whole." JPII, *SRS*, 46.

this life-giving going beyond oneself, is not only the path to development, but it also the path to justice and peace between peoples and nations.[153]

In conclusion to this section, John Paul applied his theory of justice in his social encyclicals, using the dignity of human persons as the critical criterion by which to judge all systems and institutions in which humans live and act. In his work as John Paul, this criterion had a specifically theological grounding, in the creation, redemption, and sanctification of humanity by God. Each of these acts corresponds to a special dignity in human persons. In creation, the person is revealed to be created in the image of God and endowed with human reason. In the incarnation and salvation of Christ, humans are raised to a dignity beyond compare, revealed in this act of ultimate love.

Conclusion to Part One

While John Paul could have agreed with the various "secular" documents defending the dignity and the rights of humanity, we have argued in these three chapters that his *basis* for such agreement is uniquely theological. In other words, the whole basis for John Paul's social doctrine was his theological anthropology. Although philosophical inquiry can start one down the correct path, John Paul believed, one cannot arrive at a full understanding of the human person in society apart from the Christian doctrine of God the Father, God the Son, and God the Holy Spirit.

For John Paul, fully comprehending human persons meant recognizing the intrinsic dignity of humanity, received in the *imago Dei*, raised to new meaning by Jesus Christ, and renewed in the Holy Spirit. From Wojtyla's early childhood experience with the pain of death, the horror of war, and the demoralization of oppression, Wojtyla witnessed the resilience of specific persons who were able to rise above such destruction. The faith of his father, the spirituality of Tyranowski, and the love of the priests and bishops who became his new family fostered Wojtyla's hope in humanity. His Thomistic training offered new insight into human dignity, revealed in the human capacity for transcendence both with regard to truth and with regard to the "germ of eternity"[154] in each human person that longs for communion with God. Thomism gave Wojtyla the weapons to fight against the materialist and naturalist ideologies that prevailed in Poland by reminding his flocks of this transcendent reality. His work in phenom-

---

153. Ibid., 39.
154. A phrase taken from Lubac, *Catholicism*, 202.

enology gave him the tools to explore the human person more deeply and to argue that the existence of the consciousness and the formation of human consciousness through good acts entails a higher good, the common good toward which humans in society must strive. Finally, his mature theological work as John Paul II affirmed his belief in the surpassing value of human persons and confirmed the critical criterion by which political and economic systems must be judged: the criterion of human dignity.

Within these three chapters, we have examined some of the key assumptions that underlie John Paul's optimistic humanism. First, the doctrine of the *analogia entis* lies behind his epistemology, his doctrine of God and of sin, his moral theology, and his hope for justice in society. Because humans share in the being of God, they have dignity and they possess (to some degree) a "human goodness" that gives them access to natural law and an authentic freedom to choose good or evil. This key assumption meant that neither epistemic access to truth nor the capacity to behave justly were rendered useless by human sin. Rather, by means of natural law all humans can know some degree of moral truth and can behave in accordance with this truth. Thus, John Paul took a very optimistic stance regarding the possibilities for human justice.

Secondly, John Paul assumed that Christ's justification before God, "is the main foundation of all justice."[155] By giving of himself, Christ overcame justice with mercy; he revealed the love of God for humanity in a radical new way. This overwhelming love and mercy of God in Christ initiated a relationship of love through which the human enters a new relation with the Father. In Christ, the dignity that was lost by sin is reestablished and human persons have been adopted to live in a redeemed relation of participation with God. According to John Paul, the life and death of Jesus are a powerful new model for Christians in their relation to society. Christians live in this new morality of love through the help of the Holy Spirit and with the highest goal consisting in the act that corresponds with solidarity, the gift of self on behalf of the other.[156]

The third key assumption regards God's providential establishment of his kingdom, into which humans have also been brought to participate. By participating in the dominion of the creator, humans experience their own autonomy and responsibility before God. In Christ, humans have been become sharers in the mission of God to establish his kingdom by proclaiming divine truth, which entails affirming the dignity of humanity,

---

155. JPII, *SC*, 84.
156. JPII, *SRS*, 39.

declaring the justice of God, and asserting the moral law in society. The kingly mission calls Christians to practice solidarity by giving of themselves in service to others through dominion over the self and through unreserved giving of one's whole person to Christ and to humankind.

These key assumptions of John Paul II, will serve as a starting point for dialogue with Protestant theologian, Karl Barth. Before engaging in this dialogue, however, we must now turn to examine the theological foundations for social justice in the writings of Karl Barth. Like John Paul II, and perhaps more vehemently, Karl Barth argued that human justice must derive from a theological interpretation of human personhood. We will now investigate Barth's anthropology both in its early development and in its mature form, as it engages and informs his social ethic.

PART TWO

Karl Barth

4

An Early Passion for Justice

LIKE KAROL WOJTYLA'S, KARL BARTH'S INTEREST IN SOCIAL JUSTICE was ignited by a concern for particular people. When he witnessed the members of his Safenwil congregation suffering under unjust working conditions, Barth was compelled to involve himself in the struggle for workers rights. As Hungarian Jews were being massacred at Auschwitz, Barth successfully advocated for a change in national policy so that Jews might find asylum in Switzerland.[1] One would assume that this compassion for persons would have driven his theological interests toward key tenets for social justice, similar to those of John Paul: the dignity of human personhood and natural law. Both of these beliefs have formed the basis for Christian defenses of human rights and responsibilities since the time of Thomas Aquinas.[2] Yet Barth's concern for persons took him in what appeared to be the exact opposite direction. In his early years, Barth became a bold advocate for the divinity of God, as contrasted with human creatureliness, and he rejected natural law (and natural theology) as a basis for ethics. In his reflection on the social and political oppression surrounding him, Barth came to believe that the anthropocentrism and humanism of his contemporaries had become impotent in the face of injustice.[3] Thus, he felt compelled to speak, "God," and to preach of a kingdom and a righteousness that is "wholly other."[4]

---

1. Busch, *Unter dem Bogen*, 515–17; Kranzler, "The Swiss Press Campaign," 156–70.

2. Strauss, *Natural Right and History*, 144–45. For examples in the Protestant tradition: John Calvin, *Institutes*, 2.8.1-2; or Arthur Dyck, *Rights and Responsibilities*, 24–28. Examples in the Catholic tradition: Aquinas, *Summa Theologiae* II-Iiae, q. 91, a. 2; John Paul II, *VS*, 10.

3. Barth, *The Humanity of God*, 17.

4. Ibid., 42.

His contemporaries were scandalized. They believed that this radical theology entailed the abolition of human creatureliness and the destruction of human dignity.[5] For a time, his theology may have pointed in that direction. But as Barth journeyed onward in his quest for the "wholly other," he soon discovered what he considered to be a more authentic source of human justice: the Word of God in Jesus Christ.

This chapter poses the question of epistemology, examining the early years that Barth's key assumptions were formed. We will trace Barth's early passion for social justice and the reasons that this interest led him to reject the epistemologies of his contemporaries. I will argue that this rejection went hand in hand with his concern for social justice, for he believed that these alternate epistemologies and theological methods potentially validated the violence of his era.

Barth's Early Life

Karl Barth was born in Switzerland in 1886, in the midst of the increasing social and political tensions that resulted from the industrial revolution. While industrialization brought new urbanization and wealth to Western Europe, these developments came at a high social cost for the lower and middle classes: dangerous working conditions, misuse of child labor, and long hours. Prior to this time, the predominant political and economic approach had been dominated by liberal, *laissez faire* ideals with little government interference in economic or social issues. With rising social difficulties, however, liberalism began to give way to a more positive view of government involvement in social problems, such as the limitation of child labor or the regulation of labor hours in certain industries.[6]

While Barth was growing up, his Christian family took a serious interest in these social concerns. As a pastor, his father helped to found a Christian Socialist society in his hometown of Berne. During his childhood, Barth also encountered the radical social theology of the Blumhardts through his Aunt Bethie who, "increasingly developed an eye for signs of the coming Kingdom of God. Rather than making her narrow-minded, her devotion kindled in her a love which went out to embrace all men."[7] This connection between the kingdom of God and love toward men remained a key tenant of Barth's thought.

---

5. Ibid., 44.
6. Joll, *Europe Since 1870*, 39.
7. Busch, *Karl Barth*, 10 and 19.

An Early Passion for Justice

During his university years, as a student of theology in Berne, Barth's own social and political interests developed both inside and outside of the classroom. One example from Barth's extracurricular activities includes his moving lecture to the Berne Association, "Zofingia and the Social Question." He asserted that, "the gulf between capital and work, between mammonism and pauperism, in short, between rich and poor . . . is continually growing larger." He saw the social question as "one link in the chain of development, or better *the* problem of mankind, which Jesus once posed to the ancient world."[8]

Like many of his fellow students, Barth wished to continue his studies in Germany. While his father advocated for the more conservative universities in Halle or Griefswald, Barth longed to study in Marburg. They struck a compromise and Barth moved to Berlin in 1906. It was in Berlin that Barth first read Kant's *Critique of Pure Reason*. As Wojtyla argued in his essays, Kant's critique of reason articulated the modern rise of a fundamentally different epistemology that limited knowledge to human consciousness. Kant argued that humans know things as they appear to us (*phenomena*); humans cannot know things as they are in themselves (*noumena*). While Kant did believe that *noumena* existed, he argued that human reason was limited to sense perception and the human categories for interpreting this experience. Thus, his critique of reason was a critique of metaphysics as well, for in metaphysics, sensory experience is lacking. Schwartz gave the following example, "The claim of free will versus determinism, a first cause and God or no God, provides equally good reasoning, because epistemological reflections do not lead us from the phenomena to the noumena, the thing in itself."[9] So for Kant objective reality of or true knowledge about a supreme being cannot be proven or disproven through metaphysics.

One can scarcely overestimate how influential Kant's critique was for German theology; it influenced the subjective turn that theology took from Schleiermacher onwards. In other words, Kant's critique of reason meant that theology's methods were likewise limited to an exploration of human consciousness—an exploration of human experience and conceptions of God—rather than an explanation of the nature of God's being. Whereas Wojtyla rejected Kant's critique, Barth seems to have accepted that reason could never ascertain God's being of its own accord or be a

---

8. Ibid., 37.
9. Schwartz, *Theology in a Global Context*, 5.

reliable source for theological knowledge. This presupposition would later influence his ethical method.

In Berlin, Barth was strongly drawn to Adolf von Harnack. When he moved to Marburg to study, he sought out Wilhelm Herrmann.[10] Both of these theologians followed the subjectivist turn of their liberal German heritage, which created a challenge for connecting the Christian faith with broader social concerns. For example, Herrmann expressed concern for the working classes but his analysis of social problems focused upon individual relations with no interest in structural or institutional forms of evil.[11] Harnack taught that the kingdom of God existed as something inward rather than outward, consisting in the union of the individual soul with God.[12] Harnack wrote, "True, the Kingdom of God is the rule of God; but it is the rule of the holy God in the hearts of individuals. . . . It is not a question of angels and devils, thrones and principalities, but of God and the soul, the soul and its God."[13] Like many theologians of his time, Harnack believed that the gospel of Jesus was concerned with the souls of individual humans and had little to say to the political or economical organization of society or to the struggle for social justice.

As a student, Barth's enthusiastic embrace of liberal theology likely made it difficult for him to bridge the gulf between the subjectivity of faith and his concern for social justice. Even upon his first direct encounter with the destitute living conditions of the working classes when he was in training as an assistant pastor in Geneva, Barth regarded "social misery as a necessary fact of nature in the midst of which faith held forth a strong but impractical hope."[14] While he did exhibit concern for social justice, his theology during this stage brought little to bear on the political rights of individuals. Soon after, however, this stance was challenged by Barth's work as a pastor in Safenwil.

---

10. McCormack, *Karl Barth's Theology*, 36.

11. See Harnack and Herrmann, *Essays on the Social Gospel*, 145–225. Although Herrmann was initially committed to the Ritschlian emphasis on historicity, he later shifted back toward an "existentialized Schleiermacherianism" that was more subjectivist in nature. McCormack, *Karl Barth's Theology*, 52ff.

12. McCormack, *Karl Barth's Theology*, 90.

13. Harnack, *What is Christianity?*, 56.

14. Barth, "Evangelium und Sozialismus" (original manuscript in Karl Barth-Archiv, Basle). The citations taken from Friedrich-Wilhelm Marquardt, *Verwegenheiten: Theologische Stucke aus Berlin*, 473, translated in McCormack, *Karl Barth's Theology*, 80.

An Early Passion for Justice

Shifting Foundations: The Red Pastor in Safenwil

In July of 1911, Barth moved to the Northern Swiss industrial town of Safenwil where he served as a pastor for ten years. As he became involved in the lives of the families in his parish, he encountered for the first time "the real problems of real life"[15] that he witnessed in the daily struggle of the low-wage factory and mill workers. He was so moved by these struggles that he began giving lectures to the Workers Association.[16] He also began reading more widely and increasingly turned to socialism as an answer to the injustices of industrialization. Barth wrote, "It was through S. that I became acquainted with socialism and was driven to more exacting reflection and study of the matter. Since that time, I have held socialist demands to be an important part of the application of the gospel, though I also believe that they cannot be realized without the gospel."[17] At this early stage of his pastoral work, Barth sought to apply his Christian faith to the social problems he was facing, and he found that his theological training did not prove adequate for the task.

Kutter and Ragaz

During this time, Barth found hope in the socialist activities and writings of Herrmann Kutter (1896–1931) and Leonhard Ragaz (1868–1945), to whom he was introduced through a fellow pastor and friend from his university days, Eduard Thurneysen.[18] Kutter's book, *They Must! An Open Word to Christian Society* gave birth to the Religious Socialist movement. In his book, Kutter argued that the churches had falsified the message of Christ by turning the gospel into a harmless, inward spirituality. Therefore,

---

15. Barth, *Karl Barth and Rudolf Bultmann: Letters 1922–1966*, 154.

16. The text of this lecture no longer exists. Busch, *Karl Barth*, 70.

17. McCormack agrees with Marquardt's assumption that S. refers to Werner Sombart (*Sozialismus und Soziale Bewegung*) but argues that Barth did not read Sombart in 1906 as Marquardt claims. Barth's copy of Sombart was not printed until 1908 and Barth himself recalled reading Sombart after his arrival in Safenwil. See McCormack, *Karl Barth's Theology*, 80n7. Though McCormack is probably correct regarding the connections Barth made between his own liberal theology and socialism at this time, Barth had previously observes socialism as it related to Christian faith through his earlier exposure to socialism in his father's work and the political climate of Switzerland during his childhood. Thus, perhaps he did recognize some tension between his own institutional ethical concerns with the conservative and individualist ethics of his professors during his university years.

18. Busch, *Karl Barth*, 73–75.

"socialism was nothing less than the 'hammer of God,' calling the churches to repentance, to renunciation of the dead God of the bourgeois classes, and to a renewal of faith in the living God of the Bible."[19] For Barth, Kutter was able to wed his social concerns with his Christian faith and to critique the church for its passivity.

Yet Barth remained on the outskirts of the Religious Socialist movement because he believed that many of its followers (such as Ragaz) took the continuity between the Christian gospel and the ideals socialism too far. He wrote, "Ragaz developed what Kutter meant to be a view of the current situation and an interpretation of the signs of the time, not a programme, into the theory that the church must regard socialism as a preliminary manifestation of the kingdom of God. In other words, he made it a true system of 'Religious Socialism.'"[20] While Barth affirmed that "socialism is a very important and necessary application of the gospel,"[21] he refused to equate either the church or the current socialist movement with what Jesus did on behalf of the poor.[22] Yet he remained involved in the socialist movement through his sermons on behalf of the poor and by supporting the trade union movement, eventually earning the nickname, "The Red Pastor."[23]

Shaken Foundations

The advancing signs of war brought an unexpected turning point in Barth's theology and in his social ethics. In July 1914, as international tensions heightened in Europe: Austro-Russian rivalry in the Balkans, Franco-German mutual resentment and distrust, and the Anglo-German rivalry. As the crisis escalated and German involvement and aggression indicated the certainty of war, the Social Democrats and the liberals united behind the Kaiser in support. By the time that the war began, the Kaiser received almost unified endorsement from society and intellectuals alike. A group of ninety-three of the most distinguished German intellectuals, some of the greatest figures in world literature, music, painting, philosophy, science,

---

19. McCormack, *Karl Barth's Theology*, 84.
20. Barth, *Kirchiliche Dogmatik*, 1:1, 75; citation from Busch, *Karl Barth*, 78.
21. Barth, *Sermons*, 1914. GA 1:365–66. Citation from Busch, *Karl Barth*, 80.
22. Busch, *Karl Barth*, 70.
23. Ibid., 83. Stanley Hauerwas told the story of his visit to Safenwil in the Gifford Lectures at the University of St. Andrews, 2001. In Safenwil, Hauerwas inquired of the townspeople, "Do you remember Karl Barth?" "Ah, yes," they replied, "the Red Pastor."

and theology issued a manifesto in support of the war, proclaiming that "the German army and the German people are one."[24]

Barth later recalled the eye-opening challenge to both his theological beliefs and his socialist activity of this time:

> A change came only with the outbreak of World War I. This brought concretely to light two aberrations: first in the teaching of my theological mentors in German, who seemed to me to be hopelessly compromised by their submission to the ideology of the war; and second in socialism. I had credulously enough expected socialism, more than I had the Christian church, to avoid the ideology of the war, but to my horror I saw it doing the very opposite in every land.[25]

On the theological front, Barth was shocked by the issuing of the manifesto that supported the war policy of the Kaiser. Included on that list were many of Barth's former professors including Harnack and Herrmann. Barth reflected that "a whole world of exegesis, ethics, dogmatics, and preaching, which I had hitherto held to be essentially trustworthy, was shaken to the foundations, and with it, all the other writings of the German theologians."[26] For Barth, the outbreak of the war was "a double madness," for "we had more or less definitely expected that socialism would prove to be a kind of hammer of God, yet all along national war fronts we saw it swinging into line."[27]

The Blumhardts

Following the outbreak of the war, an argument arose between Kutter and Ragaz, which further alienated Barth from his former guides.[28] In April 1915, a friend introduced Barth to Christoph Blumhardt. A charismatic and prophetic figure, Blumhardt had roots in pietism, which found social focus through his proclamation of the coming kingdom of God. Barth

---

24. Pinson, *Modern Germany*, 316.

25. From autobiographical sketches of Barth from the faculty albums of the Faculties of Evangelical Theology at Münster. Barth, *Karl Barth and Rudolf Bultmann: Letters 1922–1966*, 154.

26. Busch, *Karl Barth*, 81; from Barth, "Nachwort," 293.

27. Barth, *CD* 3/4:450.

28. Ragaz and Kutter fell into disagreement concerning the way forward: Ragaz pressed for political activity while Kutter called for tranquil reappraisal. At the time, Barth favored Ragaz's program whereas his colleague, Thurneysen, supported Kutter.

was attracted to Blumhardt upon first meeting, describing him as "a man who was not so sure of his affairs, because his secret awareness was beyond anything he could express. At any rate, this uncertainty was the best thing about him."[29]

Barth gained two fundamental beliefs from Blumhardt. First, Blumhardt combined an active and eager search for signs of the kingdom of God with a patient "waiting" on God and the decisive action, which God alone could perform. Barth wrote in reflection on Blumhardt, "Blumhardt always begins right away with God's presence, might, and purpose: he starts out from God; he does not begin by climbing upwards to Him by means of contemplation and deliberation. God is the end, and because we already know Him as the beginning, we may await His consummating acts."[30]

Second, Barth appreciated the connection between knowledge of God and the Christian hope.[31] According to Barth, hope became the dominant feature of Blumhardt's message:

> . . . hope for a visible and tangible appearing of the lordship of God over the world (in contrast to the simple, and so often blasphemous, talking about God's omnipotence); hope for radical help and deliverance from the former state of the world (in opposition to the soothing and appeasing attitude which must everywhere come to a halt before unalterable "relationships"); hope for all, for mankind (in contrast to the selfish concern for one's own salvation . . .); hope for the physical side of life as well as the spiritual.[32]

Barth's encounter with the Blumhardts marked the beginning of shift that took place in his thought because it provided a new emphasis on the coming kingdom of God as the source of Christian hope for justice. Over against the influence of liberal theology and the religious socialists, Barth began to emphasize both the "otherness" of God and the questionability of human attempts to establish God's kingdom through social reform.[33] In part, this doubt was a result of Barth's disappointment in both the theological and socialist support of WWI. Yet this doubt also stemmed from a new hope that God alone could establish the right for humanity through the coming of his kingdom.

29. Busch, *Karl Barth*, 84.
30. Barth, *Action in Waiting*, 23–24.
31. Busch, *Karl Barth*, 85.
32. Barth, "Past and Future," 41–42.
33. McCormack, *Karl Barth's Theology*, 125.

First Commentary on Romans

This shift toward divinity is evidenced in the extensive conversations that Barth had with Thurneysen, in which he continued to lament the failure of his former theological and ethical guides. Barth was dissatisfied with his prior approach in which "everything had always already been settled without God. God was always thought to be good enough to put the crowning touch to what men began of their own accord."[34] He later recalled, "It was Thurneysen who whispered the key phrase to me, half aloud, while we were alone together: 'What we need for preaching, instruction, and pastoral care is a 'wholly other' theological foundation.'"[35] The two pastors began by reading and interpreting the Old and New Testaments more thoughtfully. From these studies were birthed Barth's first commentary on *Romans* and his discovery of "the strange new world within the Bible."[36]

In this commentary, completed in 1918, McCormack locates the early stages of Barth's dialectical theology, noting Barth's emphasis on the radical otherness of God and the sin of humanity.[37] According to Barth's interpretation of Romans, in Adam's sin and fall, all of humanity fell from the immediacy of being with God. The distance between God and the creature took place through the fall of the creature from God.[38]

In order to establish a point of contact between God and humanity, Barth developed an eschatology of process in which the new world dawned in Jesus Christ and the kingdom of God establishes itself by renewing this world through an "organic" sort of growth. Barth chose the word "organic" to describe the growth of the kingdom in order to emphasize the work of God rather than man's attempt to build the kingdom.[39] In this sense of the

---

34. Busch, *Karl Barth*, 100.

35. Ibid., 97; from Barth, "Nachwort," 294.

36. Barth, *The Word of God and the Word of Man*, 28–50.

37. Barth's dialectical phase is most commonly located with the writing of *Romans* II. However, as McCormack argues (and the evidence outlined above seeks to demonstrate) Barth began his dialectical phase in this earlier commentary. (McCormack, *Karl Barth's Theology*, 182–83 and 208–9.) In this first commentary, Barth clearly was critiquing claims of the presence or continuity of God in history through human action. However, previous commentators misinterpreted his intention here, because of his use of language regarding the "organic" continuity and growth of the kingdom. Barth intended for this language to emphasize the action of God but commentators misinterpreted it to support the continuity of humanity with God. Thus, Barth later dropped this language in an attempt to clarify his dialectic emphasis for his readers.

38. Balthasar, *The Theology of Karl Barth*, 65–66.

39. McCormack, *Karl Barth's Theology*, 153–54.

phrase, Barth directly critiqued the teaching of Harnack and his former professors who maintained that the kingdom of God arises through the ethical action of individuals. In opposition to this idea that God's kingdom is established through autonomous human activity, Barth believed that the kingdom of God would establish itself through God's work in order to bring change to individuals and to society.

The philosophical understanding of human nature at the time that Barth was writing highlights the radical nature of these claims in *Romans* I. Friedrich Gogarten, one of Barth's contemporaries, described modern conceptions of human nature by contrasting them to the anthropology of the Middle Ages.[40] During the Middle Ages, Gogarten explained, the world was understood as an expression of God's creativity and glory, with humankind at the apex of God's purposes in creation. With the rise of modernity came a dramatic shift, commensurate with the Copernican Revolution, in which humans were no longer thought to be at the center of creation. This shift raised questions regarding the significance of human persons within the natural world. In modern philosophical anthropology, humans gained importance not through their created-*ness* but by creating meaning through their acts.[41] Human action, autonomy, and freedom took center stage in the quest for self-understanding and dignity.

Given this emphasis upon the importance of human agency within the philosophical and theological milieu, Barth's critique of human action sounded scandalous to his hearers. Both that critique and Barth's emphasis upon God's action seemed to undermine the very possibility of human dignity. The significance for political activism can be noted in his interpretation of the thirteenth chapter of Romans, where Barth criticized key tenants of Religious Socialism. According to Barth, Religious Socialism presumed the relation of continuity between divine and human action, maintaining an idealism that the human could judge, speak, and act for God, to establish God's justice in society. By contrast, Barth argued that all political action necessarily involves the human in sin and cannot be identified with the cause of God.

In this one swipe, Barth not only seemed to disrobed modern humans of the dignity of their actions but he appeared to condemn the socialist struggle for workers' rights to a place of insignificance. In addition, his emphasis upon the discontinuity between God and creature seemed

---

40. Gogarten, "Das Problem einer theologishen Anthropologie," 493–511. McCormack, *Karl Barth's Theology*, 407–8.

41. McCormack, *Karl Barth's Theology*, 407.

to destroy any hope in present justice and to undermine the basis for human ethics in society.⁴² The social impact of this radical shift toward deity resounded even more strongly in the Tambach lecture, summarized in the following section

Tambach Lecture

After completing *Romans* I, Barth was invited to give a lecture at the Conference on Religion and Social Relations held at Tambach in September, 1919. Originally Ragaz had been the keynote speaker at this conference sponsored by the Christian Socialists. When Ragaz cancelled at the last moment, Barth was invited by those who thought that he was a disciple of Ragaz. However, Barth's message, "The Christian's Place in Society," caused a great stir because it was perceived to undercut the very activities and ideals of Christian Socialism.⁴³

In continuity with his first commentary on *Romans*, Barth emphasized the transcendence of God and of God's work within society.⁴⁴ On the one hand, he argued that the reality of *Christ in us* affirms that society is not forsaken of God. On the other hand, he critiqued the beliefs of Christian Socialism by arguing that humans cannot simply apply Christianity to society or usher in the kingdom of God. The divine, he said, is wholly complete, something new and different, which stands in contrast to the world. The divine, "does not permit of being applied, stuck on, and fitted in. . . . It does not passively permit itself to be used: it overthrows and builds up as it wills. It is complete or it is nothing."⁴⁵ Thus, he warned against programmatic approaches to the building of a new society:

> Surely we shall resist this temptation to betray society; it is no easier to bring it to Christ than Christ to it. For it is God's help that we still have really in mind. . . . God alone can save the world. When we approach the execution of our program we shall not be able, as the familiar warning goes, to reckon too soberly with "reality"; and there is good reason why we should

---

42. Ibid., 178–79.
43. Gorringe, *Karl Barth*, 48.
44. Barth had already moved away from the "organic" language of the first *Romans* commentary.
45. Barth, *The Word of God and the Word of Man*, 277.

not, *rebus sic stantibus*—our ideals being impossible and our goals unattainable.[46]

In light of this dialectic of God's utter transcendence over against creation, Barth did recognize the need to establish some point of contact, through which God might act in human societies. In the Tambach lecture we note the beginnings of Barth's Christological synthesis. He located the movement of God in history in the resurrection of Jesus Christ, in whom the kingdom of God broke through and appeared in secular life.[47] This life, Barth explained, opened the possibility of eternal life for humans, reminding them that the origin of the soul is in God. This awakening of the soul to the new immediacy of relationship with God is also an awakening to the human's relation to society. The awakened soul, according to Barth, involves the "sympathetic shouldering of the cares of the whole generation."[48] The Christian's agitation regarding the concerns of this world provokes an engagement in the revolt of life against the powers of death that enclose it. The Christian reflects on the problems and horrors of this world with the hope that this despair is not the final word. "The last word," Barth argued, "is the kingdom of God—creation, redemption, the perfection of the world through God and in God."[49]

Like his commentary on *Romans*, this essay illustrates the dialectical movement of Barth's theology, as he emphasized the radical discontinuity between God's action and human action. It also demonstrates the beginning of his Christological synthesis, though primarily in eschatological terms. Once again many of his contemporaries were horrified. His former professor, Harnack found the speech appalling and commented to a friend, "The effect of Barth's lecture was just staggering. Not one word, not one sentence could I have said or thought. I saw the sincerity of Barth's speech but its theology frightened me."[50] Harnack believed that Barth's approach to theology was self-negating and apocalyptic, finding the turn

---

46. Ibid., 280. Barth echoes Christoph Blumhardt's warning: "Mark this well: The kingdom of God takes shape through nothing other than the coming of the Lord. It is not formed through any human discovery, no matter how worthy and honorable." *Thy Kingdom Come*, 79.

47. Barth, *The Word of God and the Word of Man*, 288.

48. Ibid., 290.

49. Ibid., 297. I have chosen to explicate only the first half of this essay. The second half deals with analogy, which I plan to develop more fully in the following chapter on Barth. For Barth's development of the idea during this phase, see McCormack, *Karl Barth's Theology*, 200–202.

50. Quoted in Zahn-Harnack, *Adolf von Harnack*, 415.

An Early Passion for Justice

to eschatological hope the most offensive aspect of his new theological developments.[51] Despite criticism, Barth continued to refine his theology in this dialectical and Christological direction.

Second Commentary on Romans

Within a year, Barth became dissatisfied with his first *Romans* commentary because he felt that he had not sufficiently moved past the concepts of contemporary theology, which he characterized as *"religionistic, anthropocentric, and in this sense humanistic."*[52] Barth explained his concern with this theology:

> To speak about God meant to speak in an exalted tone but once again and more than ever—about man—his revelations and wonders, his faith and his works. There is no question about it: here man was made great at the cost of God—the divine God who is someone other than man, who sovereignly confronts him, who immovably or unchangeably stands over against him as the Lord, Creator, and Redeemer. This God who is also man's free partner in a history inaugurated by Him and in a dialogue ruled by him was in danger of being reduced, along with this history and this dialogue, to a pious notion—to a mystical expression and symbol of a current alternating between man and his own heights or depths.[53]

He believed that such anthropocentrism had a devastating effect in the social realm. Without the sovereign God calling humans to account for their actions, Christian ethics became "blurred" and subsumed by the ethos of the culture.[54] In other words, if Christian theology focused primarily on humanity and human capacities for religious experience, self-awareness, or ethical action, then theologians would lose sight of the God who is "wholly other" and who stands outside of the cultural patterns and forces. Without the recognition that this God must be the object of theology, "the Christian was condemned to uncritical and irresponsible subservience to the patterns, forces, and movements of human history and civilization.

---

51. Dorrien, *The Barthian Revolution in Modern Theology*, 61.
52. Barth, *Humanity of God*, 39.
53. Ibid., 39–40.
54. Ibid., 17.

PART TWO—Karl Barth

Man's inner experience did not provide a firm enough ground for resistance to these phenomena."[55]

Barth had witnessed such subservience in the social failures of his theological mentors such as Harnack and Herrmann. They did not adequately address the human rights abuses of industrialization in Germany and they uncritically supported the aggression of the German Kaiser in WWI. In coming years Barth would also witness the failure of the German Christians to stand against the forces of Nazism. He attributed this moral bankruptcy to religious anthropocentrism: the failure to recognize that God (and not man) is God and that this God speaks within and against human societies.

Many of Barth's contemporaries found his turn to deity offensive and demeaning of human action, of human dignity. The irony, of course, is that Barth's turn to deity *did* issue in a perspective that could critique the worst justice abuses of his time, in the midst of Europe's industrialization and two world wars. While his dialectical theology during this period may have been one-sided (as Barth later admitted that it was)[56] it was a message he felt compelled to speak, especially in light of the urgent social difficulties that the German people were facing.

Barth developed the ethical implications of his turn to deity more clearly than ever in his revision of his commentary on *Romans* in 1920. Prior to this second commentary, he had continued to appeal, at times, to human reason as the means to knowing what was ethical. He had assumed that Christian ethics must first address the situation of individuals who do not know God and who ask, "What should we do?" Such an approach depended upon appeals to human reason and to a universal moral law as primary sources for ethics. However, Barth began to suspect the failure of such humanistic appeals. McCormack summarized Barth's view:

> Human beings living in time are sinners. For the sinful human being, the achievement of the good is an impossibility. But the ethical problem goes much deeper than the mere fact that human beings are unable to achieve the good that they would like to accomplish; even their self-chosen ethical goals—in that they are self-chosen—are the product of their self-relating, sinful orientation. Hence: "The will of God is wholly other and never identical with the will of human beings."[57] All of the ethical goals

---

55. Ibid., 17.
56. Ibid., 44–45.
57. Ruschke, *Entstehung und Ausführung der Diastasentheologie*, 73; quoted in

which human beings set for themselves and the attempts to achieve these goals stand in the shadow of this judgment. Seen in this judgment, ethics cannot be concerned with the promulgation of "this worldly goals" . . . but in the critical negation of all human goals and the proclamation of the forgiveness of sins.[58]

In such manner, *Romans* II demonstrates Barth's shift to an "ethic of witness—witness to the divine command contained in God's self-revelation in Jesus Christ."[59] In other words, Jesus Christ, became Barth's starting point for ethical knowledge. In such a re-conceptualization, Christian ethics was not called to first address the ethical situation of individuals who did not know God. Rather, ethics was called first to witness to what God's gracious work in Christ. Secondly, ethics concerned itself with the command, which God's grace entails.[60] Although he had not fully worked out the implications of this Christological approach in the areas of human personhood and justice, the second commentary on Romans demonstrated a definite shift toward the shape of his mature ethics. This Christological method was further developed through his immersion into the theology of the reformers.

Reformed Theology and the Justice of God for Humanity

Following the acclaim for his first commentary on *Romans*, Karl Barth was offered a chair of Reformed Theology in Germany at Göttingen. As he began preparing his lectures on Reformed theology, he found in Luther, Calvin, and other reformers a theological resting place after his period of disillusionment.[61] Barth later explained that he embraced reformed theology because it "made the discovery that theology has to do with *God*. It made the great and shattering discovery of the real theme of all theology. The secret was simply this, that it took this theme seriously in all

---

McCormack, *Karl Barth's Theology*, 275.

58. McCormack, *Karl Barth's Theology*, 275–76.

59. Ibid., 275.

60. McCormack, *Karl Barth's Theology*, 276.

61. Although Barth also devoted a great deal of study to Zwingli during this period, he primarily found himself disappointed with that reformer's work. Thus, this work will focus primarily upon the two major influences upon Barth during this period: Luther and Calvin. See McCormack, *Karl Barth's Theology*, 315; and Thurneysen, *Karl Barth—Eduard Thurneysen: Briefwechsel, 1921–1930*, 132.

its distinctiveness, that it names God God, that it lets God be God, the one object that by no bold human grasping or inquiry or approach can be simply one object among many others."[62]

Luther on God's Justice

Barth found in Luther's work his own dialectic between the righteousness of God and the sin of humanity. Luther first emphasized the offence of humanity's sin against God that characterizes every aspect of human behavior and human works. Secondly, he explained the positive proclamation about God: we are justified and we live by his grace. The hope of Christ's grace is made known, not by seeking to look at the invisible things of God (his majesty and glory) by way of spiritual vision but grace is made known by the revelation of God in the cross.[63] "True theology and the true knowledge of God lie, then, in the crucified Christ."[64] According to Barth, Luther turned from the medieval attention to a "theology of glory" to his own theology of the cross as the true theme for theology, the only hope for human sin, and the centre for "faith as naked trust that casts itself into the arms of God's mercy."[65]

Barth was drawn to the theology of Luther and he continued to study his works and to reflect on the implications of justification by faith for social justice. Upon first discovering Luther, however, Barth found himself disappointed by Luther's failure to make the outworking of ethics of primary importance, so he turned to Calvin who "made the Reformation capable of dealing with the world and history when he hammered the faith of Luther into obedience."[66]

---

62. Barth, *The Theology of John Calvin*, 39. Webster argues in *Barth's Ethics of Reconciliation* that Barth's entire dogmatics is an exposition of the existence/being of God, "God is." While it stood in contrast with the driving concerns of some German theologians, Barth found support and guidance for this starting point in the writings of the Reformers. Webster, *Ethics of Reconciliation*, 3.

63. Barth, *Calvin*, 42–43.

64. Ibid., 44.

65. Ibid., 46.

66. Ibid., 90 and 74.

John Calvin: Christ as the Starting Point for Theology

Barth's interpretation of Calvin shed special light on his epistemological assumptions. He critiqued interpretations of Calvin that divided knowledge of God between natural and supernatural revelation, as did Catholicism. He wrote:

> Hence I think it is wrong to say that Calvin did not gain his insight into God and us from Christ or that he simply forced Christian elements into a general metaphysical, philosophical view. We need to note above all else that for Calvin there is no basic distinction between the elements of knowledge, but that Christ is from the first the key with which he unlocks the whole. Christ is that unspoken original presupposition in terms of which we see God *a priori* as the ground and goal, the one who judges us and shows us mercy, and in terms of which we see ourselves *a priori*, when measured against God, as sinners, and are thus pointed to grace.[67]

This quotation demonstrates the interesting blend of reformed methodology and Kantian epistemology that ultimately characterized Barth's epistemological assumptions. Barth's acceptance of Kant's limits on reason was reinforced by a strongly reformed doctrine of sin. Barth quoted Calvin, "Strictly, says Calvin, God's law is written in our hearts. . . . But because of our arrogance, which prevents us from finding ourselves, God had to give it to us in written form as well."[68] In other words, the sin of arrogance prevents humans from finding moral law in their hearts, so humans are dependent upon the revelation of God in scripture. For Barth, human reason is limited, making natural theology, the metaphysical use of analogy, and laws of nature unreliable as means to knowledge about God and about moral knowledge.[69] Rather, God is known by his self-revelation; he is seen in the person of Jesus Christ. Barth called Christ the "unspoken, original presupposition" by which we see God and we see ourselves.

As an ethicist, Calvin helped to describe the practical import of such doctrine in daily life.[70] Barth characterized Calvin's ethics in his 1536

---

67. Ibid., 164.

68. Ibid.

69. Obviously Barth went further than Kant by refusing to locate God or moral law in practical reason. The similarity with Kant was his acceptance of Kant's limits for pure reason.

70. Ibid., 194. Barth describes Calvin's theology as "simply a new edition of Luther's with a greater stress on ethics."

PART TWO—Karl Barth

Institutes, "When at the end Calvin seeks to speak expressly as an ethicist in the more precise sense, we do not have an added second or new thing, nor the law as a second thing alongside the gospel. His concern is simply for a right use of the freedom that is opened up for us by the gospel."[71] This standpoint would provide a vital critique of Barth's contemporary situation, in which law and gospel were separated. He later claimed that such separation led to the impotence and marginalization of a distinctly Christian witness in society.[72] Finally, Barth also adopted two important theses of Calvin's ethical thought: the command of God and the freedom of the Christian, as will be analyzed in chapters five and six of this book.[73]

The Lectures on Ethics

In 1925, Barth began teaching in Münster, where he delivered a series of lectures published posthumously as *Ethics*. These lectures are significant because they demonstrate Barth's early argument in favor of a theological starting point for ethics, a manner that echoed Calvin's unification of gospel and law. While his Christological starting point remained relatively undeveloped (in comparison with his later work), he recognized the importance of it at this early stage.

Unfortunately, the early dates of the lectures raise questions about the appropriateness of utilizing them as a reflection of Barth's mature social ethics, as some interpreters have done. For example, William James assumed a continuity of thought from the 1928/9 lectures to Barth's mature theological anthropology, which did not exist as fully as James suggested. James assumed that in these early lectures, Barth was already employing his mature appeal to co-humanity as a basis for his discussion of justice.[74] Yet a careful reading of Barth's 1928/9 *Ethics* reveals little evidence for this supposition.

---

71. Ibid., 118.

72. See Barth's later essay, "Gospel and Law," and chapter 2 of this book.

73. For a further analysis of the impact of the Reformers on Barth's ethics, see Webster's *Barth's Moral Theology*, 61ff.

74. James writes, "Therefore, the neighbor also becomes the criterion for what is lawful and right for me to do. By right, says Barth, we understand the order of human life in society that is publicly known and recognized and protected by public force. Theologically, Barth argues, the concept of right (of law) falls under the concept of reconciliation not that of creation." "An Analysis Of Karl Barth's Theological Anthropology," 22.

An Early Passion for Justice

During this period, Barth was still in the early stages of developing a Christological framework for his anthropology and for his ethics. Barth's mature conception of a co-humanity that is grounded in the humanity of Christ (a starting point for his mature theory of justice) was in its developmental stages. Barth himself said that he was merely "on the way to a 'true anthropology'" during this phase.[75] This self-reflection appears accurate, for it was only later that Barth developed the *analogia relationis*, which is key to his theory of co-humanity that is grounded in Christ.[76] In addition, his social ethics reflected an ambiguity when compared with his later Christological framework for justice. In some instances he did appeal to God's Word as a basis for understanding that "we are oriented to our fellows."[77] Yet in others parts of the lectures, he hardly appealed to a Christological basis for ethics[78] and he called for solidarity with all humans on the basis of a kinship of souls, shared blood relations, or mutuality of life.[79]

Because Barth's ethics were yet to fully blossom in this period, it is of more value to examine Barth's mature works in seeking to describe his theory of justice. However, his 1928/9 *Ethics* is helpful for our purposes because it supports the argument that Barth held a keep concern for social justice and human rights. Even in this stage, in which he emphasized the dialectic of God's utter transcendence as over against creation, he continued to argue to argue for human dignity and human rights in this treatment of social ethics in this first volume.[80] However, given the relatively

---

75. Barth, *CD* 1/1:127.

76. According to Beintker, Barth's earliest form of the *analogia entis* could be seen in *Romans* II but it was not "unfolded" until Barth's 1931 book on Anselm. Beintker, *Die Dialektik in der "dialektischen Theologie" Karl Barths*, 262 and 193. McCormack argues that Barth (and Balthasar) overestimate the shift that takes place with the publication of the Anselm book by seeking to demonstrate that the Anselm book indicates a continuity in Barth's turn toward a Christological starting point (McCormack, *Karl Barth's Theology*, 422–23). Yet, while McCormack's thesis may indeed be true and the beginnings of a Christological method can be recognized in the *Ethics*, this method had not yet influenced Barth's anthropology and ethics to the extent that his development of the *analogia entis* later would (cf. Barth, *Ethics*, 57 and 336).

77. Barth, *Ethics*, 57. See also 336.

78. See especially Barth, "Chapter Two: The Command of God the Creator," in *Ethics*, 117–260. Jesus or Christ is only mentioned on six of these 144 pages. The Word is mentioned on fifteen pages. Compared with Barth's doctrine of creation in the dogmatics, such inattention to Christology is astonishing. While he certainly is moving toward a Christological basis at this phase, it certainly has not been developed fully yet.

79. Barth, *Ethics*, 180, 187, 195.

80. See for instance, *Ethics*, §12, especially pp. 367–69 and 376–90. His 1930/31 lectures added another section on church and state in §13, pp. 440–51.

underdeveloped state of his dogmatics, Barth had not yet developed the Christological foundation that would provide a more consistent grounding for this argument.

The One Word of God

The political events and Barth's theological research during the five years following his completion of *Ethics* proved extremely significant in establishing the Christological starting point that would characterize Barth's mature theological ethics. This period in Barth's development may be encapsulated in the following statement: Jesus Christ is the One Word of God. This theme is significant for our purposes because it demonstrates the culmination of Barth's rejection of anthropocentric approaches to God and to human ethics. In addition, it provides insight into the methodology that Barth would employ for his ethics. He believed that his contemporaries opened themselves to dangers by beginning with human laws or capacities to know God or to describe just action. By contrast, he argued that both theology and ethics must begin with God and God's self-revelation in Jesus Christ.

Barth's critics sensed that the "one-sidedness" of his emphasis upon deity would undermine human dignity. Yet during this period, Barth's witness to the One Word critiqued key human rights violations committed by the Nazis, violations that the German Christians overlooked: the oppression of the Christian church and of the German Jews. Barth spoke a "resounding 'No'" against both forms of oppression and the theology that supported them.[81] Yet Barth's "Yes," his constructive theology, was limited because he was in the early stages of his Christological method.[82]

The One Word: Present in History

A key partner in conversation during this period was the Polish Jesuit, Erich Przywara.[83] Barth encountered Przywara in 1923, through an article

---

81. Busch, "The Covenant of Grace," 478. Busch cites Barth's letter to Fr. Schmidt, Jan. 1, 1934.

82. For example, Barth argued that Christians must support members of the synagogue in 1934, but did not publish his fully developed theological rationale for this support until *CD* 2/2 in 1942.

83. Although Barth encountered Przywara before his 1925 lectures on ethics, I have placed this dialogue after *Ethics* because Barth's response to Przywara took place over a period of several years and culminated in his 1929 publication, *The Holy Spirit*

An Early Passion for Justice

in which he critiqued Barth's inability to sustain a concept of God's immanence in balance with Barth's emphasis on the transcendence of God. While Przywara appreciated Barth's emphasis upon transcendence, he accused Barth of an "one-sidedness" of relationship that rejected any unity of God with humankind.[84]

Przywara accounted for the immanence of God by developing Augustine's doctrine of the *analogia entis*, i.e., the analogy of being, which determines the direct relation of God to humanity through the concept of being. By simply existing, humans (and creation) share in the being of God. While humans and creation are certainly different kinds of being (for example, finite versus God's infiniteness), the being of God may be thought of analogically through an awareness of the realities of God's creation.[85]

The Jesuit theologian objected to Barth's replacement of the notion of "analogy" between God and the creature with "pure negation."[86] He wrote, "If the *analogia entis* of the Catholic concept of God means the mysterious tension of a 'similar-dissimilar,' corresponding to the tension of the 'God in us and above us,' then in the Protestant concept of God, the 'similarity' has been completely crossed out."[87] Such one-sidedness, Przywara claimed, undermined both a theology of Incarnation and an ecclesiology that accounts for the ongoing presence of God in the world.[88]

On the positive side, Przywara's critique appeared to have offered Barth a valuable means toward developing his mature Christological basis for interpreting human personhood (and justice).[89] That Barth devoted serious attention to Przywara's critique and to further research into the meaning of the incarnation, is evidenced in *The Göttingen Dogmatics*.[90] Likely spurred by Przywara's criticisms, Barth drew from the work of post-Reformationists a conception of the continuity of God's work in human persons and in society through the incarnation of Christ: the Logos' tak-

---

and the Christian Life (HSCL).

84. Przywara, "*Gott in uns oder uber uns? (Immanenz und Transzendenz im heutigen Geistesleben),*" quoted in McCormack, *Karl Barth's Theology,* 320.

85. Robin W. Lovin, in foreword to Barth, *HSCL*, xvi.

86. McCormack points out that Barth set aside the way of "pure negation" in favor of the "dialectic way" in Barth's article, "The Word of God as the Task of Theology."

87. McCormack, *Karl Barth's Theology,* 350.

88. Ibid., 321.

89. Ibid.

90. Barth, *Göttingen Dogmatics.*

ing on of human flesh as the Mediator between God and humanity. In this doctrine, Barth's Christology shifted from primarily eschatological in focus (an "organic" process) to both historical and eschatological. With a stronger doctrine of the incarnation, Barth could affirm the presence of the Logos in history, as one who enters the contradiction of human existence and overcomes it.[91] In coming years, this doctrine of the incarnation would enable Barth to reconceptualize his anthropology in distinctively Christological terms.

Yet Barth did not accept the whole of Przywara's solution to the dialectical problem. In *The Holy Spirit and the Christian Life* (1929), he reacted strongly against the *analogia entis*.[92] He sensed two dangers for Christian ethics in this doctrine. Simply stated, he believed that this doctrine affirmed that humans could, firstly *know* and, secondly *do* justice without the one Word of God, revealed in Jesus Christ and present in the Holy Spirit. First, Barth argued that the creaturely spirit cannot *produce*

---

91. McCormack, *Karl Barth's Theology*, 327–28.

92. Barth, "*Der heilige Geist und das christliche Leben*," in Karl Barth and Heinrich Barth, *Zur Lehre vom heiligen Geist*, Beiheft I of *Zwischen den Zeiten*, 39–105; Barth, *HSCL*. There is much evidence that this essay is a response to Przywara and the larger dialogue with Catholic theology, including Barth's engagement with Augustine (rather than Aquinas), the discussion of the *analogia entis*, continuity/discontinuity, and similarity/dissimilarity (see, for example, *HSCL*, 8–10, 60) as well as his repeated use of Przywara's phrase, "tranquil and assured," at key points in his presentation (see pp. 8–9 and 22). Later interpreters criticized Barth for misrepresenting Przywara's *analogia entis*. Balthasar defended Przywara: "Rightly understood, the analogy of being is the destruction of every system in favor of a totally objective availability of the creature for God and for the divine measure of the creature" (Balthasar, *Karl Barth*, 255). Balthasar conceded that Przywara did not make his answer to Barth's objections clear until his publication in the following decade (Balthasar, *Karl Barth*, 255n5). Jüngel described Barth's early notion of this doctrine as a "horrible phantom" that Barth later relinquished after he adopted a type of analogical method (*analogia fides*) as the starting point of his own theology. Jüngel, *God as the Mystery of the World*, 282–83. The work of Alan Torrance has resolved Jüngel's criticism by clarifying Barth's objection as a rejection of *analogia entis* as a metaphysical principle that provides the foundation for theological methodology. Torrance, *Persons in Communion*, 162–63. See also later discussion in chapter 7, Section titled: "Human Ontology and Epistemic Access to Justice. McCormack brought some resolution to the matter: "In all likelihood, [Barth] was simply indicating that the phrase *analogia entis* carries more freight than Przywara personally would allow. Barth saw in this phrase the ill-advised attempt to order both God and humankind into a higher concept, namely of 'being'; to make both God and humankind simply differing exemplifications of being in order then to ascend from a knowledge of creaturely being to a knowledge of God (natural theology)." McCormack, *Karl Barth's Theology*, 389. See also Barth's lecture, "Fate and Idea," for his critique of the *analogia entis*.

the word of God by presuming knowledge about his word as a result of continuity or by giving lists of moral counsels confidently taken from scripture. He wrote, "An ethics that thinks it can know and set forth the command of God, the Creator, plants itself upon the throne of God."[93] Nor can the creaturely spirit *receive* the Word of God unassisted.[94] Barth explained, "The fundamental significance of the Holy Spirit for the Christian life is that this, our participation in the occurrence of revelation, is just our *being grasped* in this occurrence which is the effect of the *divine* action."[95] Thus, in opposition to the *analogia entis* as a foundation for ethics, Barth argued that the only starting point for knowing the good is the revelation of God's Word in the Holy Spirit who meets the creature and points to him his way as creature.[96]

The second problem Barth addressed was the Augustinian doctrine of reconciliation. Barth argued that Augustine had too weak a view of human sin and of grace, "Augustine's view of sin was that it was really only a wound, a derangement within the undisturbed continuity of man with God."[97] Grace, then, was a "synergism" of "divine gift and man's creative action combined into one."[98] For Augustine, Barth said, the role of the Holy Spirit is to impart "a divine quality inhering in the soul" that "uplifts man by and by until he is made a non-sinner."[99]

Why did Barth recoil at the idea of a synergism between God and humanity? He believed that it failed to take the problem of sin seriously: "Sin is not taken in deadly earnest when it is regarded as something that can be radically overcome by the enthusiasm of 'good intentions.'"[100] In much the same way, he believed that his contemporaries, such as Karl Holl, in their appeals to the "'synthetic view' of God's act and man's experience" were actually asserting their own forms of power and pride. Even worse, such writers were doing so "under the prefix of predestination and the loftiest of humility."[101] To truly listen to the One Word of God is to know the claim

---

93. Barth, *HSCL*, 10.
94. Ibid.
95. Ibid., 6.
96. Ibid., 11.
97. Ibid., 23.
98. Ibid., 22.
99. Ibid., 23.
100. Ibid.
101. Ibid.

of grace that binds us in service to God and to our neighbors.[102] To reject this grace is to exalt oneself in the place of power, "to hear only the echo of our own voice, in unbounded solitariness"[103] that is ultimately destructive of the neighbor. Such anthropocentrism was the danger that Barth sensed and vehemently rejected.

The parallel contrast with the work of Wojtyla/John Paul II should be clear. Whereas John Paul II wanted to attributed two sources of knowledge (nature and revelation) to his account of justice, Barth insisted on only one. In the next chapter, I will argue that Barth retained his critique of the *analogia entis* in a manner that differentiates his ethical methodology from that of John Paul II. His dialogue with Przywara played a key role in developing this critique. Yet it also helped him to recognize the centrality of the doctrine of the incarnation for bridging the divide between the Logos and human existence.

Faith Seeking Understanding

In 1930 Barth accepted a new teaching position in Bonn. That summer, he taught a seminar on Anselm of Canterbury (1033–1109), whose method of theological inquiry so riveted Barth's attention that he soon published a book on Anselm's *Proslogion*. His interpretation of Anselm provided a clear articulation of the conceptual framework for his own theological method: *Fides Quaerens Intellectum*, (*Faith Seeking Understanding.*) Barth argued that Anselm was not seeking to prove the existence of God in order to lead men to faith. Rather, "*Credo ut intelligam* means: it is my very faith itself that summons me to knowledge."[104]

Using this approach, Barth sought to undermine the traditional task of rational theology, which attempted to establish, by use of reason, the existence and sometimes the attributes of God. "For Barth, this is unnecessary, if not positively misleading, because God has given himself in this revelation in such a way that we can speak rationally of him on the basis of this very revelation. Rational theology is the description of what is in fact the case . . ."[105] In other words, God's being and his reality, which is revealed in his Word, grounds every attempt at understanding. Thus the task of

---

102. Ibid., 34.
103. Ibid.
104. Barth, *Anselm*, 18.
105. Gunton, *Becoming and Being*, 126.

theology is not to prove God's existence (e.g., Aquinas)[106] or to unfold the contents of the human religious consciousness (e.g., Schleiermacher).[107] Rather, it is to "explicate the meaning of faith as it is given to us in the incarnation."[108] Once again in this work, Barth rejected any attempts to begin with humanity or human rationality to get to God. Rather, the task of theology is to describe and witness to the God who exists and who has revealed himself in Christ. Thus, all theology begins with God's one word in Christ.

On the Political Front (1933–1934)

Two years after Barth completed his book on Anselm, his Christological approach found its expression in the political sphere. In 1933, Hitler rose to power as chancellor of Germany. In a speech given on January 31 of that year, he pledged that the "national government . . . will take under its firm protection Christianity as a basis of our morality."[109] From that time onward, Hitler sought to bring all German institutions under governmental control, including the church. In April of 1933, the Nazis established the Civil Service Law, which included "The Aryan Paragraph," which barred non-Aryans from civil service (including education and church service). In fall of that year, the German Christians acted to "rid the church of Jewish influence" by forbidding those of Jewish ancestry to hold church offices or to serve as pastors and by confining non-Aryans to their own separate parishes.[110]

The Aryan Paragraph became the major catalyst for the formation of the Pastors' Emergency League and the Confessing Church in 1933. At the first meeting of the League, speaking on the treatment of the Jews, Barth argued that the church must not remain silent for "the one whose duty it is to proclaim the Word of God *must* address such events with what the Word of God declares."[111] In a letter dated January 1, 1934, he said that the word is a resounding "No" and that the Evangelical church must "enter the fray in earnest support of the members of the synagogue."[112]

106. Aquinas, *Summa Theologica* 1a. 1–26.
107. Schleiermacher, *A Brief Outline of the Study of Theology*, division one.
108. McCormack, *Karl Barth's Theology*, 427.
109. Lindsay, *Covenanted Solidarity*, 22.
110. Baranowski, "The Confessing Church and Antisemitism," 101.
111. Busch, "The Covenant," 480.
112. Ibid., 478. Barth's letter to Fr. Schmidt, Jan. 1, 1934.

PART TWO—Karl Barth

From a theological perspective, Barth believed that the root of the problem for the church was the posing of a human message "alongside God's revelation."[113] He believed that the German Christians were adding to God's revelation in Christ an additional source of revelation, which provided the foundation to support human theories about "race, blood, soil, people, state, etc."[114] Such theories could be conceptualized using the Lutheran idea of a first revelation of the law (OT) that preceded the second revelation of the gospel of grace (NT).[115] Or they could be thought of in terms of a natural theology that is revealed in the orders of creation, orders that support the separation of races. Barth sensed danger that such natural laws or orders merely served to label human preference (i.e., anti-Semitism) as the will of God (i.e., established through creation or law).[116]

For example, the pro-Nazi theologian, Emanuel Hirsch argued that the nation is an order of creation that is composed by a particular *volk* (people) of common biological-racial, cultural, ethnic, and religious heritage.[117] Because the nation is an order of creation, rather than a human creation, Hirsch believed that Christian duty entailed upholding and preserving the state in its strength and distinctiveness over against the threat of oppression by foreign and domestic elements.[118] Any weakening of the state (as during the Weimar era, following the Versailles Treaty of WWI) threatened the very identity of her citizens.[119] In this manner, a belief in *volk* as a primary order of creation, willed by God, paved the way for Hirsch's embrace of Nazi ideology, including aspects of its anti-Semitism.[120]

---

113. Busch, *Karl Barth*, 241.

114. Ibid., 243.

115. See Jüngel's argument that such an interpretation is a later development in Luther's theology, rather than attributable to Luther himself. *Karl Barth*, 105–16.

116. Busch, *Karl Barth*, 243.

117. Hirsch, *Deutschlands Schicksal*, 109–25. Cf. 143–44.

118. Reimer, *The Hirsch and Tillich Debate*, 142 and 150.

119. See also, Ericksen, "Assessing the Heritage," 26–33.

120. According to Reimer, Hirsch separated himself from the more radical anti-Semitic polemic that labeled Jews as racially inferior and he advocated friendship with those of Jewish descent. Yet Hirsch's *volk* theology supported racial segregation in the church and in society. Reimer writes, "It is here where he in effect provided fertile soil for anti-Jewish policy both in the state and in the church. His sympathy for individual cases cannot exonerate him for this underlying structural discrimination against the Jewish converts, let alone the German Jewish community at large about which he, like most Evangelical Christians even in the Confessing Church, remained silent" (Reimer, *The Hirsch and Tillich Debate*, 86. Cf. 97–98).

An Early Passion for Justice

In May of 1934, Barth composed the Barmen Declaration, which proclaimed: "Jesus Christ, as he is attested for us in Holy Scripture, is the one Word of God which we have to hear and which we have to trust and obey in life and in death."[121] Barth's concern was to defend the right of the church to religious freedom over against Hitler's desire to make the church subservient to the state. For Barth, this proclamation entailed the rejection of another ruler of the church (e.g., Hitler) and of another source of proclamation by the church (e.g., orders of creation or natural theology). The declaration was unanimously accepted by the Confessing Synod of the German Evangelical Church.

As Barth witnessed the destruction wrought against the Jewish community in Germany in coming years, he regretted that he had not made "the Jewish question" a decisive feature of the declaration. In 1934, he chose not to because of the extreme conservatism of the participants of the synod and his expectation that the declaration would not be accepted if it addressed anti-Semitism. In his later regret, he wrote, "but that does not excuse me for not having at least gone through the motions of fighting."[122]

---

121. http://www.sacred-texts.com/chr/barmen.htm.

122. Busch, *Karl Barth*, 248. Barth has been widely accused of anti-Semitism by various interpreters. I have interpreted Barth differently due to the remarkable evidence to the contrary, brought to light by the research of Eberhard Busch and Mark Lindsay. In this footnote and in a later footnote in this chapter, I will state the accusations and the reasons I have interpreted Barth as having supported the Jewish race. Klaus Scholder accused Barth of anti-Semitism because he focused the Barmen Declaration on the preservation of the church rather than on a challenge to the Nazi state and the Aryan Paragraph. Scholder, *The Churches and the Third Reich*, 546–59. While Barth admitted his own failure to bring "the Jewish question" to the fore in the Declaration, this was not due to his personal anti-Semitism but to the conservatism of the church, which would not have passed such a pro-Jewish document (see previous footnote). In September 1 of that year, Barth wrote, "The Jewish question is certainly, seen theologically, *the* exponent of the entire event of our time . . . Here, if anywhere, one must draw the line which, if crossed, can only be considered a betray of the Gospel" (Barth's letter to Fr. Dalmann, Sept. 1, 1933 documented in Busch's "The Covenant of Grace," 479). Such statements, as well as his participation in the Pastors' Emergency League, whose manifesto condemned the Aryan Paragraph, indicate Barth's personal support of German Jews.

PART TWO—Karl Barth

The Barth-Brunner Debate

In that same year, Emil Brunner wrote a pamphlet condemning the "false conclusions" of Barth's theology.[123] Over against the "one-sidedness"[124] of Barth's argument that Christ is the one Word of God's revelation, Brunner wanted to posit natural theology as a basis for ethics. Brunner questioned Barth's ability to find a point of contact with non-Christian ethics that would allow for dialogue. He argued that Barth should not communicate to non-Christians an ethic that depends upon the grace of God to be understood. He claimed that natural theology provided that necessary point of contact.

Barth replied to Brunner with an angry, "Nein!" and rejected natural theology, which he defined as "every (positive *or* negative) *formulation of a system* which claims to be theological, *i.e.* to interpret divine revelation, whose *subject*, however, differs fundamentally from the revelation in Jesus Christ and whose *method* therefore differs equally from the exposition of Holy Scripture."[125] Many scholars believe that Barth overreacted to Brunner's essay. Yet it is important to note the background against which Barth wrote. In the midst of such a volatile political context, Barth perceived Brunner's essay as "an alarm signal" indicating the danger of compromise that threatened the purity and unity of the theology of the Evangelical Church.[126] In addition, the seeds of this split between Brunner and Barth had already been sown in the early 1920s, during a disagreement between the two on the relation of law and gospel. During a visit with Barth in 1924, Brunner argued for a "dialectic of law and gospel,"[127] in which there was one level of the knowledge of God that came through the law and a one that came through the gospel. "For the knowledge of the law we need no revelation whatsoever," Brunner wrote.[128] The law is "*innata*, rational." Through knowledge of this innate law, the person recognizes that he is placed under judgment by God and he encounters his despair. At

---

123. Brunner, "Nature and Grace," 15.

124. Ibid.

125. Barth, "No!" 74–75.

126. Ibid., 69. He writes, "The real danger seems to me to lie in a future attitude of the Church and of theology which is informed by the spirit of the many on both sides to-day who are undecided and ready for compromise and which might stand at the end of all that we are now going through."

127. McCormack, *Karl Barth's Theology*, 397–98. Letter from Brunner to Barth, undated, original in Karl Barth-Archiv.

128. McCormack, *Karl Barth's Theology*, 397–98.

this point, the person becomes open to the revelation of God's grace and acceptance.

For the same reasons that Barth rejected Przywara's doctrine of the *analogia entis*, he rejected Brunner's appeal to natural theology.[129] For Barth, the rational capacity within the human person did not yield reliable knowledge of God—whether of God's law or of his grace. Rejecting any "point of contact" within the creature, Barth argued that the Word of God does not rely upon human capacity in any sense. Rather, the Word overcomes humanity's resistance and opposition to God.[130] In addition, God does not speak two words, one of judgment under the law and one of grace in Christ. Rather, Christ is the One Word of grace and judgment, claim and command.

The ethical and political implications of Brunner's claims were perhaps the greatest impetus for Barth's uncompromising reply. Barth feared the imminent danger of natural theology as a foundation for ethical and political decisions. He sought to reinforce the absolute impossibility for a human to hold up history or society as a foundation for discovering God-implanted orders in creation, which shape political and ethical programs. By holding history and society and nature as valid foundations for knowledge about God, Barth believed that German Christians limited the freedom of the gospel to proclaim God's grace and his commands for humanity.

Writing from Switzerland, perhaps Brunner did not realize the implications of his argument for the existence of natural "ordinances which are the constant factors of historical and social life."[131] Though Barth conceded that such ordinances may indeed exist, he insisted that humans are unable to discern them or to use them as a basis for speaking about God or ethics. He wrote:

> No doubt there are such things as moral and sociological axioms which seem to underlie the various customs, laws and usages of different peoples, and seem to appear in them with some regularity. And there certainly seems to be some connection between these axioms and the instinct and reason which both believers and unbelievers have indeed every reason to allow to function in the life of the community. But what are these

---

129. Barth, "No!" 96.
130. Ibid., 89; and Hart, *Regarding Karl Barth*, 162–63.
131. Brunner, "Nature and Grace," 29.

axioms? Or who—among us, who are "sinners through and through"!—decided what they are?[132]

Thus, Barth radically opposed him by arguing that Brunner's *theologis naturalis* provided a foundation for human law that was naïve regarding the noetic impact of sin. Using such an approach, human ethics claimed a validity that Barth believed should only belong to the one word of God in Christ.

Because of this concern with Brunner's approach, Barth came down even harder upon his own good friend than he had come against Catholic natural theology. He wrote:

> I can hardly say a clear "No" to Hirsch and his associates, but close my eyes in the case of Brunner, the Calvinist, the Swiss "dialectical theologian." For it seems clear to me that at the decisive point he takes part in the false movement of thought by which the Church today is threatened.... My polemic against Brunner is more acute than that against Hirsch, because his position is more akin to mine, because I believe him to be in possession of more truth, *i.e.* to be closer to the Scriptures, because I take him more seriously—because for that very reason he seems to me just now to be much more dangerous than a man like Hirsch.[133]

Because he saw Nazism as the primary enemy, Barth viewed his rejection of Brunner's natural theology as more critical than his rejection of Hirsch. Barth sought to oppose any methodology that opened the door to the projection of human ethics onto the command of God. His opposition to Brunner demonstrates that Barth's critique of natural theology was not anti-Catholic[134] but that his overriding concern was to oppose the methodology, arising from either tradition, which set another source alongside revelation.

In his responses to Brunner and Przywara, Barth did not explicitly answer the valid questions that were implied in their critiques: Does Barth's Christological ethic have a point of contact with common humanity? What does the gospel of grace have to do with the morality of a non-Christian society? Does the church, without a point of contact in natural theology or the *analogia entis*, lose her voice altogether? Barth's answers to

---

132. Barth, "No!" 86.

133. Ibid., 68.

134. For example, see Barth's affirmation of Söhngen's conception of the *analogia entis* in CD 2/1:81.

these questions came more explicitly in his *Church Dogmatics*, which we will expound in the following two chapters.

Conclusion

This chapter sought to explore the development of Barth's epistemology as it specifically related to his account of social justice. It articulated what Barth was against, in order to clarify Barth's own method for discerning an account of justice. Namely, Barth was *against* any philosophical or theological system that set up human consciousness, human reason, or natural theology as a viable source of knowledge alongside the self-revelation of God in Jesus Christ. I sought to demonstrate that his very concern for social justice went hand-in-hand with his critique, for he believed that the violence of his era was substantiated by such sources.

Ironically, each of the systems of thought he opposed proved compelling precisely because they appeared to dignify human persons: Religious socialists defended the rights of workers; the Nazis sought to restore dignity to their native peoples; the beliefs of theological liberalism, the *analogia entis*, and natural theology sought to establish human dignity by emphasizing continuity with God and the autonomous capacities of human persons. Yet Barth contended that an evil lay inherent in each of these systems: the failure to recognize one's own tendency towards pride and destruction of the neighbor or towards sloth and apathy toward the neighbor. Because of this danger, Barth argued, human systems and human beliefs must always be laid bare to the critique of the one word, Jesus Christ. Thus, for Barth, the revelation of God in Jesus Christ formed the basis for epistemic access to justice.

5

Barth's Epistemology and Ethical Method

CHAPTER 4 EXAMINED THE HISTORICAL DEVELOPMENT OF BARTH'S EPIStemological basis for justice, primarily explaining the ethical methods that Barth was reacting against and the reasons that he centered his methodology on the revelation of God in Jesus Christ. This chapter continues to explore the question of ethical method, but from a theoretical perspective. It seeks to answer the same question that was posed to the thought of Wojtyla/John Paul II: How is knowledge about justice posited? Chapter 4 provided Barth's initial solution, as seen in his claim that Jesus Christ is the source of ethical knowledge. This chapter explores the significance of that claim for Barth's idea of justice.

Barth's Epistemology: The Theological Basis for Knowing Justice

Like John Paul II, Barth argued that the source of Christian ethics is God. In opposition to a deistic or non-theistic starting point that would seek to derive a theory of justice from cultural norms, human ideals, or rationality independent of God, both men argued that God must be the source of human ethics. Specifically, Barth said that the ethical question finds its starting point in God rather than in human existence.[1] He appealed to God as the source of good and the source of good human action.[2] For Barth, this good and responsible human action is revealed in God's command. Although John Paul appealed to natural law, he argued that this law is not independent of God or of co-existence with God but grounded in God's very being. God's being, which is good, determines what is good in

---

1. Barth, *CD* 1/2:792–93.
2. Barth, *CD* 2/2:546–47.

Barth's Epistemology and Ethical Method

human existence. God's very being determines the moral laws that guide good human behavior.

In this sense, Barth and John Paul II have striking similarities because they both rested their ethics upon God's being. It is for this reason that Carl Braaten pointed to their apparent convergence, suggesting that Barth's critique of natural law played a role in shifting Catholic ideas of natural law away from any deistic tendencies or attempts to detach natural law from the principles of theology. Likewise, other commentators have pointed to Barth's favorable movement toward Roman Catholic thought, citing his apparent change after his early critiques of natural law and the *analogia entis*.[3]

Yet when one examines their epistemic bases for justice, the divergence of their thought becomes more evident. While they would agree that God's being is the basis for ethics, they believe that humans obtain knowledge of this being (and thus of ethics) in different ways. John Paul II believed that God revealed himself both in creation and in Christ. By implication of this starting point, John Paul II believed that ethics, and justice in particular, is grounded in nature, so that social justice means treating another in accordance with the good of his or her nature and acting in harmony with the common good. For John Paul, the revelation of Christ offers a more complex account of justice by further revealing the dignity of human nature and by showing that, at times, mercy must overcome justice.

In contrast, Barth argued that God revealed himself definitively in Christ. Because of human sinfulness, God's revelation in creation is rightly interpreted only from a Christological starting point. In Christ, Barth suggested, humans discover justice in the acts of God in Christ: in election, in creation, in reconciliation, and in redemption. By implication, Barth discussed justice most often in terms of righteousness—the righteousness of God revealed in Christ that established right relations between humans. While both men appeal to God as the one from whom justice is derived, I will suggest that there is a marked divergence in epistemologies, which gives rise to differing theories of justice.

---

3. In the 1950s Brunner said that Barth's position on the *analogia entis* changed, thus settling the controversy between himself and Barth. Brunner, *Christian Doctrine of Creation and Redemption: Dogmatics*, 42–45. This was likely due to Balthasar's interpretation of Barth's conception of the *analogia entis* in *The Theology of Karl Barth*.

PART TWO—Karl Barth

Barth's Critique of the Analogia Entis

According to Barth, the Roman Catholic grounding of both moral philosophy and moral theology in creation, specifically in the metaphysics of being, differentiates Catholic ethics from his own. While he felt positively toward the Catholic ethical orientation, he also noted a substantial criticism regarding the dependence upon the *analogia entis*. Barth wrote:

> For this Roman Catholic co-ordination of moral philosophy and moral theology is based on the basic view of the harmony which is achieved in the concept of being, between nature and super-nature, reason and revelation, man and God. . . . According to this view, the fall does not alter the fact that man's imitative knowledge is capable and to that extent partakes of true being even without grace, and therefore—*analogia entis*—of communion with the supreme essential being, with God, and therefore with the supreme good, although on account of the fall a special illumination by the grace of revelation is needed actually to prevent it from falling into error.[4]

In other words, through the *analogia entis*, human knowledge of God and of the good is possible after the fall, because of the continuity of being between humanity and God. Barth argued that it is only the revelation of Jesus that makes possible human knowledge of God's good command because the command is grounded prior to creation and human nature, in God's being that is revealed in the election of Christ.[5]

Many scholars assume that Barth dropped his critique of the *analogia entis* following his dialogue with Catholic theologians Gottlieb Söhngen and Hans Urs von Balthasar. Yet research by Keith Johnson provides evidence that such an assumption is mistaken. According to Johnson, Barth did accept an adaptation of the *analogia entis* as articulated by Söhngen and developed further by von Balthasar and he agreed with Roman Catholic theology inasmuch as it embraced this modification, but he never relinquished his basic concern.[6]

This question of Barth's critique of the *analogia entis* is especially significant in seeking to engage Barth with John Paul because it raises the question, Would Barth have accepted John Paul's conception of the *analogia entis*? I contend that Barth would not have accepted it. In seeking

---

4. Barth, *CD* 2/2:530.
5. Ibid., 531.
6. Johnson, "*Analogia Entis*," 297–98. Barth, *CD* 2/1:82.

Barth's Epistemology and Ethical Method

to make this argument, I will first examine the adaptation proposed by Söhngen, which Barth found acceptable. Then I will compare Söhngen's proposal with John Paul's conception of the *analogia entis*, to seek to demonstrate that the latter did not make the proposed adaptation in his own work, so that Barth's criticism would still stand. Finally, I will seek to articulate Barth's alternate proposal for the knowability of God and ethics, namely the *analogia relationis*.

Söhngen's Interpretation

In his work, Söhngen argued that Barth could not reject the *analogia entis* because some correspondence must exist in order for the being of humanity to relate to God's being. In other words, the Christian life involves a faithful participation in the divine life, which must entail a participation in being. Thus, for Barth to reject any analogy of being, Söhngen suggested, rejects the very participation of the Christian in the being of God.

For Söhngen, the *participatio fides* in the Christian life must include a *participatio entis*. The two should not be opposed, otherwise, faith is only extrinsic to the human being and does not form the Christian in any significant way.[7] Through the incarnation, such a *participatio entis* is possible because Christ draws the human into participation in the divine life. He argued that Barth neglected to see that this participation in being is absolutely necessary if he wants to speak meaningfully of reconciliation between God and humanity. Yet Söhngen also argued that the *participatio entis* is only possible because of the *participatio fides*. In other words, faith provides the avenue by which such a participation in being might take place.

Along parallel lines, Söhngen proposed that the *analogia entis* is subordinated to the *analogia fides*.[8] He argued that humans cannot attain knowledge of God on the basis of metaphysics because "[human] nature does not participate at all in divine nature."[9] In metaphysics, Söhngen said, the human is merely directed to himself and the experience of his

---

7. Söhngen, "*Analogia Fidei,* Gottähnlichkeit allein aus Glauben?," 124. The majority of the following argument is indebted to Keith Johnson's excellent examination in "Analogia Entis."

8. Söhngen was also critiquing Barth on this account, arguing that Barth must take seriously the real human participation in the being of God or else salvation and the Christian life are merely external to the creature. Barth agreed with Söhngen on this point, stating that God's act of grace does imply a *participation fidei*. Barth, CD 2/1:82–84. Cf. Johnson, "*Analogia Entis*," 253.

9. Söhngen, "Analogia Fidei: Die Einheit in der Glaubenswissenschft," 201.

existence.¹⁰ By implication, philosophy cannot yield knowledge of God. Thus, the *analogia entis* must be conceptualized theologically rather than philosophically.¹¹

In his response, Barth acknowledged the warning that Söhngen posed to him and he agreed that "If there is a real analogy between God and man—an analogy which is a true analogy of being on both sides, an analogy in and with which the knowledge of God will in fact be given—what other analogy can it be than the analogy of being, which is posited and created by the work and action of God Himself, the analogy which has its actuality from God and from God alone, and therefore in faith and in faith alone?"¹² From this statement it is clear that Barth began to affirm the necessity of the *analogia entis* as a part of knowledge and life with God. Yet he carefully bounded the analogy of being within the analogy of faith, echoing Söhngen's concern that the *analogia entis* is subordinated to the *analogia fides*. Barth admitted, "If this is the Roman Catholic doctrine of *analogia entis*, then naturally I must withdraw my earlier statement that I regard the *analogia entis* as 'the invention of anti-Christ.'" However, he continued, "I am not aware that this particular doctrine of the *analogia entis* is to be found anywhere else in the Roman Catholic Church or that it has ever been adopted in this sense."¹³ Because Barth believed that Söhngen was unique among Catholics, Barth continued to criticize Roman Catholic metaphysics, echoed in his critique of ethics that was quoted previously.¹⁴

After von Balthasar took up similar lines of argument a few years later, Barth became relatively silent on the topic so that many thought that he withdrew his criticism entirely. Yet Barth did not relinquish his concern about the *analogia entis*. Rather, he believed that Söhngen had been the forerunner of "a new Catholic theological learning" that had adapted the *analogia entis* along similar lines.¹⁵

This fact is demonstrated in the response that Barth gave to a question posed to him in 1962, near the end of his career, inquiring how he had modified his use of the *analogia entis*. Barth answered that he "began to

---

10. Söhngen, "Analogia Fidei: Die Einheit in der Glaubenswissenschaft," 198.

11. Johnson, "*Analogia Entis*," 248–49.

12. Barth, *CD* 2/1:83.

13. Ibid., 82.

14. Barth, *CD* 2/2:530. Note that this critique followed his engagement with Söhngen earlier in the same volume.

15. This quotation is from a letter to Markus Barth in 1957, cited in Busch, *Karl Barth*, 428. Cf. Johnson, "*Analogia Entis*," 252.

see that the notion of analogy cannot be totally suppressed in theology."[16] For this reason, he explained, he began to speak of analogy in terms of the *analogia relationis*, the analogy of relation between God and humanity established in the God-human, Jesus Christ. Then Barth described his response to the critiques of Söhngen and von Balthasar. Barth explained, "Some of my critics said: 'Well, after all, an *analogia relationis* is also some kind of *analogia entis*.' And I couldn't deny it completely. I said: Well, after all, if *analogia entis* is interpreted as *analogia relationis* or analogy of faith, well, then I will no longer say nasty things about *analogia entis*. But I understand it in *this way*. So I have not changed my mind."[17] Here Barth restated his earliest response to Söhngen and allowed for *analogia entis* if it were reinterpreted in light of the analogy of faith.

Söhngen and John Paul II Compared

Having depicted the form of the *analogia entis* with which Barth agreed, we now raise the question, Would Barth have accepted John Paul II's conception of the *analogia entis*? I contend that Barth would have rejected it. In part one of this book, I sought to demonstrate that the *analogia entis* formed a primary basis for the ethics of John Paul II. From this research it became evident that John Paul II grounded his theory of justice in nature because he assumed that humans could attain knowledge of God and of the laws of nature apart from Christ. Christ served to further and perfect Christian ethics. Specifically, humans could know justice through both nature and through the revelation of Christ. For this reason, John Paul II defined justice as that which accords with human nature.

From this research, it is evident that John Paul II did not embrace the concept *analogia entis* that Barth found acceptable. John Paul II maintained the belief that some knowledge of God and of justice is possible through nature, and thus through philosophy, whereas Söhngen explicitly rejected this possibility. In addition, John Paul II believed that the correspondence of human nature with God's nature (in the *imago Dei*) made knowledge of justice possible apart from Christ, and indeed formed the basis of his definition of justice. Söhngen, rejected any natural participation of humanity in God, thus relegating knowledge of God and ethics to theological rather than natural knowledge. So while Barth may have accepted Söhngen's understanding of the *analogia entis*, the approach of

---

16. Barth, *Gespräche*, 499.
17. Ibid.

PART TWO—Karl Barth

John Paul II employed this key metaphysical concept in a manner that Barth continued to reject.

Barth's Alternative: The Analogia Relationis

This argument becomes even more convincing by comparing their bases for knowing justice, for at this point the difference between Barth's *analogia relationis* and John Paul II's *analogia entis* demonstrates itself. John Paul defined social justice as that which accords with human nature. In knowing what human nature is, one discovers what justice is. John Paul II grounded his definition of human nature in creation, arguing that humans were created with a goodness that corresponds to the goodness of God, with a capacity for reason, freedom, and transcendence. He appealed to the Boethian definition of the human as individual substance of rational nature and emphasized the capacity for humans to relate to others in freedom and love. While the fall impacted the will, it did not destroy the goodness of human nature or the *capacity* for humans to have knowledge of themselves and God. The fall did, however, impact the human will and thus the *willingness* of the human to seek God and to know what his image means. For this reason, Christ came to bring humans back to this truth of their dignified nature before God and to restore man to his proper value. Thus, for John Paul II, fallen human nature stands in continuity with the nature that Christ perfects.

For Barth, by contrast, there is no seed of goodness in human nature, by which we may know and do the good. Our knowledge of justice is not grounded in our existence as creatures. Rather, for Barth, the grounds for knowing God and justice precede creation. This knowledge is grounded in election, for the election of Christ to be the God-human, forms the basis for the unfolding relation of God and humanity and, by analogy, for intra-human relations. A brief description of Barth's doctrine of election may assist readers who are unfamiliar with Barth's thought.

The Doctrine of Election

In 1936, Barth heard Peter Maury give a lecture titled, "Election and Faith," which influenced Barth's doctrine of election. In this essay, Maury proposed that the doctrine of election could not be treated in abstraction from Jesus Christ for "outside of Christ we know neither of the electing

Barth's Epistemology and Ethical Method

God, nor of His elect, nor of the act of election."[18] Maury reasoned that if election is in Christ, it means that Christ has taken human rejection upon himself and, as a result, the purposes of God for humans are positive. Rather than electing some and rejecting others, God in Christ rejects all and elects all.[19] Thus, both the election and the rejection of humanity were realized in Christ, revealing God's love for humanity.

Barth incorporated Maury's thesis into his own thought, applying it in his doctrine of God, as the first step towards understanding the link between God and humanity: the love of God for human persons revealed in the election of humanity in Christ. According to Barth, the subject of election is the Son of God with the Father and the Holy Spirit. Christ is the subject because he is the elect, chosen by God to bear the sin of the human race and to accept the wrath that is the consequence of sin. Christ is also the object of election as the elected human person, the eternal son in human nature. Thus, Jesus Christ was elected to be the object of divine retribution and rejection: he accepted the consequences for sin that humans deserved.[20] Because of this election, Christ bridges the gap between God and all humanity, "Himself God and Himself man, and so mediating between the two. In Him man sees and knows God."[21] In Christ, all humans have been elected to participate in his glory.[22] In this way, Jesus fulfils the eternal will and decree of God and he discloses God's covenant toward all humanity: the divine election of grace.[23]

For the purposes of our inquiry, Barth's doctrine of election has two key facets. First, the covenantal relationship was established prior to God's act of creation by God's election of Christ as the mediator between God and humanity. By implication, human nature is only given in Jesus Christ because, in Him, Barth said, "we have to do with the eternal basis and temporal fulfilment of the covenant and therefore with the ground and basis of all the natural and historical relationships in which the covenant is reflected as the basic relationship between God and man, God and the world, and in which it has therefore analogies."[24] In other words, Christ's

---

18. Maury, *Erwahlung und Glaube*, quoted in McCormack, *Karl Barth's Theology*, 457.
19. Maury, *Predestination*, 65.
20. Barth, *CD* 2/2:94.
21. Ibid.
22. Ibid.
23. Ibid., 95.
24. Barth, *CD* 4/2:58.

election as the mediator and his temporal reconciliation between God and humanity forms the basis for all relations. Only in Christ do we have "the basic reality which underlies the possibility of the basic relationship of the covenant, and therefore all the natural and historical relationships."[25] Thus, Christ is the basis of the *analogia relationis*, the relations between God and humanity or between humans themselves.

Second, Barth asserted that God elected humans for a purpose: to be partners in the covenant. This covenant is two-sided. It includes (a) election, in that God elected himself *to be God* of his people, and (b) command, because God elected his people *to be his people*.[26] As partners of the covenant, all persons are ruled over by God, whether they recognize it or not.[27] In other words, because God has elected all persons in the election of Christ, his command extends to all as well. Thus, human action stands under God's command and has the character of either obedience or disobedience.[28]

For Barth, the reality of this command is not grounded in nature, as in Roman Catholic idea of natural law. Rather, God's command is revealed by his act of election in Jesus Christ. In other words, for Barth, the fact that God has graciously elected himself to be in covenant with humans immediately entails responsibility on the part of humans. Barth wrote, "It is as He makes Himself responsible for man that God makes man, too, responsible."[29] In other words, God's taking responsibility for humanity, in Jesus Christ, both relativizes and authenticates human act and responsibility. We are responsible because God has taken our responsibility for us. Our responsibility lies in a corresponding acceptance of God's self-responsibility in our stead. For this reason, Barth continued, "Ruling grace is commanding grace. The Gospel itself has the form and fashion of the

---

25. Ibid., 58. Cf. 2/2:52, in which Barth wrote, "It is undoubtedly the case . . . that the election does in some sense denote the basis of all the relationships between God and man, between God in His earliest movement toward man and man in his very earliest determination by this divine movement. It is in the decision in favour of this movement, in God's self-determination and the resultant determination of man, in the relationship which is enclosed and fulfilled within Himself, that God is who He is."

26. As Gunton stated, "Election is to a particular kind of life." Gunton, "The Triune God and the Freedom of the Creature," 51. See also Webster, *Ethics of Reconciliation*, 48–50; and Matheny, *Dogmatics and Ethics*, 166–270, on the ethical implications of Barth's doctrine of election.

27. Barth, *CD* 2/2:512.

28. Ibid., 535.

29. Ibid., 511.

Law. The one Word of God is both Gospel *and* Law."[30] By making God's covenant that is revealed in the election of Christ the ground and moment of human ethical life, Barth sought to rework the Lutheran ordering of law and gospel that gave rise to the natural theology that he critiqued in Brunner.[31] This revised means of knowing what is right also brought him into conflict with the Roman Catholic appeal to natural law.

The Analogia Relationis as the Basis for Knowing Justice

Now we come back to our earlier question of how knowledge of justice is possible. For Barth, it is not possible by looking at human nature or through natural law, as in the case of John Paul. For Barth, justice is known only through Christ. God reveals to us what justice is through Christ's very being that is revealed by his work of justice in our world.

Such a view stands in contrast with the anthropology of John Paul II in which the *imago Dei* implies a substantial, rational capacity for humans to know God and a continuity between the human and God. For Barth, the human has no such capacity or continuity of his own. The capacity and continuity is completely determined by the divine movement of election, God's decision to be for humanity in the person of Jesus Christ. This decision made the God-human relation possible; from this decision, "the existence and being of the creature and therefore of creation" was made necessary.[32] Thus, human nature is discovered not in a capacity or continuity but in God's revelation in Jesus Christ, which is known by faith.

Because of his grounding of humanity in God's election rather than in nature or creation, Barth advocated his alternate analogy, the *analogia relationis*, which is the analogy of relation between God and humanity established in the God-human, Jesus Christ. According to Jüngel, Barth's conception of the *analogia relationis* is "a correspondence of relationships which are constituted by a 'Yes': a 'Yes' which thereby renders possible in the very first place the existence of the being to whom 'Yes' is said. It is the 'Yes' of the free love of God, which the Trinitarian God speaks to Godself and which God then also speaks to God's creature, thereby creating its correspondence."[33] This concept marks Barth's reaction against

---

30. Ibid.

31. See Barth's essay, "Gospel and Law" in *Community, State, and Church*, 71–100.

32. Barth, *CD* 3/1:97.

33. Jüngel, *Barth-Studien*, 221–22. Cf. Barth, *CD* 3/2:147; Nimmo, *Being in Action*, 89; Price, *Karl Barth's Anthropology*, 128.

PART TWO—Karl Barth

Aristotelian substantivalism by emphasizing that being follows action (*Esse sequitur operari*).[34] While there is some dispute over what this means for *God's* being in Barth's thought,[35] the implication for *human* beings is clear: humans correspond to God's Trinitarian relationality because of the "Yes" spoken to them. The human correspondence is not grounded in nature but grounded in the action of God. For this reason, Barth would never appeal to human nature as grounds for a justice that corresponds to God's justice, as did John Paul II.[36] Rather, Barth argued that the election of Christ created both the ground and the moment of our ethical life. Creaturely correspondence to the being of God is located, not in human nature, but in the covenant of God toward humanity that was initiated by the "Yes" of God toward humans. From that "Yes" issues the command of God for humanity.

Barth's Ethical Method

In the prior section, we sought to establish the grounds for knowing justice. According to Barth, justice is known through the revelation of God in Christ, which creates a claim upon all humans to correspond to God's good action. In this section, we pose a second set of questions: How do humans perceive this command? How do humans discern justice in particular situations?

---

34. Price, *Karl Barth's Anthropology*, 134; cf. Gunton, *Becoming and Being*, 143.

35. Recently in this debate, Nimmo argued that Barth employs an actualistic ontology, in which "the action of God in electing to be God for humanity in Jesus Christ is *not* the act of an already existing agent. Rather it is an act in the course of which God determines the very being of God" so that "election is constitutive of the being of God." Nimmo, *Being in Action*, 8. Price, on the other hand, suggests that Barth's ontology did not leave out the action that follows being (*operari sequitur esse*) but that he emphasized being follows action (*esse sequitur operari*) in his reaction against Aristotelian substantivalism. Price, *Karl Barth's Anthropolology*, 134. See also the discussions on being and election between George Hunsinger, Bruce McCormack, Paul Molnar, and Kevin Hector. Hunsinger, "Election and the Trinity"; McCormack, "Election and the Trinity," and "Grace and Being"; Molnar, *Divine Freedom*, and "The Trinity, Election and God's Ontological Freedom"; and Hector, "God's Triunity and Self-Determination."

36. In support of this point, Webster said that, for Barth, "'Nature' is thus detached both from phenomenological history and from non-theological metaphysics and defined out of the eschatological reality which is established in the history of the covenant, supremely in Jesus Christ and the Holy Spirit." Webster, *Karl Barth*, 157.

Three Ethical Methods that Barth Rejected

Barth opposed three common methods for deriving human ethics. The reasons for these criticisms highlight the distinctiveness of Barth's approach. First, he condemned *casuistry,* which understands the command of God as a prescribed text, "made up of biblical texts in which there are believed to be seen universally binding divine ordinances and directions, of certain propositions again presumed to be universally valid, of the natural moral law generally perceptible to human reason, and finally of particular norms which have been handed down historically in the tradition of Western Christianity and which lay claim to universal validity."[37] Essentially, God's command is regarded as a legal text known to the ethical teacher, expounded and applied to individual cases, instructing others what is to be chosen as good or rejected as evil. He opposed this approach for three reasons:

a. The moralist wishes to become the commander of God's will, wishing to set himself in God's place and distinguish good from evil and making himself lord, king, and judge in God's place.

b. This approach assumes that the command of God is a universal rule. Barth wrote, "Casuistry thinks it can and must abstract from the Bible a collection of general moral rules which it is then the task of ethics to expound and apply in particular."[38] The commands, Barth insists, are specific directions that concern the behaviors and deeds of humans in particular historical contexts and cannot be divorced from the concrete situations, which they addressed.

c. The moralist destroys Christian freedom by replacing God's free gracious relationship of father to his child with a universal moral principle. The human's action under God is not to decide what is the command; God's commandment leaves no room for application or interpretation—it leaves only room for obedience or disobedience.[39]

Second, Barth said that he opposed the ethical methodology based upon *natural law,* as exemplified by Emil Brunner. Though Barth appreciated Brunner's rejection of casuistry, he opposed Brunner's ethical method

---

37. Barth, *CD* 3/4:6. Barth claims that this approach arose at the time of the transition from the first to the second century "when there developed a lack of confidence in the Spirit (who is the Lord) as Guide, Lawgiver, and Judge." Ibid., 7.

38. Ibid., 12.

39. Ibid., 13–15.

for its appeal to natural law as a basis for just behavior in society. Barth objected to Brunner's conception of "divine orders," i.e., the orders of society established in creation.[40] Though Brunner rejected the universal ethical guidelines of the moralist, he favored presuppositions and structures in nature that created a basis for ethics. Rejecting any foundation apart from Jesus Christ, Barth repudiated Brunner's divine orders, his notions of earthly and human justice in family, industry, and state, for their basis in natural law.[41]

Barth rejected both of these approaches to determining human justice because, he argued, Jesus Christ alone is the judge. God determines right and wrong because he alone is righteous. Barth argued that the fact that Jesus died totally for the reconciliation of all humans means that human corruption is "both radical and total."[42] Barth spared no space in the human person that was not affected by sin, no seed of unredeemed human goodness by which humans could have epistemic access to true justice.[43] He wrote:

> The Word of God—and the atoning work of Jesus Christ as the Representative of man, of the whole man—brings against man the accusation that at the very core of his being—the heart, as the Bible puts it—he is not good but evil, not upright but corrupt, not humble but proud in one or other of the forms known to us, wanting to be God and Lord and the judge of good and evil, and his own helper, and therefore hating God and his neighbor.[44]

In the desire to judge good and evil, the human misunderstands herself. If she wants to make a decision between right and wrong where the judgment of God has already decided and his knowledge has discerned good from evil, she arrogantly overestimates her ability and her position. By renouncing confidence in God's judgment, she loses her freedom to stand as a witness of what God has decided. For she is free only when she "thinks

---

40. Brunner defined these orders of creation as "those existing facts of human corporate life which lie at the root of all historical life as unalterable presuppositions, which although their historical forms may vary, are unalterable in their fundamental structure, and at the same time, relate and unite men to one another in a definite way." Brunner, *Divine Imperative*, 210.

41. Barth sought to expose Brunner's dichotomy between the justice to be apprehended from natural law and the command of God for individual ethics. Barth, *CD* 3/4:21.

42. Barth, *CD* 4/1:492.

43. See the entire argument in ibid., 492–95.

44. Ibid., 494–95.

and decides and acts at peace with God, when [her] decision is simply and exclusively a repetition of the divine decision."[45]

Barth illustrated the implications for ethics in his exegesis of Genesis 3. In this story, Eve was tempted by the serpent to become like God, knowing good and evil. "What the serpent has in mind," Barth argued, "is the establishment of ethics." The following quote of Barth displays the radical nature of his interpretation and approach to justice:

> It is surprising that in the Christian Church more offence is not taken at the fact—or have we simply read it away?—that in Gen. 3 the desire of man for a knowledge of good and evil is represented as an evil desire, indeed the one evil desire which is so characteristic and fatal for the whole race. The consequences for the theory and practice of Christian ethics—and not only that—would be incalculable if only we were to see this and accept it instead of regarding this very questionable knowledge—whether sought in the Bible or in the rational nature of man or conscience—as the most basic of all the gifts of God. The armor behind which the real evil of the pride of man conceals itself is obviously thicker and more impenetrable at this point than at any other.[46]

This quote reveals Barth's fundamentally different approach to ethics. He claimed that Christian ethics must begin, not with reflection, but with hearing.[47] Human persons answer the question of justice and good not by a philosophy or worldview or program but by thinking through what God has already thought about human activity. Christian ethics merely repeats what God has already spoken to the human about his activity.[48] The human has not been left to reflect upon and judge between abstract notions of good and evil. As the just judge, God in Christ has declared justice; he has spoken his command. The human need only act accordingly.[49]

---

45. Ibid., 449.

46. Ibid.

47. Barth, *God Here and Now*, 87.

48. Ibid., 87. See, for instance, Barth's exegesis of Naboth's vineyard in Kgs 21. Barth affirmed that human knowledge of right and wrong is not based upon categories of good and evil or upon human judgment of just or unjust. The knowledge of righteous behavior issues directly from the commands of God. God has already made the ethical judgment. In attempting to assert justice which counters God's command, as Ahab did, the human finds himself an arrogant and unjust judge. Barth, *CD* 4/1:453–54.

49. Barth, *God Here and Now*, 87.

PART TWO—Karl Barth

If this is the case, does Barth then expect the Christian to be *guided by the Spirit* hour by hour? This third approach Barth also rejected because the command of God is not a "disconnected multiplicity of individual demands, claims, directions and prohibitions, but a single and unitary command which moves the divine plan of history toward completion."[50]

Barth's Method

Having explained why he rejected these three methods, we now turn to describe the method that he advocated. According to Barth, ethics is the inquiry into good human action. Human action is good when it is commanded by God.[51] The question of ethical method for Barth is the question of right knowledge of and obedience to God's command.

The command is perceived in the encounter between God and humanity, an encounter that has two dimensions. First, there is the vertical dimension, which comprises "the event or rather the many events of the encounter between God's command and human action in a singularity and uniqueness which cannot be anticipated and with scorn regimentation."[52] In other words, there is a specific event of encounter when God commands right human action for a specific situation. Yet such an encounter does not take place in a vacuum, as is the case in the third ethical method that Barth rejected. There is a second, horizontal dimension, which is the history of encounter in the covenant of grace. The specific encounter is part of the history of encounter between God and humanity. This horizontal dimension serves as "instructional preparation" for the particular ethical event because it becomes a "formed reference (*geformter Hinweis*)" for it.[53] It

50. Barth, *CD* 3/4:17.

51. Barth, *Christian Life*, 3.

52. Barth, *CD* 3/4:17.

53. Ibid., 18; and *The Christian Life*, 6. The formed reference provides guidance so that his analogical method is not "arbitrary" as his critics concluded. Thielicke said that Barth's method could be used to defend a variety of practices, *Theologische Ethik, Band I*, 411–13; Brunner wrote, "anything and everything can be derived from the same principle of analogy: a monarchy just as well as a republic (Christ the King), a totalitarian state just as much as a state with civil liberties (Christ the Lord of all, man a servant, indeed a slave, of Jesus Christ)." Brunner, *The Christian Doctrine of Creation and Redemption, Dogmatics*, 319. See also Will Herberg's introduction to Barth's essays in *Community, State, and Church* in which he calls Barth's method "most arbitrary." He writes, "The objections to the Barthian teaching on analogy are so obvious and so compelling that we are hard put to it to understand why Barth himself has not seen them from the very start." Barth, *Community, State and Church*, 35. Willis countered

is a formed reference for the particular ethical event because it answers the key questions that frame the "moral field"[54] in which we exist: Who is God? Who is the human? According to Barth, beginning with these questions and the question of their relations provides the reference for ethics.[55] By answering these questions, we can pose the "counter-question" of the command of God and right human action. Yet even the answers to these questions provide no more than "a series of directives, which give guidance to the individual in the form of an approximation to the knowledge of the divine command and right human action."[56] For Barth always wants "to leave the final judgment to God."[57]

For Barth, then, the command is not an order of creation or a demand for submission, it is an event of encounter between the God who commands and the human who acts within covenant history. On the part of the human, the command is a vocation: a call to act in correspondence to the grace of God. In this manner, the history of grace and encounter between God and humanity forms the reference for discerning the unique event of the particular command. It also makes Jesus Christ the

---

these criticisms by explaining, "In the event of reconciliation, man is restored to his original and proper place as the covenant partner of God, and is set on the way to authentic co-humanity and fellowship all men and women. The only legitimate use of analogy, therefore, will be in providing suggestions as to the consequences this might carry for an ordering of man's common life within the political order," Willis, *Ethics of Karl Barth*, 402. For more discussion on the recent critique and a defense of Barth's use of analogy, see Aboagye-Mensah, *Social-Political Thinking of Karl Barth*, 102–23.

54. Webster utilized this language of "moral field" to describe Barth's ontology. The moral field is "the space within which moral agents act," and "the shape of their action, a shape given above all by the fact that their acts take place in the history of encounter between God as prime agent and themselves as those called to act in correspondence to the grace of God" (Webster, *Barth's Ethics of Reconciliation*, 4).

55. Barth wrote, "It is possible and even imperative to trace the historical outline always particular to the ethical event, to give an indicatory if not a complete picture of it piece by piece, to gain at least a prospect of the field or fields of the encounter of God and man, and then from this standpoint to put the counter-question what is the command of God and the corresponding right human action in this or that sphere and relationship and as reflected in this particular mirror. A definite lead in the direction of the answer which is finally asked of each of us individually and in his relationship to God and his fellows will become possible and necessary in proportion as we perceive this historical outline: not the answer itself; not a definition or determination of the event." Barth, *CD* 3/4:30.

56. Ibid., 31.

57. Ibid.

starting-point for all ethics, for he is the one who reveals this history between God and humanity.[58]

In sum, justice is perceived through faith in Christ. For Barth, knowledge of good ethical action finds no basis in nature or culture or reason. In his own experience, such appeals led to disastrous consequences in Nazi Germany and compromised theology. For Barth, the answer to the question of justice is only perceived in the creature's acknowledgement of the moral field in which he has been set by God's encounter with humanity, in the person of Jesus Christ. Barth explained

> In the determination and limitation given them in their intercourse with God they are men of unconditional and unlimited capacity. They can think rightly (*richtig*) and desire rightly, wait rightly and hasten rightly, obey rightly and defy rightly, begin rightly and end rightly, be with and for men rightly and by themselves rightly. They can do all these things . . . because in faith they have the freedom of God's partners.[59]

Thus, through faith in Christ one thinks *richtig*, rightly or justly; one perceives justice. Yet faith not only impacts reason, faith impacts human action as well. As the "anthropological counterpart" to God's grace, faith frees humans to perceive God's justice and to act in accordance with it.[60]

Critical Reflections on Barth's Ethical Method

Barth has come under a great deal of criticism for his ethical method on numerous fronts. On the one hand, critics argue that his approach implies that knowledge of justice is exclusive, attainable by Christians alone, and leaves no point of contact with non-Christian ethics. Chapter Seven will address that criticism. On the other hand, Christian ethicists criticize Barth's neglect of the empirical context in his ethical method.[61] For instance, Charles West argued that Barth's doctrine of grace led him "to neglect his responsibility for that difficult empirical analysis of real human

---

58. Barth, *Christian Life*, 5.
59. Barth, *CD* 4/2:242.
60. Ibid., 243.
61. Willis, West, Biggar, and Hauerwas have criticized Barth's neglect of the empirical context and description of the ethical event. Willis, *Ethics*, 199; Biggar, *Hastening that Waits*, 140; Hauerwas, "On Honour: By Way of a Comparison of Barth and Trollope," 149. Cf. Nimmo, *Being in Action*, for a summary of these critiques.

relations."[62] Paul Nimmo suggests to these critics that Barth's method does not imply that context has no bearing on ethics. "Rather," he proposes, "at the very centre of Barth's actualistic understanding of the command is precisely its uniqueness and contextuality."[63]

My primary question for Barth is the following: How is the human to discern justice in ambiguous situations? For example, in his ethics, Barth argued that humans have responsibilities within spheres of human relations. In *Church Dogmatics* 3/4, He provided the following guidance: it is right for parents to care for their children; it is right for a person to uphold her own life; and it is right for a person to uphold the life of the neighbor. Yet here is a dilemma: if one person is both parent and a neighbor of a starving child and she receives a limited amount of food, then which action is right? To eat that food for herself, so that she might live and find means to provide to others; to give that food to her child; or to give that food to her neighbor's child? How does one discern justice in that situation? How does the woman choose one right action among the three potentially good acts?

Barth argued that right action is obedience to God's command. Yet how does one know God's command in such a situation? For Barth, God's command is a dynamic reality; it is a specific command by God for particular circumstances. Barth wrote, "God accompanies man's way with ever new and living and specific direction. He is always the free God who has chosen the good for man and made it known to him as a matter for his choice too. What free man has always to do is to receive God's command as his concrete claim, decision, and judgment, and thus to repeat God's choice, practicing what God has elected as the good."[64]

Barth seemed to assume that if a person asked, "What shall I do?" with a true openness to the command of God, that God would indeed communicate this command.[65] How does this take place? Barth rarely answered that question. He simply affirmed that it does take place. In

---

62. West, *Communism and the Theologians*, 313.

63. Nimmo, *Being in Action*, 75. Nimmo's argument is supported by Barth's very definition of special ethics. Barth writes, "Special ethics looks at man as this particular man at this particular time and place, who yesterday selected and decided and acted on the basis of the possibilities available, who does the same today in different circumstances, and who will do the same tomorrow in different circumstances again. It is concerned to see and show how far this specific, concrete, special, and even very special action of man can or cannot be called good action" (*Christian Life*, 4).

64. Barth, *Christian Life*, 33.

65. Barth, *CD* 2/2:648.

PART TWO—Karl Barth

The Doctrine of Reconciliation, however, he attributed this knowledge to the Holy Spirit, "He is the One—and this is His instruction—who actually reveals and makes known and imparts and writes on our heart and conscience the will of God as it applies to us concretely here and now."[66] He said that the instruction is precise and authoritative and that it "may always be distinguished from all fanatical self-instruction by the fact that it shows itself to be the instruction of the living Jesus Himself, obviously awakening and summoning us to participation in his exaltation."[67] In this passage, Barth seemed to indicate some criteria by which we know that the command is the command of God, such as the outcome of the command (that it awakens and summons) and the motivation of the person (to uphold the Lordship of Christ rather than being "our own lords and rulers"[68]) yet such criteria appear simplistic and inadequate in light of real moral dilemmas, such as the one we have posed.

As Gustafson said, "Barth's confidence in the objectivity of a particular command of God that can be heard, and thus can provide a moral certainty" is not warranted.[69] Barth seemed to assume that the encounter with God in the ethical event provides clear and precise direction for human action. Yet if this is the case, then why would so many faithful Christians arrive at such different conclusions about the ethical dilemmas of the contemporary era, like abortion and euthanasia? Barth said that "the obscurity of God's will in a particular case always arises on man's side, not on God's."[70] So does that mean that faithful Christians who disagree are failing to listen or to be open to God's command? Are they being their own lords and rulers? How does one really know when she has heard the command of God and her fellow Christian has not? These questions raise a fundamental problem for Barth because they ultimately throw the human back upon her own capacities to reason and to discern the will of God.

In addition, according to Barth, God's action is always prior and his command is always clear and precise. What if there are times when God simply does not speak a command? That does not seem a possibility for Barth, yet it is a real possibility. For Barth, the election of God appears to commit him to a transparent, precise, clear encounter of command. Yet must this clarity necessarily be the case? Can God in his freedom choose

---

66. Barth, *CD* 4/2:372.
67. Ibid., 373.
68. Ibid.; and *CD* 2/2:608.
69. Gustafson, *Ethics from a Theocentric Perspective*, 33.
70. Barth, *CD* 3/4:12.

not to speak and to leave decision to the human? Or may choose to hide himself? And if it does happen that God does not speak in a concrete situation, how might the human act rightly? In Barth's attempt to preserve the freedom of God to speak his Word by preventing the human from institutionalizing or controlling God's commands, Barth has inadvertently limited God's freedom by assuming that God will always speak in the ethical moment.

Conclusion

This chapter examined Barth's answer to the question: How is justice known? It sought to demonstrate that Barth's epistemology is grounded in his conception of the *analogia relationis*, which is the analogy of relation between God and humanity established in the God-human, Jesus Christ. In Christ, the triune God elects and reconciles humanity in Christ. Because God's election extends to all people, his command does so as well. Humans are to correspond to this relationship.

Therefore, justice is known through faith in the triune God who was revealed in Jesus Christ. It does not rest on human nature but upon the just nature of God and His revelation of this justice in the person of Jesus Christ. In order to discover how Barth defined human justice in the spheres of politics or economics, we must first turn to examine the manner in which he defined the justice of God.

6

Barth's Theological Framework for Justice

THE PREVIOUS TWO CHAPTERS OUTLINED BARTH'S ANSWER TO THE FIRST question that we have posed for each author: How is justice known? This chapter will examine Barth's answers to our two final questions: "What is social justice?" and "How is it cultivated in society?" As we noted in Chapter Five, Barth's ethical method led him to define human justice by examining God's just action that is revealed in Jesus Christ. Thus, for Barth, human justice is that which corresponds to God's justice.

This definition stands in clear contrast to the John Paul's view of justice, which means treating people in accordance with their nature. From John Paul's perspective, the *analogia entis* provides epistemic access to the truth of human nature and the dignity of that nature. By means of natural law, all humans can know some degree of moral truth and behave in accordance with this truth. The Christian revelation adds to this vision of truth by revealing that human nature has a "dignity beyond compare" and revealing God's radical love for humanity. For John Paul, God's love is so radical that his mercy overcomes the natural norms of justice.

In Barth's thought, the human does not reflect the justice of God in her rational nature; her idea of justice must stand corrected by the righteousness of God revealed in Christ. Such an approach negates the *analogia entis* as a starting point for defining justice. Rather, the *analogia entis* only finds significance within the *analogia relationis*. Only because of God's election, creation, and reconciliation can persons discover what God's justice is. Likewise, only in that relation of God and Christ does a correspondence between God's act and creaturely action take place.

This ethical method led Barth to a different conception of justice. He began not with natural norms but with the righteous being and acts of God, first asking the question, "Who is the just *God* who commands?"

Second he posed the question, "Who is the human who acts?"[1] The answers to these two questions describe the moral field in which humans act and provide directives that witness to the divine command that God speaks to the person in his concrete situation.[2] The first part of this chapter will seek to articulate Barth's theory of social justice by examining his answers to these two questions, as formed by the three doctrines that he considers key to ethics: the doctrines of God (*CD* 2), creation (*CD* 3), and reconciliation (*CD* 4).[3]

Doctrine of God: God's Justice as Right Relations and Mercy

In his doctrine of God, Barth gave two primary characteristics of God's justice: God's justice is distributive and it is relational. These two characteristics are key aspects of justice woven throughout his discussions of God's justice and of human justice in the *Church Dogmatics*. He introduced these themes in a key discussion on the justice of God in *Church Dogmatics* 2/1. In order to understand the significance of this text for his definition of justice, it is important to be aware that the German language differs from English and Latin. Much like the Greek language, the words that are here translated "justice" (*Gerechtigkeit*), "justification" (*Rechtfertigung*), and "righteousness" (*Rechtschaffenheit*) share the same root: *richtig* or *recht*, which mean "right." When used the noun form, Barth most often employed the word, *Gerechtigkeit*, which literally means "justness" and is most often translated in the English text as "righteousness."[4]

In this section, Barth defined God's righteousness. He wrote, "God is righteous [or just, *gerecht*], that, founding and maintaining in this way fellowship with another, He wills and expresses and establishes what

---

1. Barth, *Christian Life*, 6.
2. Ibid., 7.
3. In ibid., Barth states that the structure of his special ethics includes "the knowledge of God as Creator and man as his creature; the knowledge of God as Reconciler and man as a sinner referred to his grace and participant in it; the knowledge of God as Redeemer and man as his future heir" (7). Barth did not have time to develop the final doctrine, so it will not be examined in this chapter. In addition, I am adding the doctrine of God to the doctrines that we will consider because (a) it shaped his "general ethics" and (b) it includes a key passage on God's justice and mercy that sets the stage for his theory of justice.
4. He used *Rechtschaffenheit* only once in this section in Barth, *CD* 2/1:389 (*KD* 2/1:437.)

corresponds to His own worth."⁵ In other words, in creating fellowship with humanity, God does so in a way that is worthy of Himself, despite the contradiction and resistance of human persons. According to this definition, God's justice is relational at its core. It is about establishing right relations that correspond with his worth. God's righteousness is determined by his love.

Barth criticized Protestant theologians like Quenstedt and Schleiermacher for characterizing God's righteousness as merely exacting: rewarding obedience and punishing disobedience.⁶ He contrasted this definition with the Lutheran insight that the righteousness (*Gerechtigkeit*) of God is his mercy. For Barth, this did not mean that God grants clemency, suspends the law, or "limits his justice by gentleness."⁷ In scripture, "it is everywhere stated that He unconditionally maintains right as right and wrong as wrong, judging, rewarding, and punishing according to this standard. . . . Only when we admit this unreservedly do we understand what it means that God's justice is also in fact a determination of His love, and his judgement is an expression of his grace."⁸ This righteousness is not merely exacting, it is *iustitia distributiva*.⁹ In other words, God's righteousness is that by which he makes sinners righteous, not by suspending the law, but by imputing to sinners that righteousness by which he is reckoned right. In this act, God reveals that "there is no righteousness of God which is not also mercy and no mercy of God which is not also righteousness."¹⁰

In this manner, Barth tied together mercy and justice. In God's act of judgment against human unrighteous, God makes humans right in Christ. As God speaks his "No" of judgment against Christ, he likewise speaks his "Yes" of mercy through Christ. Barth wrote, "For God's righteousness (*Gerechtigkeit*) is that the man in covenant with Him should be righteous (*Gerechten*), that he should be such a one as is justified (*recht hat*) in God's sight because God has addressed him and dealt with him in righteousness (*Gerechtigkeit*)."¹¹ God's justice is the merciful justification of sinners. This act does not suspend his just judgement or weaken it by extending mercy.

5. Barth, *CD* 2/1:377.
6. Ibid., 378.
7. Ibid., 382.
8. Ibid.
9. Ibid.
10. Ibid., 380.
11. Ibid., 385.

Rather, God satisfies his justice through the death of Christ. Thus, God's righteousness is also his mercy.

Barth contrasted God's idea of justice with human ideas of justice, arguing that people cannot "appropriate and understand his love and grace and mercy without at the same time hearing and considering the summons with which he lifts us out of all being and doing in which we try to follow our own ideas of justice (Gerechtigkeit)."[12] Rather, it is through faith that people choose to accept righteousness of Christ as their own.

At this point, Barth demonstrated his method clearly, for he argued that human justice must correspond to God's justice. He explained, "human righteousness (Gerechtigkeit) required by God...has necessarily the character of a vindication of right in favour of the threatened innocent, the oppressed poor, widows, orphans and aliens."[13] In the same way that God's righteousness is established through mercy to humans who could not save themselves, so human justice entails mercy to those who are unable to help themselves.[14] For Barth, human justice corresponds not to that which is known about human nature (as in John Paul) but to the justice that is revealed in the just and merciful action of God in Christ Jesus.

This passage provided the initial answer to our first question: Who is the God who commands? The God who commands practices justice that is distributive and relational. It is distributive because God extends his righteousness to those who could not procure it for themselves. It is relational because God does so in fellowship and covenant with humanity, establishing right relations on the behalf of humanity. Having tentatively answered this question of the God who commands justice, we now turn to the doctrine of creation, primarily exploring the question of the human who acts.

Doctrine of Creation: Social Justice as Co-humanity

According to Barth, creation is the context in which God's election and commands transpire. Barth called creation the external basis of the covenant because creation prepares and establishes the sphere in which the institution and history of the covenant can take place.[15] On the other hand, the covenant is the internal basis of creation, for "the wisdom and om-

12. Ibid., 386.
13. Ibid.
14. Ibid., 387.
15. Barth, *CD* 3/1:97.

nipotence of God the Creator was not just any wisdom and omnipotence but that of His free love. Hence what God has created was not just any reality—however perfect or wonderful—but that which intrinsically determined as the exponent of his glory and for the corresponding service."[16] In this intricate relationship between creation and covenant, we understand God as Creator and Lord over all, freely loving his creation through his covenant.

God the Creator and Lord of Humanity

In his *Church Dogmatics* 3, Barth answered the question, "Who is God the Creator?" According to Barth, God created human persons as his own creatures and covenant-partners with Him in Christ. The Creator relates to his creature as a sovereign and loving Lord who exercises providence toward his creation in accomplishing his will and covenant in Jesus Christ.[17] God fulfils his providential ordering, or his fatherly Lordship, over his creature by *preserving, accompanying,* and *ruling* the course of its earthly existence. He *preserves* the creature by upholding and sustaining its individual existence for covenant in Jesus Christ. He *accompanies* the creature by surrounding the creature with his presence as Lord, *ruling* over him or her in a way that gives freedom and maintains the autonomy of the creature in relation to Creator.[18]

Next he examined the second question, "Who is the human as his creature?" According to Barth, these questions taken together provide a formed reference for the question of human justice in the social sphere.[19]

---

16. Ibid., 231.

17. Barth, *CD* 3/3:3.

18. Ibid., 92. With regard to the earlier question regarding human freedom, Barth uses this point to espouse a sort of synergism or participation. God "affirms and approves and recognizes the autonomous actuality and therefore the autonomous activity of the creature as such. He does not play the part of tyrant towards it." Gunton explains, "We do not have to do here with 'things' that interact as part of some automatic cosmic machinery, but with a gracious and personal divine accompanying of the creature." God's person, ruling by his Word and Spirit, confirms and establishes the freedom of the human creature. Gunton argues that those who reject this accompanying as an aspect of human freedom do so because their presuppositions are deist or Pelagian. They either suppose an impersonal bond between God and man or none at all. Gunton wrote, "Such positions, however, are not so much criticisms of Barth as root and branch rejections of his view that human autonomy is given by God and remains only so long as God continues to be its support." Gunton, "The Triune God," 56–57.

19. Barth, *Christian Life*, 6.

Like John Paul, Barth will suggest that knowledge about human persons forms a vital criterion for determining justice in the social sphere. However, Barth defined humanity solely in reference to Christ and this definition led him to the belief that human justice is that which corresponds to the just acts of God in Christ. We will first examine his theological anthropology and then its implications for justice.

Christ the Criterion for Real Humanity

Rather than starting with a universal understanding of humanity and moving toward the particulars of social ethics, Barth began with the particular human Jesus Christ to determine true humanity, which is being-in-encounter with God and humanity. He argued that humanity may be known only in the particular person of Jesus Christ.[20] He critiqued speculative theories of human beings for the over-confident presupposition that one can know oneself without the revelation of God. For example, a scientific approach such as naturalism, while it can be helpful for speaking about humanity, ultimately deals only with the sum of specific and partial phenomena rather than the being of humanity.[21]

Not even the revelation of God in the Old Testament shows us true humanity, for it discloses "man as a betrayer of himself and a sinner against his creaturely existence."[22] This radical depravity of humanity hides the true nature of the person and the light of God's revelation enables humans to understand their self-contradiction. Revelation also reminds men and women that they are objects of divine grace, partners in the covenant, and creatures of God.[23] Yet the revelation about humanity in scripture does not reveal humanity without sin, except in the vicarious humanity of Jesus Christ. To understand authentic humanity, Barth argued, we must begin with the human personhood of Jesus Christ.[24]

---

20. He wrote, "In its [theological anthropology's] investigation of the nature of man in general, it must first look away from man in general to concentrate on the one man Jesus, and only then look back from Him to man in general." Barth, *CD* 3/2:53.

21. Ibid., 22–24 and 80–87. Barth also critiqued existentialism and theological anthropology but we will leave the details of this discussion to our final chapter in dialogue with John Paul's anthropology.

22. Ibid., 26.

23. Ibid., 31–32.

24. Ibid., 132. Barth acknowledges the manner in which Christ is not like real humanity by nature of his divinity and his unique relation to God, which will never exist between God and the human, for "he alone is the Son of Man and the Son of God.

Such a declaration immediately raises the question of the relation of Christ's humanity with his divinity. If Jesus is also God, which aspects of Christ exhibit the humanity that is similar to our humanity? Which are the human characteristics and which are the divine characteristics of Christ? These classic questions of Christian theology begin with the assumption of a "general *humanum*" into which Jesus fits and the highest qualities of which Jesus models.[25] The radical implications of Barth's starting point are manifest precisely at this point. Christ does not share in our humanity or take on the characteristics of a universal humanity in addition to his divinity. Rather, He is the one in whose humanity we share. Christ alone, because he is the Creator and the one who is both God and human, can posit, reveal and explain human nature.[26]

What then does Christ reveal about human nature? Christ reveals that real humanity finds its basis in relationship with the divine.[27] Bromiley summarizes, "Real man is to be seen as conditioned by his relation to God, his deliverance by God, his determination to God's glory, his standing under God's lordship, his being in history and freedom, and his service of God and being for him."[28]

Real humanity is being-with-God. He is man elected and summoned by God. According to Barth, to see the human as "summoned"[29] is to un-

---

Our fellowship with God rests upon the fact that He and He alone is one with God." In the following chapter, I will argue that this very dissimilarity makes possible Christ's vicarious humanity that frees humanity from the sin that separates us from right relationship with God. Through his vicarious humanity, Christ restores humanity to fellowship with God. In this manner, the divinity of Christ restores real humanity.

25. Ibid., 59.

26. Barth wrote, "It is not the case, however, that He must partake of humanity. On the contrary, humanity must partake of Him. It is not the case, then, that He is subject to these specific determinations and features of humanity. It is not that he is conditioned and limited by them, but in so far as humanity is His it is He who transcends and therefore limits and conditions these features and determinations. As the nature of Jesus, human nature with all its possibilities is not a presupposition which is valid for Him too and controls and explains Him, but His being as a man is as such that which posits and therefore reveals and explains human nature with all its possibilities." Ibid., 59. Cf. Webster, who substantiates my assumption here that the decisions that Barth makes in his anthropology regarding the prioritizing of the humanity of Christ in defining human nature and action has profound implication for his later ethics. Webster, *Barth's Ethics of Reconciliation*, 61–66.

27. Ibid., 66.

28. Bromiley, *Introduction*, 125. Summary of Barth, *CD* 3/2:73–75.

29. He defines summoned: "to be heard, to have been awakened, to have to arouse oneself, to be claimed." Bromiley, *Introduction*, 150.

derstand human nature in its entirety. "Who am I really?" Barth asked, "If I understand myself in the light of God or His Word, then I must answer that I am summoned by this Word, and to that extent I am in this Word. And the same answer is equally true of others. They are men, and may be addressed and seriously regarded as such, because primarily and fundamentally they are summoned by this Word. This is a universal truth."[30] In this manner, Barth drew out of Christ, the elected one, the implications for general humanity; they are elected and characterized at the root of their nature as claimed by the divine address.

Barth contrasted his view with Brunner's anthropology, which is similar to John Paul's, in which the very essence of humanity is "freedom as rationality and responsibility, and therefore as personality, historicity and capacity for decision."[31] Barth rejected anthropology that characterized human being as "potentiality" with a neutral capacity for choosing in loyalty or disloyalty to God. Rather, Barth argued that "if man has his being in the Word of God, he can do only that which corresponds to the Word of God. The actuality in which he has his being is from the very first orientated in that direction. It is the actuality of man caught up in the act of divine revelation and human obedience."[32] In other words, the anthropology that appeals to humanity as potentiality or human freedom as a neutral capacity fails to refer to the ontic basis of humanity but appeals only to a formal disposition in which the being of humanity has not yet been positively characterized or orientated. Barth argued that grounding humanity in the loving election of God meant that the human finds her being in the covenant; she is newly characterized by the divine address of God; in Christ, humanity has been transformed at an ontological level as being-with-God.[33]

If humanity is indeed characterized at the ontological level by this divine address, then why do humans turn away from God? Why do they sin? By grounding humanity in the election of God, Barth claimed that sin is for the human person "an ontological impossibility."[34] The human was not created with a neutral capacity to choose good or evil. The human person was created for relationship with God and obedience to him.

30. Barth, *CD* 3/2:150.

31. Brunner's anthropology, his description of human freedom and capacity, is strikingly similar to John Paul's. Barth, *CD* 3/2:128.

32. Ibid., 131.

33. Ibid., 131–32.

34. Ibid.2, 146.

The person does not decide against God because the possibility has been rooted in his nature. "On the contrary," Barth wrote, "when [man] chooses evil he grasps that which is made impossible for him and from which he is preserved."[35] Thus, there is no excuse for sin and the human can be remade righteous not by his own choice but by that state of right that God alone can effect through his divine forgiveness. Humanity was created for relationship with God, not with a neutral capacity for good and evil. This creation, election, and summoning by God characterizes that which is the very core of humanity. Turning against this core can only be conceived as impossible for the human as creature.

For this reason, when he sins the human contradicts himself. Yet even when he sins he can deny and conceal but he cannot remove or destroy the fact that he is oriented to be the covenant partner with God. "He cannot escape God, or lose his being as the creature of God, or the nature of his being. He can trifle with the grace of God, but he cannot make himself wholly unworthy to be in covenant with God. He does this too. But he is found and rescued by the free and totally undeserved grace of God."[36] By the faithfulness and grace of God to humanity, then, all humans are determined as covenant-partners to God, even when they refuse to acknowledge this reality.[37]

Real Humanity Ontologically Relational

Barth believed that the image of God in humanity means that real humans are relational as the core aspect of their being. The image of God in Christ does not indicate direct identity with the essence that exists between God and God (i.e. between the Father, the Son and the Spirit.) Rather, the *imago* indicates correspondence and similarity.[38] In Jesus Christ the connection between God and humanity is realized in an *analogia relationis*, an analogy of the relation between the Father and the Son in the relationship between God and humanity. In other words, the similarity of the two relationships exists in the love that the Son and the Father have for one another. This love is addressed to the human by God. "Hence the factuality, the material necessity of the being of the man Jesus for his fellows, does not really rest on the mystery of an accident or caprice, but on the mystery

---

35. Ibid., 147.
36. Ibid., 319.
37. Ibid., 318–20.
38. Ibid., 119.

of the purpose and meaning of God, who can maintain and demonstrate His essence even in His work, and in His relation to this work."[39] Thus, the *imago Dei* in Jesus Christ consists in the fact that, as he is for God, He is also for his fellow-humans.[40]

In describing what the *imago Dei* consists in, the conception of similarity as an *analogia relationis* once again contrasts with the *analogia entis*. Barth argued that the being of God cannot be compared with the being of humans (as in the *analogia entis*) because he rejected the concept that the *imago Dei* could reside in an individual without regard to the relation to others.[41] In the same way that God is relational in his very essence, the *imago Dei* in Christ entails ontological relationality between God and humanity as an analogue of that relation of love, which exists between Father, Son and Spirit.[42] For God created the human "in His own image in the fact that he did not create him alone but in this connection and fellowship. For in God's action as the Lord of the covenant, and even further back in His action as the Creator of a reality distinct from Himself, it is proved that God Himself is not solitary, that although he is one in essence He is not alone, but that primarily and properly He is in connection and fellowship."[43] Likewise, in his image, the human is created-with-God as man and woman-with-others.[44] Barth located human relation, therefore, in the very essence of human ontology.

Real Humanity as Neighbor

Barth argued that the *analogia relationis* means that as humans are covenant partners with God by nature, they are also neighbors with one another by nature. He based this claim upon the humanity of Christ. Whereas Christ's divinity means that he is the human person for God, his humanity means that he is a creature among others. What interests Jesus exclusively is the humans who need him, the humans who are the objects of his saving work. He is sent and ordained by God to deliver his fellow-humans.[45] Christ's work reveals that he is ontologically the Neighbor and

---

39. Ibid., 220.
40. Ibid., 222.
41. Ibid., 220.
42. Ibid., 323–24. Cf. Anderson, *On Being Human*, 75–76.
43. Barth, *CD* 3/2:324.
44. Ibid., 243.
45. Ibid., 208–9.

Savior of humans.[46] Like John Paul, Barth described Christ as gift. He gave of himself in fulfillment of the task given him by God.[47] His humanity is characterized by being the Human for other humans.

Our corresponding being is being in encounter with other human persons.[48] Barth ruled out anthropologies such as Nietzsche's, which bracketed out fellow-humanity by seeking to understand the human as individual. Barth argued that such isolation is inhumanity.[49] Humanity means encounter with other humans in which humans look one another in the eye, speak and listen to one another, render mutual assistance, and exist with others in gladness.[50] As the human for fellow-humans, then, Jesus Christ provides the criterion for social justice by determining humanity as co-humanity.[51]

Real Humanity as the Criterion for Justice

In an essay, "Justification and Justice in Barth," William Werpehowski criticized Barth's failure to give political expression to this notion that humanity is co-humanity. Werpehowski sought to "correct and complete Barth's political writings" by arguing that human activity corresponds to the kingdom of God "in the humanization which is co-humanity."[52] He is correct that in Barth's earlier political essays (which were the essays that Werpehowski examined)[53] Barth provided only glimpses that suggest that such correspondence is consistent with his thought. But I suggest that Barth did, in fact, develop co-humanity as a criterion for justice in his *Church Dogmatics*. One may observe it in *CD* 3/4, in his sections on Freedom in Fellowship[54] and on Freedom for Life. In the latter, Barth writes,

---

46. Ibid., 133 and 210.
47. Ibid., 217.
48. Ibid., 320.
49. Ibid., 251.
50. Ibid., 250–71.
51. In this section and the following I am indebted to Anderson's article that links Barth's concept of neighbor with his political ethics. Anderson, "The Concept of Neighbor in the Ethics of Karl Barth," in *The Shape of Practical Theology*, 132–60.
52. Werpehowski, "Justification and Justice in Barth," 635.
53. These essays that are included in *Against the Stream* and *Community, State, and Church* were first published prior to *CD* 3/4 and *Christian Life*.
54. For example, Barth wrote: "As God the Creator calls man to Himself, He also directions him to his fellow-man. The divine command affirms in particular that in the encounter of man and woman, in the relationship between parents and children

Barth's Theological Framework for Justice

"As God the Creator calls man to Himself and turns him to his fellow-man, He orders him to honor his own life and that of every other man as a loan, and to secure it against all caprice in order that it may be used in this service and in preparation for this service."[55] Such a statement points toward the humanization to which the church is called to witness in the state on issues that Barth addresses, like abortion and capital punishment. In his book, *The Christian Life*, which was published after his death, Barth drew these connections even more clearly, suggesting that the humanism that corresponds to God's kingdom is the ethical *a priori*.[56] I will explore this idea further, at a later point in this chapter. But the point to note here is that the notion of humanity as co-humanity is clearly imbedded in Barth's later ethics, more explicitly than Werpehowski suggests.

However, I agree with Werpehowski that Barth did not spell out the full political ramifications of this idea of co-humanity. (Unfortunately, one of Barth's final works, compiled as *The Christian Life*, ended abruptly just as Barth was developing this idea more fully.) Werpehowski attempts some further applications, which he believed would be faithful to Barth's concept of co-humanity, such as "co-equal fellowship for members of the state."[57] Werpehowski writes:

> In their active commitment to norms of justice which regulate their major political and economic institutions . . . citizens may help one another in the advancement of their life plans under conditions of freedom and equality. Through their common deliberations about how they, as persons with different visions of the good life, may live together justly, citizens may as well move toward an ideal of public virtue that expresses their nature as free and equal.[58]

Perhaps the brevity of Werpehowski's suggestions mislead his reader to criticize what was not his intent, but they do provide a point of clarification on the manner in which Barth applied the criterion of co-humanity. In seeking to be faithful to Barth, Werpehowski skates dangerously close to the very precipice that Barth warned against in his ethics, if he does not fall over it entirely. Barth attempted to build an ethic that resisted regulative

---

and outwards from near to distant neighbours, man may affirm, honour and enjoy the other with himself and himself with the other," Barth, *CD* 3/2:116.

55. Barth, *CD* 3/4:324.
56. Barth, *Christian Life*, 267–68.
57. Werpehoski, "Justification," 635.
58. Ibid., 635–36.

"norms of justice," to which Werpehowski appeals. In addition, Barth indicated that he could only speak a Yes and a No to an "ideal of public virtue," such as Werpehowski proposes. For Barth, co-humanity means that the "total and definitive decision is for man and not for any cause."[59] Barth loathed principles, ideals, or causes that were absolutes, because they are ultimately only the "works and produces of human perversion which can only increase the evil which suppresses and oppresses people."[60] Because it could so easily be torn asunder from the command of God and turned into a norm or ideal that forgets its very purpose (humanity) and its very author (God), Barth appears to have had a certain nervousness about using a criterion of co-humanity in the political sphere. He did use it, but not in the sense that Werpehowski suggested that he should. The following section will examine an example of this use in *CD* 3/4.

Humanity as the Criterion for International Relations

In his section, "Freedom in Fellowship," Barth employed the criterion of co-humanity. He argued that when God summons the person to serve him, he addresses that person concerning his or her vocation to be a covenant-partner with himself and he directs the person to his fellow-human. According to Barth, God calls men and women to fulfill their beings through encounter with another, to allow one's humanity as fellow-humanity to be his nature.[61] Thus God calls the human person into freedom in fellowship with others. In this manner, the divine command is the invitation to real humanity. Barth explained, "Humanity, the characteristic and essential mode of man's being, is in its root fellow-humanity. Humanity that is not fellow-humanity is inhumanity. For it cannot reflect but only contradict the determination of man to be God's covenant partner, nor can the God who is no *Deus solitarius* but *Deus triunus,* God in relationship, be mirrored in a *homo solitarius*."[62] As God offers humans co-humanity, he also calls them to live in his image, which is relational. According to Barth, humans are called to do so in three different spheres, as man and woman, as parent and child, and as neighbor near and far. The third sphere has direct political implications for Barth.

---

59. Barth, *Christian Life*, 268.
60. Ibid.
61. Barth, *CD* 3/4:117.
62. Ibid.

In this third sphere are those who Barth called *near neighbors*, those of one's own race or people, share a common language, geographical location, and history. By *distant neighbors*, Barth means wider humanity to which he and his people are also bound.[63] In his attempt to prevent the sort of mistakes of Nazi Germany in which the idea of *Volk* or one's own people elevated too highly, Barth made an important differentiation between this sphere and the two prior spheres.[64] The spheres (1) of man and woman and (2) of parent and child belong to human essence as a human creature. In contrast to those spheres, the sphere of neighbor is only provisional and temporary. One's particular nationality or citizenship is simply the place in which one exercises his fellow-humanity.[65] Barth says that the state is not an order of creation but an order of the covenant, to be considered in the doctrine of reconciliation. He illustrated this in his exegeses of Genesis 11–12 and Acts 2.

He argued that according to Genesis 11:1–9 a single race came to build a tower with intention of exalting itself and becoming its own Lord—making itself equal with God on the basis of its work. God came and, knowing that a sinful race in unity could cause great evil, he judged their arrogance by taking away their gift of unity, giving them many languages, and dispersing them throughout the earth. Barth concluded that this act of the Creator was an act of preservation for his creation, instituted to preserve the continuance of the world. On the one hand, the Christian gives thanks to God for preserving Creation for the covenant. On the other hand, a homesickness is evoked by this separation of people into neighbors near and far. Thus, the person remains loyal to their nation (or near neighbors) while maintaining an openness to far neighbors.

Barth took this argument a step further through his exegesis of Acts 2, in which the Holy Spirit manifested a universal offer of salvation by giving the peoples one language, creating peace, and making them one in Christ Jesus (Eph 2:13ff.). Because of Christ, the loyalty of the believer in the Creator God does not entail loyalty to a particular nation. The loyalty of the believer belongs first and foremost to Jesus Christ as the head of the new *polis*, the kingdom of God.[66]

---

63. Ibid., 286.
64. Ibid., 305.
65. Ibid., 302.
66. Ibid., 316–17. Further implications of this encounter of the kingdom of God with the state will be developed in the following chapter.

Inasmuch as co-humanity is part of the doctrine of creation, Barth did not use it as the basis for his political theory, for he grounded the notion of "the state" not in creation but in reconciliation.[67] Perhaps this explains the reason that he appealed in his earlier political writings to the kingdom of God (which he normally associated with the doctrine of reconciliation) as the *polis* that determines the state rather than a theory of co-humanity that determines statehood. In other words, states are established by God as an act of preservation so that he might complete his work of redemption in creation. Yet they are not fixed. God can easily replace one state with another. What is important for Barth is that the state is not merely a human institution established by humans to maintain our common existence, our co-humanity. It is a matter of God's providential rule.[68]

Yet as I have demonstrated here, Barth did utilize the criterion of co-humanity at key points in determining what justice looks like within the state and in international relations. He used this idea of reconciled co-humanity to inform the way Christians should act in the political sphere, the righteousness of God to which they should witness. For example, Barth wrote of the encounter between the human and his fellow citizens within a state, "this confrontation is simply the place where he has to exercise his fellow-humanity."[69] According to Barth, the human can be fellow-human without the state. The state only exists to preserve humanity and it is one context in which the human must act as fellow-human; one's co-humanity is not limited by the state. For example, as a member of the new *polis*, one's allegiance Jesus Christ means that co-humanity is lived with neighbors both near and far. Thus, co-humanity serves Barth as a vital criterion for justice in the state, but it does not establish the state. For this reason, co-humanity will always trump loyalty to the state. Barth argued for such an understanding of the state so that the threat to statehood would not be perceived as a threat against one's own being and nature.[70] Rather, by arguing that fellow humanity extends to neighbors both near and far, his ethic entails a commitment to all humans, across national and ethnic boundaries.

---

67. Ibid., 303.
68. Ibid., 304.
69. Ibid., 302.
70. Ibid., 305.

Summary of Doctrine of Creation

In this chapter, we are exploring Barth's answer to the question, "What is social justice?" According to his ethical method, Barth defined human justice as that which corresponds to the justice of God. In providing the framework for this question of justice, he posed two primary questions that we have sought to expound in this chapter: "Who is the just God?" and "Who is the human?" According to Barth's doctrine of God, God's justice is a distributive justice that is closely tied to mercy: God gives righteousness to sinners. Thus, God's justice is defined in terms of right relations between God and humanity that are grounded in the grace of God. In answering the question of humanity in his doctrine of creation, Barth argued that humans were created in the image of the triune God, created by God for fellowship with him and others. As a result, they are fundamentally persons-in-relation with God and fellow-humanity. Having explored the answers to these two fundamental questions, we now turn to Barth's doctrine of reconciliation, in which he described the reason that we rarely experience this justice of co-humanity in daily life. In these three volumes, Barth provided a more in-depth description of the moral field in which we exist as humans with God and with one another.

Doctrine of Reconciliation: Justification, Sanctification, and Witness

In his doctrine of reconciliation and his lectures on the ethics of reconciliation that are found in *The Christian Life*, Barth described both the cause of social injustice and human forms of justice that correspond to the justice of God. The key idea that frames his discussion is the kingdom of God. According to Barth, human societies exist in a state of disorder that do not reflect the intent of God when he created the world. This disorder arose from "the unrighteousness of the fall of people from God," the rejection of his Lordship and order.[71] In other words, the sin of humanity against God entailed a rejection of their co-humanity. In offending God, humans necessarily offend one another as well. Barth wrote, "They cannot deal righteously with one another, nor be liberal with one another, nor live at peace with one another. In and with the sin of Adam, who wanted to be as God, there is already enclosed the sin of Cain, the murderer of his brother. . . . Where we are against God, the hand of each can only

---

71. Barth, *Christian Life*, 211.

be against that of others."⁷² The rejection of God's Lordship means that humans have likewise rejected their co-humanity by sinning against their neighbor as well.

Barth provided the following example of his claim: People may reject the Lordship of God in order to serve an empire. Yet by giving the idea of empire so much power, as in the case of Hobbes' Leviathan, power is necessarily seized by some, in the subjugation of others. In exalting empire and rejecting the order of God as the Lord, the rights of individual persons will inevitably be trampled upon. Thus, rejecting the Lordship of God to serve an empire also results in sin against fellow humanity.⁷³

According to Barth, this disorder that "both inwardly and outwardly controls and penetrates and poisons and disrupts all human relations and interconnections"⁷⁴ is only overcome through the breaking in of God's kingdom. The kingdom is the revelation of God's justice, by which humanity is judged and established. Through the rule of God over humanity, human relations and interconnections are re-ordered according to the intent of God. Barth wrote, "The kingdom of God is God himself in the act of normalizing human existence."⁷⁵ This "normalized" existence reflects human creation as co-humanity, humans in relationships that love, respect, and uphold the rights of the other.⁷⁶

Barth contrasted his own conception of the kingdom of God with that of his contemporaries on a key point. According to Barth, the kingdom of God is initiated only by God himself, never by human persons. Humans can never bring in the kingdom of God through their own work. It is "God's own action, which does not merge with the best of human action."⁷⁷ Rather, human justice is different from the justice and order of God because it is, "even at best, an imperfect, fragile, and highly problematical righteousness."⁷⁸ For this reason, it is necessary that Christians pray

72. Barth, *Christian Life*, 212, Cf. CD 4/1:399. "I can only live at unity with myself, and we can only live in fellowship with one another, when I and we subject ourselves to the right which does not dwell in us and is not manifested by us, but which is over me and us as the right of God above, manifested to me and us only from God, the right of His Word and commandment alone, the sentence and judgment of His Spirit." Ibid., 451.

73. Barth, *Christian Life*, 220.

74. Ibid., 211.

75. Ibid., 212.

76. Ibid., 270.

77. Ibid., 240.

78. Ibid., 265.

with Christ, "Thy Kingdom Come" and wait with hope for the coming of God's justice in society.

According to Barth, the fact that humans cannot establish the kingdom of God, which restores justice in human relations, does not mean that Christians should merely be passive in the face of human injustice. The kingdom of God has already been inaugurated by Jesus Christ, in his work on behalf of humanity. In Christ, humans have been reconciled with God and with one another.[79] As a result, the belief in Christ and prayer for the justice and order of God sets the Christian life in motion toward this end. In this time between the beginning of the history of Christ and the age of his final manifestation, Christians have to be concerned about justice.[80] While their work for righteousness will always be "far below divine righteousness," their actions should witness to what God has done for man. Barth wrote, "Christians may and can and should reflect and practice God's being and acting for man."[81] Thus, human justice corresponds to the justice of God that was inaugurated by Christ.

This section has provided a brief outline of the key facets at work in Barth's theory of justice: the root of social injustice, which is human sin; the source of social justice, which is the kingdom of God that is revealed in Christ; and the manner in which human justice corresponds to the order that God's kingdom inaugurated in Christ. In order to provide more substance to this outline, one must explore Barth's specific conception of the justice of God revealed in Christ and the corresponding implications for human justice. Barth provided this exposition in his *Doctrine of Reconciliation* in three parts that reflect the threefold movement of Christ: Downward in Justification, Upward in Sanctification, and Outward in Prophetic Witness. The following sections will briefly summarize the three movements as they inform Barth's conception of social justice.

---

79. Ibid., 252.
80. Ibid., 264.
81. Ibid., 267.

PART TWO—Karl Barth

The Downward Movement: Reconciliation through Justification

Barth framed his soteriology in terms of reconciliation: the act of God to be with us in Jesus Christ.[82] This concept of *God with us* plays a key role in Barth's understanding of God's justice and corresponding human justice. As himself God and Lord, Jesus Christ became human in solidarity with sinful humanity. Barth expounded four aspects in which Christ was "for us." First, he was for us by taking our place as our judge. In the first sin of Adam and Eve in Genesis 3, the temptation that led to human obedience was the evil desire to know what is good and evil. The sinner tries to become God by arrogantly making himself the judge of ourselves and other. Yet in revealing himself for us, Christ likewise knows and decides for us, revealing at the same time our arrogance to try to make ourselves like God and our liberation from the tyranny that we impose on ourselves and others.[83] By implication, Christ, and not humans, is the source of judging what is just in society. For this reason, we must turn to God's revelation in Christ to know what social justice is.

Second, Christ is the one judged. He accepts the responsibility that we shirk. Barth explained,

> He as One can represent all and make Himself responsible for the sins of all because He is very man, in our midst, one of us, but as one of us He is also very God and therefore He exercises and reveals amongst us the almighty righteousness of God. He can conduct the case of God against us in such a way that He takes from us our own evil case, taking our place and compromising and burdening Himself with it. And as He does that, it ceases to be our sin.[84]

Christ is the unrighteous and condemned among those who are pardoned because the sentence of judgment is directed against Him.[85] He is judged, condemned and rejected. He is the enemy against God in whom we recognize our own sin only because he frees us from the intolerable responsibility of it.[86]

---

82. Barth, *CD* 4/1:14.
83. Ibid., 231–34.
84. Ibid., 236.
85. Ibid.
86. Ibid., 238.

Third, Christ is for us in suffering and dying on our behalf. As the judge, he takes the place of those who ought to be judged. According to Barth, this act of suffering and death was effective to reconcile God and humanity. By taking our place as man, "the man of sin, the first Adam, the cosmos alienated from God, the 'present evil world' (Gal. 1:4), was taken and killed and buried in and with Him on the cross."[87] Christ made atonement and gave all humans peace with God.

Fourth, Christ is for us because he has done right. He was the one man who was obedient to God. In fulfilling all righteousness, His day of divine judgment was "the birthday of a new man."[88] While Christ accepted the "No" of judgment against human sin, he likewise became the "Yes" of God who was resurrected and brought new life to all humanity. It is at this point that Barth developed his doctrine of justification. In Christ, the man of sin is destroyed and set aside. Because Christ does this as a righteous man, his righteousness becomes our righteousness.[89] In Christ the old, sinful man has been put to death; in Christ the new man, who is reconciled with God and fellow-humanity, is resurrected.[90] This new humanity is declared righteous before God and becomes righteous in the righteousness of Christ.

JUSTIFICATION AND THE STATE

Barth himself believed that it was important to demonstrate the link between this justification by God and social justice. In his 1938 essay, "Church and State," titled in the original *Rechtfertigung und Recht* ("Justification and Justice") Barth sought to draw the connections between justification and social justice. According to Barth, Calvin and Luther presented a picture of the church and state as two distinct realms, which were not in conflict and could exist side by side. Barth agreed with this claim but added a further question as to the connection between the two realms. He asked, "What is the relationship between human justice and divine justification?"[91] If divine justification has nothing to do with human justice, then churches would either become exclusively spiritual communities, ceasing to deal with societal problems or they might become

---

87. Ibid., 254.
88. Ibid., 259.
89. Ibid., 550–55.
90. Ibid., 557.
91. Barth, "Church and State," in *Community, State, and Church*, 101–2.

communities that work for human justice based on human law, devoid of the divine Word and revelation to humankind.[92] Barth sought to forge a third way by arguing that the church and state should recognize their deep connection in Jesus Christ. While the church was obviously established by Christ, Barth argued that the state likewise "belongs originally and ultimately to Jesus Christ."[93] Elsewhere he explained that the state is an instrument of divine grace because is an act of divine providence, "to protect man from the invasion of chaos" and to provide time for the preaching of the gospel, for repentance, and for faith.[94] He believed that the state serves the person of Christ and therefore the justification of the sinner.

Barth illustrated this idea by examining the confrontation between Jesus and Pilate in John 19.[95] After being whipped by Pilate's soldiers, Jesus was brought before Pilate a second time and questioned. When Jesus did not answer Pilate asked, "You will not speak to me? Do you not know that I have power to release you, and power to crucify you?" Jesus answered him, "You would have no power over me unless it had been given you from above; therefore, he who delivered me to you has the greater sin." Thus, Jesus confirmed Pilate's claim to have power over him. Barth argued that this dialogue demonstrated two things. First, the passage shows the power of God's justice in allowing human injustice to be the instrument of justification for sinful man through the cross.[96] Secondly, the failure of Pilate to assert what Pilate himself recognized was human justice when he said, "I find no crime in him"[97] led to the "demonization" of the state.[98] However, if Pilate had chosen what he recognized as true justice,

92. Barth, "Church and State," in *Community, State, and Church*, 104.

93. Barth, "Church and State," in *Community, State, and Church*, 118.

94. Barth, CCCC, 156.

95. Barth, "Church and State," in *Community, State, and Church*, 109–14.

96. Barth wrote, "What he means is that what actually took place in this use of the statesman's power was the only possible thing that could take place in the fulfilment of the gracious will of the Father of Jesus Christ! Even at the moment when Pilate (still in the garb of justice! and in the exercise of the power given him by God) allowed injustice to run its course, he was the human created instrument of that justification of sinful man that was completed once for all time through that crucifixion" ("Church and State," in *Community, State, and Church*, 110). Thus, Barth argued, this passage finds significance by declaring the solidarity of paganism with the sin of Israel, by demonstrating the "demonic" state is ultimately constrained to do good, and by showing that, in this case, the "demonic" action of the state was attributed to *failing* to assert human justice and giving into the demands of men.

97. John 18:38.

98. Barth, "Church and State," in *Community, State, and Church*, 111.

his choice would have favored Christ, recognizing the right of Christ to proclaim the kingdom of God. Barth argued that the power of God brings divine justification both through the injustice of humans within the state and through actions of the state that accord with human justice. Therefore, the state is used by God as an order of redemption. The just state provides the church the freedom to proclaim the justification of the kingdom of God and promotes human justice.[99] Yet even when the state is unjust, God brings his justification into the world through that state. For this reason, the church should uphold the state while it also calls the state to justice.

Justification and Human Justice

Two years after publishing that essay, Barth drew a further link between justification and human justice in his exegesis of Isaiah 11:1-5. In this passage, he continued to grapple with the connections between divine and human justice. He argued here that the doctrine of justification demands that Christians have a particular political attitude: a driving concern for human rights.

In this passage, Barth's starting point is his doctrine of justification, which reveals that God's righteousness is merciful; his justice is a distributive justice that gives righteousness to those who do not deserve it. God's righteousness is revealed in Christ as help and salvation. When human persons encounter that righteousness, they recognize that it is not something that they can procure on their own. "The righteousness of the believer consists in the fact that God acts for him—utterly, because he cannot plead his own case and no one else can represent him."[100] The person of faith who recognizes the righteousness that has been given to him by God in Jesus Christ is likewise made responsible to all who are poor and wretched as he was before God. He is summoned to procure the rights of those who lack them. Barth writes, "He cannot avoid the question of human rights. He can only will and affirm a state based on justice. By any other political attitude he rejects the divine justification."[101] For Barth, therefore, the failure to take up the question of human rights is a rejection of one's very salvation.

This passage is significant because it again demonstrates Barth's connections between justification and human justice. Because God's justice is

---

99. Barth, "Church and State," in *Community, State, and Church*, 126 and 147.
100. Barth, *CD* 2/1:386.
101. Ibid., 387.

a distributive and merciful justice, the human justice that corresponds to it is likewise distributive and merciful. By their very justification, Christians are called to procure justice for those who do not have it by defending the rights of the oppressed. This positive form of human righteousness is shaped by the righteousness of God and "has necessarily the character of a vindication of right in favor of the threatened innocent, the oppressed poor, widows, orphans and aliens." Therefore, Barth's understanding of human justice, as informed by the justice of God revealed in his merciful justification of sinners, is a distributive and merciful justice.

In the human form of this justice, Christians do not act as if they are gods, reaching down to help those who need their aid, like the philanthropist who creates dependence and humiliates the one he claims to serve.[102] Rather, the "small righteousness" of Christians is their solidarity with the poor and oppressed.[103] All persons are powerless to obtain justice and are equally in need of God's justification. The poor serve as witnesses to the righteousness of God, manifesting this powerlessness of all humans in the sight of God.[104] One may critique Barth on this final point, for glorifying or justifying material impoverishment or oppression, which in reality can be deeply dehumanizing. Yet it appears from this passage that his intent was (a) to affirm the dignity of the oppressed by establishing the solidarity of believers with the marginalized and (b) to procure justice for those who are oppressed.

In this manner, Barth illustrated the human justice that corresponds to God's justice in his work of justification. In this movement the nature of God's justice is distributive and relational. God established right relations with humans through Jesus Christ. He came as God with us and reconciled humanity with himself in the personhood of Christ. Through his own death, he procured justice for those who could not obtain it. The human justice that corresponds to this revelation must necessarily be distributive and relational, acting as persons who have received justice and who may work to uphold the justice of others, regardless of apparent national or economic boundaries. We now turn to examine the justice of God in the second movement of Christ's work of reconciliation.

---

102. Barth, *CD* 4/2: 440.
103. Barth, *Christian Life*, 270.
104. Barth, *CD* 2/1:387.

Reconciliation through Sanctification

While Barth associated the first movement of Christ as servant with the revelation and distribution of God's justice to individuals, he associates the second movement of Christ with his Lordship. As Lord, Christ inaugurated the kingdom of God and freed his fellow humans to act in accordance with God's just order. As noted earlier, this concept of the kingdom of God is key to Barth's ethics of reconciliation because it is in his kingdom that Christ reveals and establishes the order of God on earth. This order is just because it accords with the justice of God. Human justice in society corresponds to the just order of God's kingdom.

In this second movement, Christ draws humanity upward in obedience to God. This upward movement is initiated by the incarnation, in which Christ assumes human essence and unites in himself divine and human essence. In doing so, he draws human essence upward in participation with God. He is the obedient human who exalts our human essence to gracious fellowship with His divine nature and to common action with his divinity.[105] Barth wrote, "In Him the homecoming of the Son of Man has already taken place. . . . In spite of all that we are, and must be called, without Him, the divine promise that we shall be like Him has already been pronounced. In Him, in His being as man, the reconciliation of the world with God has already taken place, the kingdom of God has already come on earth, the new day has already dawned."[106]

Yet in Christ humans are not turned only to God but also to fellow-humans. Barth wrote, "In the actualization which it has found in Him humanity means to be bound and committed to other men."[107] For Christ himself, in his royal freedom, is fellow-man of his fellows, neighbor, helper, and advocate for humans. In him, we are "elected and created and determined for fellow-humanity, for neighbourly love, for brotherhood."[108] In Christ, humanity is exalted as Royal Man. This exaltation is "a summons to participate, as thankful recipients of his grace, in the humanity actualized in Him, to share this humanity with a concrete orientation.[109]

Yet Christ's fellow-humanity reveals a second aspect of human sin: sloth. Humans isolate themselves from God and neighbor, they resist

---

105. Barth, CD 4/2:37–38, 117.
106. Ibid., 117.
107. Ibid., 432.
108. Ibid., 433.
109. Ibid.

obedience to God and relationship with the neighbor. In doing so, humans contradict their own natures, though they can never destroy the fact that we are bound up with others at this ontological level.[110] Yet humans persist in this "inhumanity," through isolation, self-will, and inactivity, at the very point where we should be moved in the direction of our neighbors.

Barth used the prophesies of Amos as an illustration of this sloth. Amos brought the word of God's judgment against the Northern Kingdom of Israel. Barth called his message peculiar because Amos did not address about idol worship or monarchs who are behaving badly. Rather, his accusation "is simply and solely the inhumanity of the social relationships."[111] God's concern is the "the affair of the fellow-man who is so severely and constantly hurt by man"[112] and his reason for judgment is that "in this state one man does not live and deal with others as he ought to do according to the will of Yahweh."[113] At this time, the Northern Kingdom was peaceful and prosperous yet the leading citizens oppressed the poor and did not give them justice. According to Amos, they concealed their injustices not in the worship of other gods or idols, but of Yahweh. For example, the high-priest of Yahweh resisted the accusations of Amos and sought to make him flee from the land.[114] Amos said that despite their sacrifices and feast days and gifts, God was not pleased. He demanded that they treat one another justly.[115] This passage illustrates the form of sloth that Barth described: the tendency of humans to isolate themselves, to not extend themselves to their fellow-humans as they were created to do.

Yet through the cross, Christ embraced the human situation and he radically transformed it as our brother by also becoming the Royal Man who is reconciled with God.[116] He reconciled humans with one another in himself. He lives as the new man in whom all humans "may discover that they are known and proclaimed as regenerate."[117] The sanctification of humanity in Christ is God's fashioning of a holy people that serve God and their fellow-humans.

---

110. Ibid., 281–82 and 433.
111. Ibid., 447.
112. Ibid., 448
113. Ibid., 447.
114. Ibid., 450.
115. Ibid., 451.
116. Ibid., 293 and 297–98.
117. Ibid., 395.

In addition, the Holy Spirit grants us "a very definite freedom" to become holy people.[118] God recreates humanity in Christ as obedient children and speaks to us, "Be what thou art."[119] This view of Barth stands in contrast to the modern notion of freedom found in an author like Sartre, in which freedom is "the nothingness which is *made-to-be* at the heart of man and which forces human reality *to make itself*."[120] For Barth, freedom is not in this potential for the human to make itself into what it is to be. Rather, the human has already been determined by God's act in Christ, in creation, reconciliation, and redemption. Barth's idea of freedom is the acknowledged occupation of this reality, the discovery of selfhood as determined by the works of God, and the action that corresponds to this reality.[121] In sanctification, our being is transformed by God and we are set in a new direction. This direction is one of freedom in Christ in which humans are liberated from the compulsion of continuing in disobedience into living as the brother of the one exalted, obeying the command of God, and loving fellow-humans.[122]

Like John Paul, Barth defined love as the giving of the self.[123] Love thus entails relation with the neighbor.[124] Love for the neighbor springs from the love, which God has given to humans. It is not a general love for humanity but a specific love for neighbors and enemies which is given as a witness of God's own love.[125] Christians are thus called and set in the direction of Christ in giving of themselves to witness to the love that God has already given to humanity. For the time, however, we see that Barth's overwhelming emphasis is upon the participation that believers are given in Christ's relation with the Father. This participation creates human freedom to love the neighbor and to fulfill the criterion of co-humanity that is core to Barth's social ethics.

118. Ibid., 363.

119. Ibid.

120. Sartre, *Being and Nothingness*, 567.

121. Webster, *Barth's Ethics of Reconciliation*, 224–25. It is not within the bounds of this chapter to handle the extensive question of human freedom and agency in Barth's ethics. Recent authors such as John Webster and Archibald Spencer have addressed this issue in detail, arguing that there is a moral space for human action in Barth's thought. See Webster, *Barth's Ethics of Reconciliation*, 223–30; Webster, *Barth's Moral Theology*, 1–40 and 151–78; and Spencer, *Clearing a Space for Human Action*.

122. Barth, *CD* 4/2:312.

123. Ibid., 728–31 and 786.

124. Ibid., 733.

125. Ibid., 802 and 812.

From this doctrine of sanctification, it becomes clear that key to a theory of justice is Barth's notions of obedience and solidarity. Humans are called to act in accordance with the just order of the kingdom of God that was inaugurated by Christ. This means that they are summoned to live with their fellow-humans in love and justice. In *The Christian Life*, Barth asked: What is the human action that corresponds to the kingdom of God? What is the human righteousness that corresponds to the Christian's prayer that God's kingdom come? He answered, "According to the measure of what is possible for them, their action must in all circumstances take place with a view to people, in address to people, and with the aim of helping people." He explained further:

> Christians can look only where they see God looking and try to live with no other purpose than that with which God acts in Jesus Christ. This means, however that the true and serious and finally important object of their attention, love and will, and therefore of their thought, speech, and action, in agreement with their prayer and in correspondence with what they pray for, can only be man.[126]

They are able to act with and for man because they have been freed to do so by the sanctification established for them in Christ and developed in them through the Holy Spirit. Barth wrote, "As Christians, obedient to the command that they are given . . . they confess solidarity at every point with man himself, they show themselves to be his companions and friends . . . , and they make his cause their own."[127] This solidarity is central to the exaltation of humanity in Christ. It is the social act of obedience for which humanity is freed.

In this movement of reconciliation as sanctification, Barth developed more fully the implication of God's relationship with humanity. In Christ, humans begin to see that they have become who they were created to be: humans in relation with God and one another. As Lord, Christ inaugurated the kingdom of God in which God's just order reigns because humans have been reoriented to God and to one another. The human justice that corresponds to this order follows the direction that Christ re-established through his sanctification: solidarity with God and with fellow-humanity.

---

126. Barth, *Christian Life*, 266.
127. Ibid., 270.

Reconciliation through Prophetic Witness

According to Barth, Christ's third movement of reconciliation was his movement outward as prophet. His work of reconciliation overcomes the distance between God and human persons; humans perceive this work through this proclamation that "The Kingdom of God is at hand."[128] This proclamation declares the reality of the new human person and the new freedom in the kingdom of God through Christ's vicarious work. Yet in opposition to this revelation of Christ, the world clings to the old reality and resists Christ with anthropocentric worldviews. However, at the conclusion of history, Christ will be proven the final victor in truth and light.

In this time between Easter and the end, Christ comes near to humans in his Spirit, encountering us, proclaiming his truth, and giving to us the time and space to live in this new human freedom. His revelation of truth exposes the falsehood of humans as they seek to evade his prophesy by establishing false "truths."[129] God opposes this falsehood through the living and present reality of Jesus Christ, the self-declaration of the grace and truth of God.

What are the implications of this declaration for the human? In proclaiming and activating the reconciliation of man with God, Jesus calls the human out of darkness into light. This particular person, Jesus, frees all humanity from falsehood by rising and living for the world and by proclaiming God in the Word of grace and reconciliation and in the promised Spirit.[130] In this time between, the primary difference between Christians and non-Christians is not their reconciliation but their recognition of the truth that Christ has done this work on their behalf. Both have been given freedom under the conditions of this effected but not fully manifested reconciliation, but Christians are more aware of this freedom because they know that Christ is the hope of the world in the midst of continuing injustice. Barth wrote,

> The reconciliation of the world with God, and in it the justification and sanctification of man, have taken place and have been publicly declared in the resurrection of Jesus Christ. But this

---

128. Barth, *CD* 4/3:180.

129. Ibid., 475. Gorringe draws a relation between this comment and economic concerns, "The allusion to Adam Smith is unmistakeable. Over ruling through advertising and the inducement of false desire, is the counter hand of God witnessing to the alternative truth of cooperation and true desire." Gorringe, *Karl Barth*, 251.

130. Barth, *CD* 4/3:486. Barth related this calling to election in 486ff. See Webster on the universality of this particular human in *Barth*, 133.

declaration is not yet complete. The reconciled nature of creation has still to be revealed, i.e., its redemption and consummation. This means, however, that the declaration is still exposed to the power of evil, which is broken in the accomplished reconciliation, but which can still mount its assaults and temptations and acts of violence.

It is vital for Christians to acts as witnesses to this vertical reconciliation between God and humanity and the horizontal reconciliation between humans. They do so through proclaiming God's kingdom in word and in act. This is the service to the world to which Christians are called.[131]

Again, Barth came back to this theme of solidarity. He said that solidarity means that the church is committed to the world, participating in its situation, in the promise given to it, in the responsibility for the arrogance, sloth, and falsehood that reign in it, in its resulting suffering, and in the grace and hope in Jesus Christ.[132] The church community is called to live with the world in compassion rather than fleeing from the world or holding oneself aloof.[133] For the church has a special calling in solidarity with "the least of these," of Matthew 25, those who are marginalized, hungry, thirsty, naked, homeless, sick, feeble, mentally confused, orphaned, seeking refuge, and imprisoned.[134]

In cases of injustice, in particular, the church cannot remain "neutral" by withholding her witness but she is called to pray and to fight for just peace.[135] Barth argued that the Christian community cannot turn a blind eye to social injustice or evade its responsibility as a member of that society. Rather, the church must "raise its voice and with its proclamation of the Gospel summon the world to reflect on social injustice and its consequences and to alter the conditions and relationships in question."[136] Thus, the church is called to act and to speak for justice in society.[137]

---

131. Barth, *CD* 4/3:598. Cf. Barth, *God Here and Now*, 66; and *CCCC*, 158–59.

132. Barth, *CD* 4/3:773. Jüngel relates Barth's notion of solidarity with the world to church and state in *Christ, Justice, and Peace*, 61–62.

133. Barth, *CD* 4/3:774–75.

134. Ibid., 890–91.

135. Barth, "First Letter to the French Protestants," in *A Letter to Great Britain from Switzerland*, 30.

136. He wrote, "The diaconate and the Christian community become dumb dogs, and their service a serving of the ruling powers, if they are afraid to tackle at their social roots the evils by which they are confronted in detail." Barth, *CD* 4/3:893.

137. Barth, *Christian Life*, 270.

Barth's Theological Framework for Justice

This calling highlights the special role of the church with regard to the state. Barth's primary concern is that the church be given the freedom to act as witness to the order of God's kingdom. Barth wrote, "all that can be said from the standpoint of divine justification on the question (and the questions) of human law is summed up in this one statement: the Church *must have freedom to proclaim divine justification*. The state will realize its own potentialities, and thus will be a just state, in proportion as it not merely positively allows, but actively grants, this freedom to the church."[138] He goes so far as to argue that the preaching of justification by the church founds the true system of law, the true state.[139] He rejected any notion that the church should try to set itself up as the true state on earth. Rather, the church acts as the preservation and basis of the state; the state cannot establish or protect true human law without the proclamation of the church for the church knows the basis for all human laws, the person of Jesus Christ.[140] Barth wrote,

> The right of the Church to liberty means the foundation, the maintenance, the restoration of everything—certainly of all human law. Wherever this right is recognized, and wherever a true Church makes the right use of it (and the free preaching of justification will see to it that things fall into their true place), there we shall find a legitimate human authority and an equally legitimate human independence; tyranny [and anarchy] . . . will be dethroned; and the true order of human affairs—the justice, wisdom and peace, equity and care for human welfare which are necessary to that true order—will arise.[141]

Thus, the responsibility of the just State is to provide freedom for the church's proclamation so that the state might know what justice is and so that just human laws, which correspond to the gospel of Christ, might rule the state.

---

138. Barth, "Church and State," in *Community, State, and Church*, 147. Barth wrote, "The State is called to establish human law, and it has the capacity to do so. We cannot measure what this law is by any Romantic or Liberalistic idea of 'natural law,' but simply by the concrete law of freedom, which the Church must claim for its Word, so far as it is the Word of God."

139. Barth, "Church and State," in *Community, State, and Church*, 126. Barth makes this assertion as an implication of his argument that the gospel precedes the law.

140. Barth, CCCC, 162.

141. Barth, "Church and State," in *Community, State, and Church*, 147–48.

PART TWO—Karl Barth

Conclusion to Part Two

In Part Two of this book, we have examined Barth's answers to the three questions posed to each of our dialogue partners: (1) How is justice known? (2) What is social justice? and (3) How is justice cultivated in society? Chapters 4 and 5, sought to describe Barth's ethical method as it provides an answer to this question. For Barth, justice is known by the action of God revealed in Jesus Christ. The election of humanity in Christ creates a claim upon all humans to correspond to God's just action. The command of God provides the content of this correspondence. The knowledge of God and "the moral field" in which humans act provide direction for the content of this command.

In order to answer the two final questions, chapter 6 examined this moral field that is determined by God's work and revelation in Jesus Christ. According to Barth, social justice is that which corresponds to the justice of God. He defined God's justice as a distributive justice, for it is a justice that extends to those who were without the means to obtaining justice of their own. By implication, the human justice that corresponds to this justice is a justice of mercy toward those who cannot obtain justice. Second, he defined God's justice as a relational justice. Just as Christ became God with us and reconciled humanity with one another, humans are to live in solidarity with fellow-humanity. This solidarity is grounded in our creation as humans-in-relation, in our reconciliation with our fellow-humans, and in the hope of God's redemption in which God's kingdom is consummated and his just order is restored in full. We correspond to this relational justice established by God by seeking to live in solidarity with our fellow humans and upholding their rights, their lives, and their worth.

This definition of justice immediately leads to the answer to our third question, "How does society become just?" According to Barth, society becomes just through the in-breaking of God's kingdom. Only through the work of God can the justice of God be established. However, the Christian community is still called to act for human justice. They do so in relation to the state and the world as prayerful witnesses, pointing toward the justice of God's kingdom that was inaugurated in Christ. The state that is just, therefore, gives the church the freedom to witness and it takes seriously the content of this witness by establishing laws that correspond to God's justice. In addition to the verbal witness, the Christian community also witnesses through their actions. Because of Christ's work of reconciliation, the Christian community is directed toward their neighbors in solidarity and love. The Church is called to care for the oppressed and marginalized through acts of solidarity and through prophetic witness to the justice of God's kingdom that has come and that will bring justice to human societies. Having examined the theories of justice in the works of Barth and John Paul II, we now turn to critically compare the two on these three questions: How is justice known? What is justice? How is justice cultivated in society?

PART THREE

Critical Dialogue with a Female Interlocutor

7

Sources of Justice

JOHN PAUL II AND KARL BARTH STAND AT THE CENTER OF THE MODERN Catholic and Protestant traditions as towering figures who powerfully shaped the trajectory of their respective traditions. Parts One and Two of this book expounded the philosophical, theological, and ethical thought of each man by posing three primary questions: How is justice known? What is social justice? How is social justice cultivated in society?

Part Three critically examines Barth and John Paul in critical dialogue regarding their answers to these questions. We will not only critique the intellectual strength and consistency of their theories, we will also examine the implications of their theories for groups at the margins of the traditions they represent: the poor, the infirmed, women, and the dispossessed. Justice toward those at the margins of society played a central role in the social ethics of the Jewish and Christian traditions, from the Torah's repeated commands to care for the widows, the orphans, and the poor to the advocacy of the prophets on behalf of the impoverished. Chapter Seven will evaluate John Paul and Barth's answers first question: How is justice known? Chapter Eight will assess the final two questions: What is justice? How is justice cultivated in society?

How Is Justice Known?

With regard to our first question, both Barth and John Paul II believed that knowledge of justice begins with God. For Barth, God's justice is revealed in Jesus Christ: in election, creation, reconciliation, and redemption. For John Paul II, God's justice is revealed in nature (in natural law and human nature) and in Christ.

In evaluating these sources of justice in prior chapters, I sought to demonstrate that John Paul's two-fold approach created an unresolved tension in his theory of justice because the natural norms of justice at times differ from the revealed norms of justice. The natural norms of justice are more retributive in orientation ("an eye for an eye") whereas the revealed norms of justice bring a restorative aspect to his theory of justice, in which Christ demonstrates mercy for sinners. This disjunction potentially results in two theories of justice for John Paul: one known in the natural world and one for the church.

By contrast, Barth held a single source for justice: the revelation of God in Jesus Christ. Barth argued that the law does not precede the gospel, so that there are two forms of command ("law and gospel," or to use similar terminology by John Paul, "nature and Christ"). Rather, Barth argued that there is one form of the command of God because the gospel precedes and includes the law. The good news of the election of Christ to salvation precedes and includes the command of God for those who are elect. The covenant of God with humanity, which is indicated by the statement, "I will be your God" precedes and includes the command of God for humanity that is implied by the second statement "you shall be my people."

Sources of Justice: Consistency

Barth's Christological method appears more consistent for a number of reasons. First, it presents a portrait of God that is more unified and consistent in the Old and New Testaments. It is not the portrait of a God who first enforced a form of retributive justice and only later revealed that justice should be tempered by mercy. Rather, the law of God for Israel, "an eye for an eye," is within the larger context of God's covenant promises for Israel. As argued in Galatians, the covenant of God with Abraham preceded the law, which came "four hundred thirty years" later.[1] His method affirms the righteousness and mercy of God throughout scripture.

Second, Barth's method takes seriously the Christian affirmation that Christ preceded creation and that creation took place in Christ.[2] Using his Christological method, Barth reworked his ethics in light of this belief that we do not have first (a) nature and then (b) Christ, who provides further revelation about nature (either human nature or natural law). Rather, Christ is co-eternal with the Father and his will for creation is revealed in his covenant that preceded creation. This covenant is further revealed in

---

1. Gal 3:17.
2. Col 1:16.

reconciliation and the promise of redemption and creation is interpreted in light of Christ.

Third, Barth's single source for justice provides a theory of justice that is more consistent. Whereas in John Paul's thought, one is left wondering when to practice the justice of nature and when to practice restorative justice of Christ, Barth's theory of God's justice incorporates God's covenantal mercy from the beginning. For Barth, God's justice is consistently directed toward right relations. There is no standard of justice by which God must act or of which God must overcome. Justice itself is God's gracious gift of right relationship with humans and of human persons with each one another.

John Paul's Inconsistencies Illustrated

Barth's theory of justice is grounded in the relationship of God with humanity rather than norms of nature and the revealed norms of Christ. One can see the benefit of this single source in promoting a more consistent theory of justice. For example, on the question of capital punishment, Barth and John Paul sound remarkably similar. They both make their arguments against capital punishment based upon two appeals: (1) human life is given by God and must be upheld and (2) the gospel provides hope that the perpetrator will be redeemed.[3]

---

3. Barth, *CD* 3/4:442–44. Barth argued that retributive justice had already found expression in Christ's death and that "if this righteousness is what we are really to attest, the punishment of the criminal must take a form in which the forgiveness won for him in Jesus Christ is revealed to him and to the less wicked by being concretely offered to the more wicked. His punishment should not shorten the allotted time which still remains to him but afford him the opportunity of filling it better than he has done in the past" (443). He also wrote, "If the command to protect life is accepted and asserted in some sense in a national community, then it is impossible to maintain capital punishment as an element of normal and continuing order" (445). Note that Barth does make some exception to his general rule in extreme cases (446–50). John Paul wrote: "Nowadays, in America as elsewhere in the world, a model of society appears to be emerging in which the powerful predominate, setting aside and even eliminating the powerless: I am thinking here of unborn children, helpless victims of abortion; the elderly and incurably ill, subjected at times to euthanasia; and the many other people relegated to the margins of society by consumerism and materialism. Nor can I fail to mention the unnecessary recourse to the death penalty when other 'bloodless means are sufficient to defend human lives against an aggressor and to protect public order and the safety of persons. Today, given the means at the State's disposal to deal with crime and control those who commit it, without abandoning all hope of their redemption, the cases where it is absolutely necessary to do away with an offender 'are now very rare, even non-existent practically' (229). This model of society bears the stamp of

PART THREE—Critical Dialogue with a Female Interlocutor

Yet when examining a different justice issue, HIV/AIDS, John Paul chose to take a "natural law" approach. In addressing the spread of HIV/AIDS in a generalized population like Africa, John Paul continued to argue against the use of contraceptives, even between discordant couples in which one spouse is HIV positive. In *Humanae Vitae*, he spelled out reason for opposing contraceptives on the basis of "natural law, which . . . teaches that each and every marital act must of necessity retain its intrinsic relationship to the procreation of human life."[4] In many traditional African cultures, it is common for an older man (whose wife has passed away) to take a young girl as a bride. If the man is infected with HIV, the young bride has no defense to protect herself from infection if she cannot use contraceptives. In addition, young brides most often lack the power to remain abstinent. When John Paul made these declarations, at a time prior to the widespread availability of ARVs, he almost certainly sentenced many obedient Catholic brides to death.

Here is where the contradiction between natural law and the revealed norms of mercy that uphold human life stand in stark contrast. In the first case of capital punishment, John Paul appealed to revealed norms of justice in order to uphold life and in the second case of HIV/AIDS he appealed to natural norms (sex for the sole purpose of procreation) that were likely to destroy the life of the young bride. These two sources for justice create a clear inconsistency in his thought.

As a female reader, one cannot help but ask why John Paul would not value the actual life of the bride over and above her potential as child bearer. Such a stance appears to devalue female life, especially in a context in which a young bride lacks the power to negotiate abstinence. Does her potential to bear a child really outweigh her current value as a human person? Is the source of her value so concentrated in her potential for childbearing that the dangerous decision to have unprotected sex with her husband is worth the gamble?

Why does John Paul appeal to revealed norms in the case of capital punishment and natural norms in the case of contraceptives? At minimum, the appeal to two sources for justice may prove confusing. At maximum,

---

the culture of death, and is therefore in opposition to the Gospel message. Faced with this distressing reality, the Church community intends to commit itself all the more to the defense of the culture of life." JPII, *Ecclesia in America*, 63.

4. *Humanae Vitae*, 11. In *CD* 3/4:414–70 Barth argues that all life should be protected. Only in extreme cases and as a last resort, should human life be taken or persons allowed to die.

the natural norms for justice may disguise norms that perpetuate a frightening form of patriarchy that devalues life.

In theory, drawing from two sources of justice could be consistent if John Paul had clear criteria for when he appealed only to natural norms vs. when he appealed to revealed norms. He did recognize a difference between the two, as discussed in Chapter Two, and argued that theology provides a more expansive context for knowing truth. He wrote, "A purely philosophical interpretation is not adequate. In order to arrive at a wholly adequate interpretation, we must turn to theology and draw upon the full context of revelation."[5] At what point does the ethicist make that turn? What are the criteria for making that turn? This lack of clarity creates inconsistency in his method and leads to serious ethical mistakes in which John Paul's social ethics defended the lives of serial killers while at the same time sentencing a generation of young Catholic brides in areas of high HIV prevalence to an almost certain death.

By contrast, Barth's Christological method leads more consistently to one goal: human action that reflects the justice of God as revealed in Christ. According to Barth, God's justice consistently upholds human life. Because Barth died before HIV was discovered, he obviously did not address the use of condoms as a means of HIV prevention. Yet in his sexual ethics, he did not oppose the use of contraceptives within marriage.[6] In addition, Barth upheld the human right to life, which he derived from his Christological method. He argued thoroughly that all life should be protected and only in extreme cases and as a last resort should human life be taken or should humans be allowed to die.[7] As argued in further detail in a different essay, this Christological theory of human rights, including the right to life, indicates that he would have supported condom use as a means of HIV prevention.[8] In the case of capital punishment as well as prevention of HIV/AIDS, Barth's Christological method led to the upholding of human life. By using only one ethical method, Barth's theory of justice appears more consistent than John Paul's dual basis for ethics.

---

5. Wojtyla, EMT, 105.
6. Barth, CD 3/4:273–76.
7. Ibid., 414–70.
8. Smith, "Justification of Human Rights and the Implications for HIV Prevention."

PART THREE—Critical Dialogue with a Female Interlocutor

Sources of Justice: Epistemic Access

Barth's method, however, is not without its apparent challenges. Namely, the problem posed for Barth's epistemology is its apparent exclusivity. Those who interpret Barth as an exclusivist would conclude that if Barth believed that Christ is the revealer, then the logical conclusion is that only Christians can know the justice of God. It is at this point that John Paul's theory appears superior because he does not limit knowledge of justice to Christianity. According to John Paul, all persons have epistemic access to the norms of justice through natural law. These natural laws direct people to do the good and give enough information about human nature so that people can treat one another in accordance with the norms of justice without the need for belief in Christ.

For Barth, by contrast, good human action is not determined by compliance with norms and laws. Rather, it is determined by reality, by "that which is."[9] According to Barth, the command and law arise from this reality. In Christ, a person discovers that the Other is neighbor; she recognizes that she exists not in isolation but in fellowship as co-humanity. From this gospel reality of reconciliation, the command arises: Love your neighbor.

Does Barth's approach demand that a person have faith in Christ's Lordship in order to recognize the co-humanity of the other? I argue that his method does not require faith in Christ; Barth's theology allows for the knowledge of co-humanity to be a possibility for a non-Christian. Naturally, for Barth, the basis for this knowledge was the revelation of Christ. Yet this knowing could take place whether or not the non-Christian (a) is aware of this source or (b) listens to the command that presents itself in the encounter with the other. Barth wrote,

> As the Word of God gives itself to be heard by man, it binds itself to the man who hears it in a way which is not just incidental, external or partial, but essential, internal and absolute . . . It takes possession of him and sets him on a new ground and in a new atmosphere and situation. In virtue of its address he is a new man, a man of God, justified, sanctified and called as such. It does not merely enlighten him concerning himself in various relationships. It does this. But it does it only as first and decisively it illumines his heart, namely, himself. Hence he does not need to fear that there is a place where it will not shine with its good news. Nor is there any place to which he might

---

9. Webster, *Ethics of Reconciliation*, 214.

flee to escape the illumination of its law and command. As a bad hearer of the Word of God he might give way to fear or flight of this kind, and therefore sin. But this does not alter the fact that it surrounds him as a hearer on all sides.[10]

According to Barth, the gospel of Christ is the basis for the new reality in which all humans are set[11] and it encounters humans in a way that not only illumines their minds concerning their relationships (i.e., their co-humanity) but it also reveals the claim that arises in these relationships. Barth differentiated this way of knowing from natural theology, which arises in human capacity. Rather, this knowledge arises from the capacity of Christ to speak his Word outside of the church, to be Lord of the world and of the church. In this manner, Barth allowed for "lesser lights," for secular words and parables that are true because they are derived from the one Word, Jesus Christ.[12] Likewise, he allowed for "natural knowledge," if such knowledge is understood to exist within the sphere of divine grace.[13] Christians may discern the relative truth of these words and this knowledge because they acknowledge the one Word and his revelation in scripture and the church.

Unfortunately, Barth did not fully unpack the implications of these affirmations for his mature social ethics. Had he done so, he could have made the argument that non-Christians can know what social justice is, even though they may not know that this knowledge is mediated by Christ. If God in Christ does reveal the reality of human nature as co-humanity and illumine the hearts of non-Christians, then when non-Christians encounter the Other, they may have insight into the reality of their co-humanity with the Other. They may recognize the claim that

---

10. Barth, *CD* 4/3:154.

11. Barth wrote, "If we recognise and confess Him as the One who was and is and will be, then we recognise and confess that not we alone, nor the community which, following the prophets and apostles, believes in Him and love Him and hopes in Him, but *de iure* all men and all creation derive from His cross, from the reconciliation accomplished in Him, and are ordained to be the theatre of His glory and therefore the recipients and bearers of His Word" (ibid., 117). He explained, "while man may deny God, according to the Word of reconciliation, God does not deny man . . . The fact that he is closed to it does not alter the further fact that it is open for him. Nor does the fact that he does not recognise the sovereignty of Jesus Christ, and if he did would perhaps rebel against it in his autonomy, result in its losing any of its validity even in relation to him" (ibid., 119).

12. See Barth's fuller discussion of the relation of these words to the Word in ibid., 114ff.

13. Barth, *CD* 3/2:277.

the Other imposes upon them, the claim to co-humanity that lies at the core of personhood. While these non-Christians may not recognize that the source of this claim is Christ, they may recognize the material reality of the Other as the source of the claim to live in solidarity. Thus, non-believers may recognize their co-humanity without knowing that the source of co-humanity is the reconciliation of Christ.

Thus, Barth's apparent limitation by his Christological method need not be a limitation at all. The new reality in Christ in which all persons are set imposes an ethical claim on all persons, whether they recognize that Christ is the source of this claim or not. Any person can recognize the co-humanity of the other and act in accordance with this claim by seeking to uphold the life of the other—whether that person be threatened by capital punishment or by HIV infection, whether that person be a male in the West or a young female in Africa. For this reason, by appealing to one source (Christ) as the basis for ethical knowledge, Barth's method appears more consistent than John Paul's and more likely to issue in a more consistent form of justice that helps to safeguard from gender or race discrimination.

Sources of Justice: The Marginalized

Having examined the consistency of their methods, we now turn to examine their methods from the perspectives of those who are marginalized within society. In order to do so, we will first briefly explore the nature of poverty and marginalization.

A classical understanding of poverty was that impoverished people lacked material goods. Recent sociological research has highlighted the fact that poverty is far more complex than the lack of goods. One key sociologist, John Friedman, describes poverty as lack of access to social power. According to Friedman, all households are embedded in a complex network of interacting systems: the state, political communities, the economy, and civil society. Friedman argues that poverty is a state of disempowerment within these social systems and a result of systemic exclusion and exploitation.[14] This lack of access to social power has a psychological impact by creating feelings of disempowerment that inhibit a sense of agency and feed a cycle of impoverishment and disempowerment. Thus, the escape from poverty involves not only the attainment of material goods but also a strong sense of personal agency and empowerment within social systems.

---

14. Friedman, *Empowerment*, 66.

Sources of Justice

Building upon Friedman, Jayakumar Christian argues that poverty also involves spiritual disempowerment. He suggests that the non-poor use religious systems, media, laws, and policies to "play god" in the lives of the poor by creating narratives, structures, and systems that justify their privileged position.[15] For example, he argues that in India the idea of *karma*, in its popularized form, disempowers the poor by teaching them that their current state is a response to their previous life and must be accepted. By contrast, the Brahmin believe that they were made from the head of God and so they are justified in their position of power and rule. Christian's work suggests that religious beliefs can reinforce the systemic disempowerment of the poor by excluding them as actors. This exclusion can become internalized and result in what Augustine Musopole calls a poverty of being. Musopole writes, "This is where the African feels his poverty most: A poverty of being, in which poor Africans have come to believe they are no good and cannot get things right."[16]

John Paul's Method: Dignity for the Impoverished

The work of John Paul II proves superior to Barth's in addressing the poor at the religious and psychological levels. First, John Paul's methodology affirmed the dignity of all humans by affirming the capacity of all persons to reason and to know the dignity of human nature. Second, his emphasis on the transcendence and freedom of humans and the self-determining nature of human action provides a further sense of dignity. As he said, persons may act freely even in the context of oppression. One may transcend the dehumanizing forces of society that threaten to form her personhood negatively. Because John Paul believed that one's action shapes personhood, then the shape that one's life takes needs not be determined by external forces but by one's own acts of courage or hope in the midst of oppression.

Such a view of personhood provides a deep sense of dignity and a capacity to affirm one's dignity despite the contextual concerns, such as the experience of poverty or marginalization. John Paul's theological anthropology promotes a theologically-backed sense of dignity and agency for the poor and marginalized.[17] Perhaps it was this message of

---

15. Myers, *Walking with the Poor*, 73. Cf. Christian, "A Different Way to Look at Poverty."

16. Myers, *Walking with the Poor*, 76, quoting from Musopole, "African Worldview."

17. In the 1980s, John Paul II came under criticism from liberation theologians for

PART THREE—Critical Dialogue with a Female Interlocutor

dignity and agency that made John Paul II widely popular with poor and disenfranchised groups.

Barth's Method: Disempowering the Impoverished

By contrast, Barth's work proves problematic for the poor or oppressed because of his limitations on reason, his suspicion of the will, and his relentless critique of self-determination. Whereas John Paul II argued that reason is an aspect that reveals and affirms human dignity, Barth placed great limitations on the capacity of reason by arguing that humans cannot attain knowledge of God or of reality apart from God's self-revelation in Christ. Whereas John Paul II believed that humans could not only know the good, but that they had the capacity (albeit weakened) to do the good, Barth argued that humans have no seed of goodness in their nature by which they may know or do good apart from Christ. In other words, Barth consistently criticized any attempts at self-determination apart from Christ.

By contrast, John Paul argued that freedom is experienced in this capacity of humans to transcend a context of oppression, to act in accordance with the good and dignity of their own natures, and thus to determine themselves as good even in the midst of evil. Free actions are self-determining. For example, acting courageously forms one into a courageous person. John Paul resisted the existentialist definition of freedom as nothingness by his affirmation that humans do have a nature or essence and a *telos* that is determined by God.[18] He located their freedom in the

---

his failure to address poverty more radically. These issues of disagreement were more centered on the role of the church in the political realm and the fusion of Marxist and Christian ideology, rather than his idea of personhood. John Paul believed that Marxist ideology was counterproductive. In a sermon in Mexico in 1990, he said, "When the world begins to notice the clear failures of certain ideologies and systems, it seems all the more incomprehensible that certain sons of the Church in these lands—prompted at times by the desire to find quick solutions—persist in presenting as viable certain models whose failure is patent in other places in the world. You, as priests, cannot be involved in activities which belong to the lay faithful, while through your service to the Church community you are called to cooperate with them by helping them study Church teachings . . . Be careful, then, not to accept nor allow a Vision of human life as conflict nor ideologies which propose class hatred and violence to be instilled in you; this includes those which try to hide under theological writings" (BBC, "Liberation Theology").

18. Specifically, this is Sartre's definition of freedom. He wrote, "Freedom is precisely the nothingness which is *made-to-be* at the heart of man and which forces human reality *to make itself* instead of *to be.*" *Being and Nothingness*, 568.

free choice of the will to act in accordance with (or against) their good nature. For Barth, by contrast, humans are already determined by God. Their freedom is not a freedom to become but a freedom to act in accordance with the persons who they already are.[19] The *telos* of humanity has been accomplished in Christ. Thus, the command of God is: "Be what thou art."[20]

This view creates problems in using Barth's thought as a theory of justice that addresses the poor and oppressed because poverty, indeed, is not merely an issue of insubstantial physical resources. The social and political marginalization of the poor entails a loss of agency; the social forces of marginalization inhibit self-determination so that their situation is threatened by the determination of others. Whereas the thought of John Paul affirmed agency, Barth appeared to reaffirm the passivity of the poor or marginalized at two levels. First, in his work, the poor are most commonly acted upon by God. They are determined by God's work in Christ. Attempts at self-determination are viewed as sinful or prideful. For example, as John Webster demonstrated, Barth would condemn any attempts to view the self as a center of judgment in resistance against social forces that oppress a person. Barth would criticize attempts to create value by acts of allegiance and he would rebuke efforts to resist the mischaracterizations of the oppressor by realigning one's moral world around the consciousness of one's situation and poverty.[21]

Second, in his work, the poor are primarily acted upon by the Christian community. They are not portrayed as agents of their own liberation from social oppression. For example, when Barth wrote on the social implications of justification in *CD* 2/1, he directed the command of God to those who were in positions of power, instructing them to care for the poor and oppressed. He argued that just as God gave justice to man, so man "is made responsible to all those who are poor and wretched in his eyes, that he is summoned on his part to espouse the cause of those who suffer wrong."[22] In this passage, those with social rights correspond to divine action whereas those without rights passively accept the rights acquired for them. Such an interpretation of the command of God is problematic because it reaffirms a lack of agency for the poor and provides theologi-

19. Torrance, "Christian Experience and Divine Revelation," 104–5; and Webster, *Ethics of Reconciliation*, 223–25.
20. Barth, *CD* 4/2:363.
21. Webster, *Ethics of Reconciliation*, 18.
22. Barth, *CD* 2/1:387.

cal grounding for the dehumanizing experience of being determined by others.

While this issue may initially appear a minor oversight by Barth, due perhaps to a limited understanding of poverty within his historical context, I suggest that it points to a more serious problem with two aspects of his ethical method. First, Barth's use of the *analogia relationis* in this passage in *Church Dogmatics* 2/1 was set up in a manner that upheld a conservative form of classism, so that the non-poor correspond to the divine (who distributes justice) and the poor class corresponds to the human (who needs justice). Although I agree with Barth's argument that higher classes should seek justice for the poor, his model is deeply problematic because it gives divine status to the actions of the wealthy class and discourages the self-determination and agency of the poor. It contradicts Barth's own conception of co-humanity, in which humans look one another in the eye, speak and listen to one another, and render mutual assistance.[23] By contrast, this application of the *analogia relationis* sets up one group as the divine who gives aid and the second as needy recipient. It fails to acknowledge the co-humanity and agency of the poor.

The second problem with his ethical method is his failure to acknowledge and provide space for the role of subjective experience in theology. According to Barth, Christian ethics derives from dogmatics; the primary task of special ethics is describing the moral field, the field of encounter between God and man, and describing the command of God that issues from this event and the right human action that corresponds to it.[24] Unfortunately, Barth appeared to assume that the field of encounter and the issuing command were the same for all humans as it was for him. For example, in his ethics of reconciliation, Barth argued repeatedly that the righteousness of God means that we must uphold the rights of our neighbors.[25]

Yet such instruction did not address the marginalized and oppressed, whose own rights are oppressed. How could the marginalized possibly uphold the rights of their neighbors if they did not even have their own rights? Barth was clearly writing from a particular socio-economic perspective and experience of empowerment, which limited his perspective and his theological ethics.

---

23. Barth, *CD* 3/2:250–71.
24. Barth, *CD* 3/4:30. Cf. Webster, *Ethics of Reconciliation*, 1–4.
25. Barth, *Christian Life*, 266–70.

Some may suggest that Barth's experience under Hitler was an experience of disempowerment and oppression against his religious beliefs. Indeed, Barth did suffer a sense of marginalization. Yet such marginalization was temporary and Barth's own behavior in fighting Hitler's oppression demonstrated a clear perception of divinely-inspired agency. When Barth left Germany, he was immediately offered employment and continued his work. Barth's short experience of marginalization did not appear to change his socio-economic perspective or his experience of empowerment. To the contrary, Barth's experience of oppression under Hitler appeared to reinforce his own sense of divinely-backed agency.

Unfortunately, it appears that Barth's Christological method failed to challenge Barth's socio-economic perspective. To the contrary, Barth appeared to use this Christological method to reinforce his position of correspondence with the divine. The poor, in Barth's thought, correspond to powerless humans in need of salvation. In his hundreds of pages written on ethics, Barth only rarely addressed poverty. By contrast, poverty is a dominant theme of scripture and the teachings of Christ. Why would Barth's use of his Christological method have missed this important theme so severely? And when Barth did address this theme, why would he have used his analogical method to reinforce the divinely-inspired power of his own socio-economic class? Is this a failure of Barth's use of his method? Or is it a failure of the method itself? Is the Christological method that claims to allow God to speak and claims to minimize the role of experience, merely a form of conservatism that provides divine backing for Barth's own class?

Because Barth's writing on poverty was so minimal, we simply do not have enough information to answer these questions. Yet a theologian's theory of ethics cannot be adequately assessed without asking these vital questions regarding treatment of social justice for the poor and marginalized. Since Barth's ethical writing regarding the poor is sparse, we may assess Barth's ethical method in light of his statements about another historically marginalized group: women.

Barth's Method: Dehumanization of Women

According to Barth, women and men are equally in dignity. They are equally elected and determined by Christ and created for fellowship with one another. In fact, Barth made positive gains by defining the image of

PART THREE—Critical Dialogue with a Female Interlocutor

God as man and woman.[26] In continuity with his relational anthropology, Barth argued that "the life of man is ordered, related and directed to that of the woman, and that of the woman to that of the man . . . This mutual orientation constitutes the being of each other."[27] The particularity of woman as woman and man as man are maintained and this relation is the prototype of the I-thou relationship between humans. Barth wrote, "As they consider one another and necessarily realize that they question each other, they become mutually, not the law of each other's being (for each must be true to his particularity), but the measure or criterion of their inner right to live in their sexual distinctiveness."[28] They are who they are in their relation to the other and in being related to by the other. To fail in this mutual relation is to call one's humanity into doubt, to contradict their very existence as persons in the image of God.[29]

Such a view of gender relations has received positive reviews from women theologians.[30] Yet unfortunately, Barth did not stop at his argument for ontological equality. He went on to argue that according to the command of God, men and women should have a social standing, function, and attitude that is ordered hierarchically. He said that in the order that God established between them, man is super-ordinate and woman is subordinate. The man is "the first, the leader, the initiator, the representative of the order which embraces them both" and the woman is "the second, the led, the one who must follow up the initiative, standing in the order represented by him."[31]

Once again, Barth based this social hierarchy on his ethical method: the *analogia relationis*.[32] He used two analogies to reinforce this hierarchy.

---

26. See Salomonsen's argument regarding Barth's and Irigaray's contribution to the essentialist/constructionist debates in gender theory. According to Salomonsen, Barth opposes both gnostic and liberal gender models by affirming that the image of God is male and female. In addition, she writes of Barth's theological contribution: "humans cease from aspiring from seeking to overcome their sexual and separated mode of being by proclaiming an androgynous or sexually neutral mode of existence" ("Love of Same," 113).

27. Barth, *CD* 3/4:163.

28. Ibid., 166.

29. Ibid., 168.

30. See for example, Salomonsen's essay arguing that Barth provides new resources for overcoming the essentialist and constructionist debates in gender studies: "Love of Same," 112–14.

31. Barth, *CD* 3/4:173.

32. Ruether, "Christian Tradition and Feminist Hermeneutics," 282.

Sources of Justice

First, he said that the relation of God and Christ serves as an analogy for the correct ordering of the male/female relationship. "On the one hand, Christ is the sum, the *kephalē* (head) of all authority and power, he is the super-ordination. Yet because God is the *kephalē* of Christ, as revealed in the humbling of Christ to become obedient, Christ is also "the basis and sum of all subordination."[33] Although only Christ is the total head and his is the surpassing inferiority, man and woman correspond to this ordering according to 1 Corinthians 11:3. Barth made this argument in order to demonstrate that both man and woman demonstrate the image of God in Christ. This hierarchical ordering of male and female was established by God's creation. Barth explained,

> It is so solidly grounded in the lordship and service, the divinity and humanity of Christ, that there can be no occasion for the exaltation of man or the oppression of woman. "If any man be in Christ, he is a new creature." It is the life of this new creature which Paul describes with the saying that the head of the woman is the man. Gal. 3:28 is still valid . . . [for] there is an equality of man and woman *en kuriō* in the order in which the one God has with equal directedness assigned this place to man and that to woman.[34]

Thus, woman "is to be led by him" and "to accept his authority" as the one who is head, meaning that he is "the one who has precedence, initiative and authority."[35] This is their equality: they are equally *in* Christ, one as the super-ordination of Christ's relationship to creation and the other as the subordination of Christ's relationship to God.

This argument bears a striking resemblance to his statements on the poor because it undermines the agency of women. Like the poor in Barth's thought, who correspond to powerless humans in need of salvation, women represent Christ in his humility and subordination. In both instances, the socially powerful (Barth's own class and gender) are representatives of the divine. To the poor, the powerful give rights. To women, men (the super-ordinate) provide leadership and direction. In Barth's moral field, the poor are at least better off than women. While their social agency is determined by other people, at least their situation is recognized as unjust. In his passages on women, Barth placed women in a God-ordained position of subordination while trying to argue that they are equal. But the only

33. Barth, *CD* 3/4:173.
34. Barth, *CD* 3/2:312.
35. Ibid., 311.

sense in which they are equal is that they are both in Christ. Unfortunately for the woman, she corresponds to Christ the servant while the man corresponds to Christ as the Lord and authority. Spiritual equality plus social inequality cannot yield full equality.

In his favor, Barth cited a second analogy taken from Ephesians 5, in which the husband is the head of the wife as Christ is the head of the church and he insisted that only Christ is the savior of men and women. He held up woman as the representative of all who are addressed by Christ. He wrote, "The advantage of the wife, her birthright, is that it is she and not the man who, in relation to her husband and subordination to him, may reflect, represent and attest this reality of the community ... The husband has no option but to order himself by the wife as she is subordinate in this way."[36] So Barth attempted to give the wife spiritual equality before Christ and suggested that she is a model of how the man should behave toward Christ.

Yet the social inequality remains. Barth interpreted verse thirty-three, which says "a wife should respect her husband," to mean that she should "respect him in his superior position, let her be the answer to his question, let her follow up the initiative assigned him ..., let her give effect to his inspiration."[37] In this manner, he attempted to establish spiritual equality with social inequality between husband and wife. The social inequality and the oversight that a man has over a woman's action is remarkably similar to oversight that God has over man's ethical action. In the same way that God determines man's action, the woman's action is determined by man's leadership.

Once again, two major problems in Barth's method are illustrated. First, his use of the *analogia relationis* made the God-creature hierarchy the analogy for male-female relations. Rosemary Radford Ruether argues that "given Barth's belief in the absolute gulf between the divine and the human, this establishes the most hierarchical model imaginable as analogue for male-female relations."[38] His use of the *analogia relationis* reaffirms the tendency of the Christian tradition to make the male "like God" with regard to the female who represents the creaturely. Ruether rightly points out that any attempts to make the God-human relation analogous to the male-female relation will necessarily be hierarchical, "unless one

---

36. Ibid., 314.
37. Barth, *CD* 3/4:175.
38. Ruether, "Christian Tradition and Feminist Hermeneutics," 283.

remove entirely any idea that the divine is superior to the human," which Barth most certainly refused to do.[39]

One could argue in Barth's favor that he did not use the *analogia relationis* to provide divinely-backed social power for himself throughout his thought. His political ethics in particular demonstrate a humility about the scope of human action. He harshly criticized any effort of humans to identify themselves with the divine in the political sphere, arguing that Christians can never claim to bring in the kingdom of God and that Christians can never claim to do God's righteousness. By arguing for a deep divide between divine action and human action, Barth indeed attempted to combat the human arrogance that would make such attempts. That Barth would take this step in gender relations, to argue that man corresponds to Christ's lordship and woman corresponds to his obedience and subordination or to argue that the rich correspond to God's justifying work and the poor correspond to human powerlessness, is disappointing at minimum. It is inconsistent with his attempts to differentiate divine action from human action. In addition, it appears to contradict his anthropology of co-humanity, which emphasizes mutual listening, speaking, and rendering of assistance.

One could argue that his dealings with these two historically marginalized groups are merely hiccups, an inconsistent use of his method influenced by the social context in which he lived. One could suggest that if in his use of the *analogia relationis* he refused to identify one group, class, or gender with the divine and one with the human, in the same way that he refused to identify political action with God's kingdom, then his problem would be solved. One could simply discard these passages, or rewrite them with a greater consistency with his political thought, while still using the *analogia relationis* to make these revisions. Certainly, such steps would improve "the moral field" for women and the poor.

Unfortunately, the argument for women's equality would not be possible even with these correctives because of another facet of Barth's theological method: his insistence that theology must stand *beneath* scripture. On the positive side, this aspect of Barth's method proved valuable for promoting political justice for his own situation and resisting the Nazi regime. In particular, his standing *beneath* scripture provided the critical critique of Hitler's action toward the church and upheld the role of the theologian who speaks that Christ (rather than Hitler) is Lord of the Church. On the negative side, without a robust understanding and critique of the patriarchal context in which scripture was written, this method proves itself

39. Ibid., 284.

extremely problematic for upholding the full humanity of women and, therefore, for promoting equality for women. Taking Barth on his own terms, I will illustrate my claim.

According to Barth's theological anthropology, humans are humans-in-relation. Barth wrote, "The minimal definition of our humanity, of humanity generally, must be that it is the being of man in encounter."[40] This encounter is "at the very root" of being.[41] The human is encountered by God and encounters fellow-humanity. This being-in-encounter consists: (1) in seeing and being seen by the other; (2) in mutual speech and hearing; (3) in rendering mutual assistance; and (4) in doing so with gladness.[42]

On the first point, Barth described this "seeing and being" as a form of openness to the other. He wrote:

> I know thee as a man, as something like myself, and I make it possible for thee to know me in this same way. We give each other something in our duality, and this is that I and Thou are men. We give each other an insight into our being. And as we do this, I am not for myself, but for thee, and Thou for me, so that we have a share and interest in one another. This two-sided openness is the first element of humanity. Where it lacks and to the extent that it lacks, humanity does not occur.[43]

There are several examples of this seeing between man and woman in scripture. In the garden of Eden, Adam sees Eve and recognizes her as "bones of my bones and flesh of my flesh."[44] In this sense, Adam recognized Eve's humanity. Scripture is curiously quiet as to Eve's response upon seeing Adam.

In addition, there are numerous instances when women are seen by the witnesses of scripture, such as when the prophets tell Israel to administer justice to widowed women or when Jesus saw his mother from the cross. Yet on the whole, women are seen far less in scripture than men. And the times that women are portrayed as seeing a man or another women are even more scant, indicating according to Barth's standards that scripture portrays women as less human. In the book of Genesis, for instance, a man "saw" a man thirteen times and a man "saw" a woman six times yet a woman "saw" a man once and another woman once. Interestingly, the one

---

40. Barth, CD 3/2:247.
41. Ibid.
42. Ibid., 250–65.
43. Ibid., 251.
44. Gen 2:23.

Sources of Justice

time a woman "saw" a man in Genesis, she covered herself with a veil, so as not to be seen by him.[45]

This pattern of dehumanization becomes even more pronounced on Barth's second point: mutual speaking and listening. There are some beautiful instances of women speaking and being spoken to in scripture, such as the time when Jesus "astonishes" the disciples by speaking with the woman at the well and by declaring to her that he is the messiah. She spoke back to him and told others so that they also believed that he was the savior.[46] But once again, the number of women who speak and are spoken to in scripture is far fewer than the number of men. When God speaks or is spoken to in scripture, it is almost always to men or by men. A Pauline text goes so far as to command women to be silent in all churches, "for they are not permitted to speak, but should be subordinate, as the law also says. If there is anything they desire to know, let them ask their husbands at home. For it is shameful for a woman to speak in church."[47] Finally, in the witness of scripture there is no indication that a female ever served to write this authoritative Word.

So as not to belabor the point, I will let Barth's first two forms of encounter serve to demonstrate that according to Barth's standards of personhood, women appear less human than men in scripture by their relative obscurity and silence. While there are some texts in which scripture may stand against this patriarchal treatment of women, there are many more texts that uncritically accept or teach that women are subordinated to men. Barth's refusal to criticize these texts and his insistence that theology must stand *beneath* these texts that are authoritative led to his own subordination of women within the male-female relationship, especially when he used Pauline texts to make his case. In addition, although Barth argued that men and women are equally human, the terms by which he defines humanity leads one to the conclusion that men and women are not equally human in relation to God. *All of this leads to the conclusion that if Barth really wanted to be true to his own ethical method, he would need to (a) develop a more nuanced reading of scripture that critiqued patriarchal assumptions within the text or (b) redefine what humanity is or (c) admit that women are not, in fact, fully human.*

Barth claimed to have an ethical method that authentically reflected the command of God as authoritative objective truth in particular

---

45. Gen 24:64.
46. John 4:1–42.
47. 1 Cor 14:34–36.

PART THREE—Critical Dialogue with a Female Interlocutor

situations. Yet Barth's method, in fact, provided divine backing for his own gender and class while using claims about "God's command." First, under the threat of Nazi Germany, Barth fought for a Barmen declaration that defended his church and remained silent on those who were marginalized by society: Jewish people. While he later regretted this decision, his regret did not appear to call his theological method into serious question. Second, in his writing, he upheld his own class and his own gender as the "divine" side of the analogy of God and humanity, whereas he subordinated the poor and women to the "human" side. Barth's ethics protected his own situation in life in the name of God's command.

Barthians may dismiss this criticism by pointing to Barth's historical context, which largely upheld the subordination of women and the poor. Barthians who want to affirm the real equality of women and men may excuse Barth for being a product of his day and age. Yet this excuse on Barth's behalf highlights the very source of the problem for his method. Barth failed to recognize how powerfully context, one's culture and one's situation in life, shapes the hearing of God's word.

Both in scripture and in Barth's own theology, the culture, context, and concerns of the hearer influence theology far more than Barth himself seemed willing to admit or to incorporate allowance and for into his theological ethics. Barth's own use of his method upheld his own social class and gender as a superior form of humanity that determines lesser forms of humanity.

To fix Barth's method so that it issued in a form of justice that upholds the full humanity of all persons (men/women, rich/poor, and powerful/marginalized), one would need to make two changes that would necessitate a thorough re-working of his theology. First, Barth needed to take seriously the *analogia entis*—the fact that all beings correspond to the divine in some way that the demands the upholding of their existence as beings. While he may have still started with the *analogia relationis*, affirming the fact that God's election preceded his creation of these beings, he must affirm the full humanity of all persons. One gender, race, or class does not correspond to the divine more than another. Each person is fully human thanks to the election, creation, and reconciliation of Christ. The existence of each person exerts a claim to look one another in the eye, speak and listen to one another, and render mutual assistance.[48]

Second, Barth's method would need to take seriously the role that culture, context and an individual's self-interest obscures any claims to an

---

48. Barth, *CD* 3/2:250–71.

authoritative hearing of God's command. This same context and experience also limited the writers of the biblical text. I suggest that theology must not stand *beneath* Scripture but *beside* Scripture in dialogue and mutual correction, as a text that witnesses to the experience of God in a particular context and history. Theology must also stand *beside* persons of varied backgrounds so that systematic theology, in particular, will not continue to be dominated by the interests of a few elite social groups.

Such changes would take seriously Barth's idea that humans cannot speak God's word or do God's work. They can only speak human words about God or act in a manner that seeks to witness to God. In the same way, humans can never claim to know God's justice as if they are divine or as if God speaks a command to them that they can clearly hear.

Conclusion

In sum, neither John Paul II nor Barth offer a satisfying answer to the question: How is justice known? John Paul's dual approach proves potentially contradictory at points and fails to explain when one appeals to natural norm of justice and when one appeals to a restorative norm of justice. At minimum, the appeal to two sources of justice may prove confusing. At maximum, what John Paul calls natural norms of justice may merely disguise arbitrary social norms that perpetuate a frightening form of patriarchy and devalues actual human life.

Barth's Christological method offers greater consistency by producing an ethic that is shaped by the revelation of God in Christ and Christ's overarching affirmation of human life as demonstrated by incarnation and reconciliation. Yet I have argued that this method consistently empowers Barth's own class and gender by identifying his own forms of humanity with the divine. Thus, in comparing the two from the perspective of the marginalized, Barth's method appears to be far more problematic whereas the biases in John Paul's method have not been shown to be as entrenched in bias against the marginalized. The following chapter, however, will suggest that what appears to be a rather minor issue of failing to safeguard against bias in John Paul's methodology grows to be far more pronounced in his theory of justice.

While it is not within the scope of this book to pose an alternative methodology that will solve the problems raised in this chapter, these problems do point to an issue that needs to be taken far more seriously within conservative and evangelical forms of systematic theology like

PART THREE—Critical Dialogue with a Female Interlocutor

Barth and John Paul's. For Barth in particular, the development of a theological method that upholds the class and gender of the group at the center of the church leadership is the antithesis of the gospel of Christ. To his credit Barth worked hard to develop a bias-free ethic that guarded against hubris and was centered in Christ. Yet he still failed to do so. His bias ultimately exalted his own race and class. To avoid such serious ethical problems, it is of utmost importance for systematic theologians like Barth to engage seriously with persons of varied gender, racial, and economic backgrounds, who can critique such biases and provide aid in developing a methodology that does leads toward a theory of justice that treats those at the margins with equal dignity as those at the center. Continuing to exclude and marginalize such voices within the halls of theology poses a serious threat to building robust theological and ethical methods that lead toward truly just theories of justice.

8

Theories of Justice

HAVING COMPARED THE TWO AUTHORS' EPISTEMOLOGY AND METHOD, we now turn to compare their theories of justice. Chapter Eight will address our final two questions for Barth and John Paul: What is justice? How is justice cultivated in society? Like Chapter Seven, their theories will be critically assessed in light of their strength as working theories and from the perspective of the margins.

What Is Justice?

There are numerous commonalities in the way that Wojtyla/John Paul II and Barth defined social justice. Wojtyla/John Paul II defined justice as that which accords with human nature or treating another in a manner that accords with his or her nature.[1] While Barth defined justice in different terms, as that which accords with the justice of God, his next step was to argue that the justice of God is co-humanity, the living together as neighbors in solidarity with one another. Like John Paul, Barth argued that the critical criterion for justice in the social sphere is the criterion of humanity.[2] Both John Paul II and Barth believed that human persons must be valued and upheld as primary within economic and political systems. Both held specific issues—from human rights abuses to the materialism rampant in capitalistic societies—up to the criterion of humanity. The ethical act that is just promotes the "true humanity" or the dignity of persons in society.

---

1. JPII, *CA*, 55.
2. Barth, *CD* 3/4:340; and *Christian Life*, 267.

PART THREE—Critical Dialogue with a Female Interlocutor

Barth: A "Co-Humanity" of Hierarchy

Unfortunately for Barth, co-humanity proves a promising determination of justice but in posing the question of justice for the marginalized, his methodology quickly loses promise in a manner that negatively undermines his theory of justice. As argued in the prior chapter, one discovers in Barth that "co-humanity" between men and women or the rich and poor are relationships of hierarchy rather than mutuality or solidarity. Such characterization of these relationships creates serious problems for his definition of social justice because it makes it impossible to uphold the full equality and full humanity of all persons. In fact, as argued previously, when one compares his definition of humanity with his statements on women, it becomes clear that Barth's theory actually leads toward the belief that women are less than human. This dehumanization of women is expressed in Barth's just society by placing them in a subservient role of listening, being spoken to, and being subservient to men.

Wojytla/John Paul: An Ontology of Passivity

As suggested in the prior chapter, the anthropology of John Paul did a better job of defining justice that is actual justice for the marginalized. John Paul argued that the dignity of human nature is revealed in the freedom to act. As Wojtyla, he argued that the human "makes himself a somebody through the action."[3] He wrote, "To say that man 'is free' means *that he depends chiefly on himself for the dynamization of his own subject.*"[4] Such arguments gave great hope to the poor and marginalized. Despite the social or historical situation, the poor person can recognize the dignity of his own nature. His own actions, not the actions of others, determine his personhood and affirm his true freedom even in the midst of oppression. For this reason, as a young man, Wojtyla could resist the political oppression of occupied Poland both psychologically and religiously: psychologically by retaining a sense of his dignity despite the dehumanizing actions of the Nazis and religiously by secretly pursing ordination to the priesthood.

In turning to the question of women's dynamization, John Paul's conception of human nature would appear to also affirm the capacity of women to resist forms of patriarchal oppression in the same way that the poor are empowered to resist economic oppression. But unfortunately,

---

3. Beigel, *Faith and Social Justice*, 16.
4. Wojyla, *AP,* 120.

Wojtyla actually described the human nature of women in very different terms than that of men, terms which severely limited the moral agency of women. In his writings, he stated that women are equal to men. But like Barth, this "equality" falters when one takes a deeper look at what John Paul said about women.

John Paul believed that "womanhood expresses the 'human' as much as manhood does, but in a different and complementary way.... Womanhood and manhood are complementary *not only from the physical and psychological points of view,* but also from the *ontological*."[5] Using his phenomenological method, John Paul described these differences and defined the "special dignity" of women, as that which is evidenced in the vocation of Mary, who is the archetype of femininity. Mary reveals the two dimensions of women's vocation: motherhood and virginity.

In describing women's vocation in these terms, John Paul explained what he meant by the physical complementarity of women to men. From the psychological point of view, John Paul described women as having a unique sensitivity. To women he wrote, "Into the heart of the family, and then of all society, you bring the richness of your sensitivity, your intuitiveness, your generosity and fidelity."[6] It is this sensitivity that "is characteristic of their femininity."[7] Finally, women express humanity in a manner that is "ontologically" different and complementary. John Paul did not spell out exactly what he meant by this "ontological" difference, but it becomes clear through a careful reading of his texts on women. Namely, words related to "action," "freedom," and "transcendence" are almost entirely absent in these texts. Woman is simply not portrayed as an active moral agent who defines herself. For example, John Paul spoke about "the truth of woman as bride" in contrast to the masculine symbol of the Bridegroom. "This masculine symbol," John Paul wrote, "represents the human aspect of the divine love which God has for Israel, for the Church, and for all people." He explained further, "The Bridegroom is the one who loves. The Bride is loved: *it is she who receives love, in order to love in return*."[8] For John Paul, this passive, feminine symbol refers not only to the specific spousal relationship of marriage but is more universal in scope, describing the shape of a woman's wider interactions in society.[9]

5. JPII, "Letter of Pope John Paul II to Women," 7.
6. JPII, "Letter to Women," 2.
7. Ibid., 30.
8. Ibid., 24.
9. Ibid.

PART THREE—Critical Dialogue with a Female Interlocutor

The contrast between his active definitions of manhood and his passive definitions of womanhood become even more striking when comparing his apostolic exhortation about Joseph, the father of Jesus, with his encyclical on Mary, the mother of Jesus. In the apostolic exhortation, Joseph is held up as the model of action[10] and work[11] as a parallel with Christ's action[12] and work[13]. By contrast, work and action are never attributed to Mary in the encyclical that describes her vocation. Rather, Mary's vocation is to be the subject of God's action and Word, which she accepts in faith.[14] By contrast, John Paul said that the Word of God was "subjected to Joseph."[15] In sum, in his definition of "womanhood," Mary and all women were dominantly portrayed as "receivers." He described them as "receivers" of faith, femininity, grace, dignity, celibacy, and love.

The passivity of the "feminine" as receiver is also one reason that women cannot serve as priests. John Paul explained,

> Since Christ, in instituting the Eucharist, linked it in such an explicit way to the priestly service of the Apostles, it is legitimate to conclude that he thereby wished to express the relationship between man and woman, between what is "feminine" and what is "masculine." It is a relationship willed by God both in the mystery of creation and in the mystery of Redemption. It is *the Eucharist* above all that expresses *the redemptive act of Christ the Bridegroom towards the Church the Bride*. This is clear and unambiguous when the sacramental ministry of the Eucharist, in which the priest acts "in *persona Christi*," is performed by a man.[16]

Elsewhere he explained that this diversity of roles is "not the result of an arbitrary imposition, but is rather an expression of what is specific to

---

10. Joseph is described as acting four times. Salvation is realized in his fatherly acts. He is said to be the model of human action. JPII, *Redemptoris Custos*, 3, 7, 25, and 30.

11. Joseph is portrayed at work fourteen times and he is the "model" of workers (n35). "Work is a human 'good' which 'transforms nature' and makes man 'in a sense, more human.'" JPII, *Redemptoris Custos*, 23.

12. Christ's acts are described three times.

13. Christ is described as working three times, primarily the work of salvation in which Joseph cooperates.

14. JPII, "Letter to Women," 4.

15. JPII, *Redemptoris Custos*, 8.

16. JPII, "Letter to Women," 26.

being male and female."[17] In other words, females are different from males at an ontological level and for this reason, only men can represent Christ. Whereas males are agents and action and love originates in their own being, females are portrayed as passive recipients, empty vessels of a sort, who do not have the capacity to initiate action or love. Rather, "the Bride is loved: *is it she who receives love, in order to love in return.*" Her ability to love is not free but it is conditioned by the love of the bridegroom. For this reason, men were chosen as representatives of Christ and the Church serves as the symbol for the feminine.

Because John Paul's moral theology rested upon his understanding of man's capacity for moral agency, this idea that women are ontologically different raises a major dilemma for his social ethics. When he wrote about the moral agency, freedom, and activity of humans or *men* (i.e. he often used masculine terms in his anthropology), most readers may assume that he was also including women. However, for John Paul, woman was merely recipient, whose actions are not freely arising from her personhood but conditioned by men. By reducing women to "receivers" he deprived women of the dignity of free and transcendent action that is the essence of human nature as he defined it, thus implying that women are less than human and lack the capacities of fully human persons.

In order to retain his ideas about personhood, he must have either admitted that women are not fully human at an ontological level or he must have attributed to women the same moral agency that he attributed to men. In other words, in his encyclical he said that "womanhood expresses the 'human' as much as manhood does." He defined human persons as rational and moral agents, with the capacity to freely know the good and act upon it. Yet there is an obvious logical contradiction in his thought because he went on to define woman, at an ontological level, as "recipient;" her action is secondary and arises from the act of a man or a masculine figure. For this reason, she cannot represent Christ in the Eucharist for she is ontologically different from a man. *In order to resolve this logical contradiction, he must either admit that women are not fully human or attribute to women the same moral agency that he attributed to men.* If he chose the latter, then the ordination of women to the priesthood must be re-examined.

Catholic feminist writers have argued that John Paul's affirmation of human freedom and his stance on liberation should have led to a thorough-going feminism. However, it did not. Women have been given equal

---

17. Ibid., 11.

PART THREE—Critical Dialogue with a Female Interlocutor

access to leadership roles in society but not in the church. Some feminists have suggested this disparity took place between his social encyclicals and his ecclesiology because of his appeal to the traditions of the Church.[18] I suggest that that this disparity is due to a fundamental flaw, a logical contradiction within his ontology. By characterizing "femininity" as he did, John Paul excluded justice for women from his social encyclicals just as fully as he excluded them from his ecclesiology.

In testing John Paul's theory of justice by posing the question of justice for women, who have been severely marginalized throughout most of the history of Christianity, we find that John Paul, like Barth, failed to develop a theory that upholds the full humanity of women. From a woman's perspective, such forms of "justice" are not justice at all. They are religiously-based gender injustices and exclusions.

This examination leads us to the conclusion that neither theologian developed a theory of justice that could adequately maintain the full humanity of all persons. While on the surface, their theological anthropologies and their appeals to justice as co-humanity appear to be promising theological developments, this in-depth exploration finds them to be wanting from the perspective of the socially marginalized. John Paul's theories prove dehumanizing of women while Barth's theories dehumanized both women and the poor. While these findings are disappointing, both men did made commendable strides in developing theories of justice that seek to uphold human personhood as a central criteria for assessing the justice of social practices and cultivating justice in society. The following section will excise these gender and class injustices in the thought of these two men and assess of the capacity of their theories to cultivate justice in society.

How Is Justice Cultivated in Society?

A theory of justice or anthropology is often too abstract to assess in a vacuum, without addressing the practical implications for society. For this reason, we have raised this final critical question for our authors: In the real world, how effective would their theories be at actually cultivating justice in society?

We have already demonstrated that justice for the marginalized may be severely compromised. Barth's use of his Christological method elevates his own gender and class and leaves open this potential for dehumanizing

18. Conn and Conn, *Catholic Feminist Theology*, 45.

social practices toward women or impoverished persons. John Paul's twofold method leaves the choice between appealing to either method too ambiguous. As demonstrated, this ambiguity opened up room for John Paul to make that choice in a way that served interests other than the humans who have the least power and who are impacted most directly. It created inconsistency in his ethical conclusions. This inconsistency possibly led him toward his dehumanizing conclusions about women.

This section seeks to set aside those critiques and assess how effectively their theories might actually work to cultivate and create just societies. It especially explores how each person's theory of justice incentivizes or motivates people to act justly within the most challenging of social contexts.

Wojtyla/John Paul and Human Potential for Just Acts

John Paul's theory of justice upheld the dignity of personhood by advocating for individual responsibility, freedom, and rationality. He believed that choice and action shapes personhood and that the good choices and actions of multiple persons shapes society for the good. These affirmations provide a high level of responsibility for the acts of individuals within society. When individuals perceive themselves having this level of responsibility and freedom to create themselves and society, people may feel incentivized to act in accordance with justice.

Yet his Aristotelian conception of the *telos* of human nature results in a level of abstraction that may prove a hindrance for the actualization of social ethics. John Paul believed that humans are individuals with potential for solidarity, a potential which is only actualized through their acts. Human persons only exist as neighbor by potential; they *become* neighbor through act. In his essay, "Participation or Alienation?" Wojtyla wrote, "The *I—other* relationship, as I pointed out earlier, does not exist in us as an already accomplished fact; only the potentiality for it exists."[19] Likewise, for John Paul/Wojtyla, persons become neighbors only through act, in accordance with the command of God to love. Their relation as neighbor is only a potential rather than an ontological reality.[20]

---

19. JPII, *Person and Community*, 201.

20. Ibid., 200. See also *SRS*, 40, where John Paul argues that the Trinity is "a new *model* for human unity of the human race, which must ultimately *inspire* our solidarity"; italics mine. The triune life of God is not a reflection of what exists between real humans, but it is merely a model for the potential of unity.

PART THREE—Critical Dialogue with a Female Interlocutor

Such a belief creates a problem for his social ethics because it tends toward an individualistic, abstract ethic that can prove problematic for acting in accordance with justice in concrete situations and encounters. He acknowledged the limits of such abstraction:

> Participation in the humanity of other people, of *others* and *neighbors*, does not arise primarily from an understanding of the essence "human being," which is by nature general and does not bring us close enough to the human being as a concrete *I*. This does not mean that understanding the essence "human being" is of no consequence for participation, that it is foreign or even opposed to participation. Far from it. An understanding of this essence opens up the way to participation, but it does not itself determine participation.[21]

He attempted to overcome this problem by arguing that understanding human essence—in its potential for solidarity with the other—opens up the way for participation. Yet, because he conceived of humanity in a general way, his Christian anthropology does not ground real persons in a relation of participation with the other or to solidarity with the other, but *only* to the understanding that solidarity is a potential of human nature. By implication, social ethics can formulate abstract principles, apply laws, and discuss rights.[22] However, because such discussions take place based on assumptions regarding general humanity, they risk missing the ethical demand inherent in the encounter with concrete persons. When one is facing a concrete ethical situation, John Paul may only appeal to an abstract "ought," a potential for co-humanity that resides in human nature.

Take for instance the conflict in Israel/Palestine. For John Paul, the Israeli ought to view the Palestinian as a *potential* neighbor and act to uphold his rights and promote justice on his behalf. However, when the Israeli parent suffers the loss of his child through an act of violence from the Palestinian sector, the group the *potential* neighbor represents has acted in manner that makes the potential neighbor an *actual* enemy. In defense of

---

21. JPII, *Person and Community*, 201. Cf. Gregg, *Challenging the Modern World*, 201–4; and *GS* 32.

22. Anderson explains: "If the I-Thou relation with God constitutes humanity in an individual sense, an act against another person does not directly touch the *imago* except in an ethical sense. Because God, as the *Thou* who constitutes the true orientation to the self, wills that I also love that which he loves, my fellow human being, I have an ethical obligation to support the life of each person whom God loves. This, however, makes love first of all an abstraction and only consequently a matter of immediate and practical concern." *On Being Human*, 75.

the intrinsic right to defend and avenge the death of the child, the Israeli parent may dissolve the ethical claim to act with justice and mercy toward his enemy on behalf of his own self-interest for retributive justice. The same, of course, is true for the Palestinian parent whose child is killed in the violence of retaliation. While John Paul could appeal to the principle of basic human rights grounded in the image of God, the idea that we create ourselves through action may contain the seeds of violence when an act of murder then characterizes the person or persons as "murderers," and thus enemies. In that situation, only an appeal to the forgiveness and mercy found in Christ may overcome future violence. In this situation, John Paul would need to refer to revealed norms of justice. Yet in the case of Palestinians and Jews, an appeal to Christ fails to carry the moral weight necessary to interrupt the pull toward retributive justice—toward equal or greater acts of retaliation.

An abstract conception of ethics and rights also proves problematic because it divides the formal law to love the neighbor from the concrete personhood of the Jew or the Palestinian. There is no concrete, personal, or material content to such a right or law. Merely an obligation exists, and such an obligation carries the seed of violence because persons carry the potential to become either neighbor or enemy. Therefore, with just humanity as an abstract essence and justice as an abstract norm, humans may justify their own acts of violence on the basis of individual rights and they may become actual enemies through acts of violence against the other.

Returning to the prior question regarding motivation, what appeal exists to Jews and Palestinians to act as neighbors if their brotherhood is only an abstract obligation, a potential? What motivation would one have to transcend her political situation by acting as neighbor, especially after a history of violence and distrust? John Paul's optimism regarding humanity may cause him to think that men and women are indeed capable of such acts of transcendence, of triumphant acts that create brotherhood.[23] However, if humans are only under obligation to abstract ideals of justice and mercy, then John Paul's anthropological ethics may also contain the potential for acts of violence and lack a strong enough motivation to act as neighbor in concrete situations.

---

23. JPII, "Letter of His Holiness Pope John Paul II to Mr. Benjamin Netanyahu"; and "Letter of His Holiness Pope John Paul II to Mr. Yasser Arafat."

PART THREE—Critical Dialogue with a Female Interlocutor

Karl Barth and the Ontology of Relation as a Source for Cultivating Justice

Barth's social ethics has the potential to take a very different approach by making his starting point the human person as determined by the personhood of Jesus Christ. In Christ, one discovers not only the formal law, "Love your neighbor," but also the concrete material reality of the neighbor as fellow-humanity. Not only does the law have an ethical claim, but the concrete person also makes an ethical claim. For Barth, the person is not neighbor merely by potential but in *concrete reality*. The concrete reality of the other generates the ethical claim to *be* neighborly. The ethical claim is not merely a principle by which one can potentially justify one's own behavior; the ethical claim is a person. John Webster helps to explain this point:

> For Barth, ethics is rooted in *nature*. By "nature" is meant, not a reality prior to or existing as a condition of possibility for "grace," nor some general *humanum* which grace perfects or completes: of "nature" in these senses, Barth's theology knows nothing. What is meant, rather, is simply nature as *that which is*. Barth believes that good human action is generated, shaped, and judged by "that which is," and that "that which is" is a Christological, not a pre-Christological, category.[24]

Like John Paul, Barth grounded ethics in the nature of the human person. However, because human nature is a solely Christological category, human nature is determined by Christ's established relation with humanity. Humans are neighbors by nature rather than by potential.

In other words, the ethics of Barth sought to describe the ontology of relation to Christ, which characterizes the ontology of relation to the other in the *analogia relationis*. According to Barth, human persons exist as neighbors because Christ has reconciled people to one another in correspondence to the divine image. For Barth, it is not a matter of choosing to become neighbor,[25] for human persons have been reconciled in Christ as neighbors. Therefore, as I have argued previously, the material reality that all human beings are neighbors constitutes a moral demand upon all persons, Christian or Jew or Muslim, whether or not they recognize this reality.

---

24. Webster, *Ethics of Reconciliation*, 214.
25. Ibid., 216.

Such an ethical appeal may be critiqued on Kantian grounds by raising the question of how there can be any obligation upon someone who does not recognize the force of the obligation.[26] In other words, can an obligation exist for the person even if one is not aware of his duty? Is a Jew obligated to act in solidarity when she does not believe that Christ reconciled humans with one another? Such a question again highlights the difference between John Paul and Barth at this very point. John Paul's ethic addresses this Kantian question because, like Kant, John Paul appeals to an abstract principle, an "ought" which persons "can" perform. For John Paul, such act is a potential because humans have access to the laws of nature through reason.[27] Barth turns this approach on its head, however, because he *begins* with the existence of human as neighbor. From such existence, the ethical appeal arises. It is from this reality (the *what is*) that the claim (the *ought*) arises; the existence of the other and encounter with the other creates a claim. Yet the question remains: How can an ethical appeal be made to persons in their concrete situation so as to hold them accountable to uphold justice and human rights?

By returning to the case of the Israeli and Palestinian conflict, we can surmise how this Barthian approach of starting with the co-humanity of persons might play out differently. Underneath all that divides human persons into categories based on culture, gender, race, religion, or national identity, lies what Ray Anderson called a "core social paradigm," a social structure of humanity that exists as a common denominator for all persons.[28] The demand upon both the Palestinian and the Israeli in this case is not, first of all, an ethical demand, but a summons to be human and thus to recognize the common humanity of the other.[29] An Israeli child who wanders into a Palestinian home presents a claim upon the Palestinian adults in that home to act for the welfare of that child. Failure to act for the welfare of that child is not only an ethical failure, but a contradiction of

---

26. Kant argued that the human necessarily "must judge that he *can* do what the law tells him unconditionally that he *ought* to do." *Metaphysics of Morals*, 186.

27. Wojtyla/John Paul differed with Kant at many levels, especially regarding the relation of ethics to human experience, act, and drives. In addition, he located the "ought" in the law of God. However, his appeal to natural law as a basis for ethics maintains this Kantian connection between the "ought," which implies "can." In Wojyla, *Persons in Communion*, see "The Role of Reason in Ethics," 67–69; "The Separation of Act from Experience," 23–32 and 40–42; "The Basis of the Moral Norm," 81–83.

28. Anderson, *Practical Theology*, 161–77.

29. Barth calls this "the criterion of humanity," *CD* 3/4:536. With regard to the neighbor, see *CD* 3/4:285ff.

one's own humanity. Ought Palestinian and Israeli parents act humanely toward each other's children? Yes, because they *are* human.

Such an ethic does not depend upon an ethical principle, whether an intrinsic sense of human justice (*analogia entis*), nor an abstract principle of moral reason (Kant). Rather, it rests upon the recognition that one's own humanity is bound up with the humanity of other persons. The person who does not respond to this demand is acting inhumanely, not merely unethically. The person who does not respond to this demand is not only harming the other person but also harming oneself because his very humanity is so deeply connected to the humanity of the other. Such an understanding of the nature of personhood as human-with-fellow-humanity exposes the weakness of anthropologies that define humanity as individual substance. Such individualistic anthropologies create a potential for conflict between individuals who believe they are faced with a false either-or (e.g. "either my rights or the rights of this child.") If humanity is co-humanity, self-interest shifts from protecting my own rights to protecting our rights.

In addition, this concept of humanity also limits one's ability to make an ethical decision that is based on the actions of the person one is facing. Even if the other does not act in solidarity, it does not negate the intrinsic connectedness of our humanity. Because we are by our very nature human-with-fellow-humanity, we remain responsible to the concrete person who is our neighbor no matter what action that person takes.

Such an appeal can work in a secular or multi-religious setting. For example, Desmond Tutu held a strikingly similar anthropological ethics in his work with the Truth and Reconciliation Commission in South Africa. In order to overcome the potential for violence and move the nation toward peace, he appealed to the Xhosa expression, "*ubuntu ungamntu ngabanye abantu*," which is translated, "each individual's humanity is ideally expressed in relationship with others." Tutu argued that social reconciliation is possible because of the reality of co-humanity. In defending himself against the critics who believed that reconciliation between the victims of apartheid and their abusers was not just, he argued to the contrary, that reconciliation was the expression of true justice, of real humanity.

Tutu provided the following rationale for seeking reconciliation:

> Our humanity was intertwined. The humanity of the perpetrator of apartheid's atrocities was caught up and bound up in that of his victim whether he liked it or not. In the process of

dehumanizing another, in inflicting untold harm and suffering, inexorably the perpetrator was being dehumanized as well.[30]

The solace for the victim in a situation of abuse and exploitation is the knowledge that the act of the other does not determine her personhood. The act of violence certainly impacts the victim but no person can ever determine the personhood of another. The determination of personhood does not rely upon individual free choice. It resides in the concrete reality of human personhood, which is fundamentally relational. In Christian terms, it resides in the choice of God to elect and create individuals as persons-in-relation. This point is an important one for cultivating justice in society because it upholds the freedom that the victim has to choose to affirm her personhood and the personhood of the other, even in a context of dehumanization. Because the core social paradigm is persons in relation, one upholds his own humanity by resisting acts that dehumanize the self and the other.

In another example, authors of a recent research paper on the men who buy sex from prostituted girls and women reported that two men of their small research sample reported that they had attempted to buy sex only once. When they came face to face with the teenage girl who they had purchased, both of them described a similar experience. Each looked into the eyes of the girl and there was only a blank gaze staring back at them. In that blank gaze, each reported that he saw himself and he stopped the act. Both of the men had been victims of sexual abuse as children. They reported that the gaze of the victim caused them to see their own humanity in the other.[31] Through the concrete encounter with the other, each man recognized that his own humanity was intricately connected with the humanity of the Other. The act of dehumanizing this girl would also dehumanize himself.

To cultivate such justice, no appeals to Christian beliefs were necessary. Rather, in the case of the men buying sex, the concrete existence and recognition of the co-humanity of the Other was sufficient to evoke an ethical response. In the case of Tutu, an appeal to the African philosophical understanding of humans as persons-in-relation provided sufficient basis to help interrupt a cycle of violence. In the situation of the Jewish mother encountering a Palestinian child, the mother need not hear an appeal to the mercy of Christ in order to see her own self, her own child in the Palestinian child before her.

30. Tutu, *No Future without Forgiveness*, 103.
31. Farley et al., "Comparing Sex Buyers with Men who Don't Buy Sex," 40.

PART THREE—Critical Dialogue with a Female Interlocutor

The cluttering of her conscience with questions of justice may actually distract her from the claim of the encounter. In the story of the good Samaritan, the question of righteousness and purity distracted the priest from the ethical claim of his injured neighbor. If the Jewish mother has the resources, of course she should feed the child in need, whether that child is Palestinian or Jewish. For humans exist as parent and child and neighbor, fellow-beings in encounter.

Obviously neither theory will result in a fully just society or motivate individuals to act with justice in all situations. In the study of the men who buy sex, only a small fraction of the men were impacted by this encounter with the other. In many cases, the most effective ethical appeal is not about the harm that one's treatment causes the other but the harm that one's treatment of the other causes the self, because of this co-humanity, this intrinsic connection between the other and the self.

This section has argued for the superiority of Barth's anthropology of co-humanity as a source for actualizing ethical action in society over John Paul's more individualistic starting point. Barth's concept of co-humanity states that one's own identity and personhood is wrapped up in the personhood of the other and the dehumanization of the other dehumanizes oneself. This anthropological conception of personhood creates a greater incentive of self-interest for non-Christian persons to behave with justice; it creates an immediate ethical obligation when encountering another person; and it can be adopted and demonstrated by Christian and non-Christian alike.

Conclusion

Through this critical examination of the theories of justice of Barth and John Paul, we have discovered strengths and weaknesses in their ethical methods and theories. By beginning with an examination of the social and historical context in which their thought developed, we sought to understand the traditions and contexts that constituted their thought so that we could lay the basis for a more accurate comparison of these men from two very different traditions and contexts. We then posed three questions to each man: How is justice known? What is justice? How is justice cultivated in society? In part three of this book, I engaged the men in a critical dialogue that critiqued the internal strength of their theories as well as assessing their theories from the perspective of historically marginalized persons. These questions and this critique was not merely an intellectual exercise but an authentic quest to develop a more robust Christian theory of justice for our contemporary era.

From this quest and thanks to these partners in dialogue, several points emerged, points that I suggest must be central to a Christian theory of justice:

1. *Method/Epistemology.* Barth's sole Christological method with his appeal to the *analogia entis* created a more consistent and clearer basis for justice than John Paul's appeal to both natural norms and revealed norms, an appeal which appeared to contradict one another at times, could be used at random for different situations, or could exclude non-Christians from having knowledge of (in the case of revealed norms). At the same time, John Paul's appeal to the *analogia entis* did uphold the value of human rationality and experience and provided a basis for affirming the dignity of all persons.

   Barth's method created the prospect of greater consistency but his application of his analogical method at times upheld a form of "divinely-backed" conservatism that marginalized and disempowered the gender and classes that were not his own. I suggest that a conception of the *analogia entis* that follows and is set in a context of the *analogia relationis* creates a superior method. The relationship of God with humanity through Christ sets the context for affirming the dignity of persons and the dignity of human rationality and experience. Certainly, Christian ethics begin with Christ and remain dependent upon the revelation of God in Christ. However, as Barth's and John Paul's mistakes clearly demonstrate, no matter how much one wants to build an truly Christian ethic, one's own social and cultural perspectives are likely to prove problematic for ever achieving an ethical method that is unbiased with regard to one's own class, gender, race, etc. Caucasian men of European descent should not attempt to create a flawless methodology or do ethics without taking the time to engage seriously with the people from differing social, economic, and cultural backgrounds. Nor should anyone. In this way, Christian ethics can guard against destructive biases by developing methods that affirm both the Christological starting point for ethics and the dignity of human reason, the reason through which people of varying perspectives can expose our hidden biases and push us toward theories of justice that promote justice for all.

PART THREE—Critical Dialogue with a Female Interlocutor

2. *Defining Justice.* For both Barth and John Paul, their definitions of justice issued from their anthropologies. The criterion of humanity played the central role in discerning what was just and what was not just. The ethical act that is just promotes the "true humanity" or the dignity of persons in society.

Defining justice in this manner is beneficial because it gives precedence to personhood rather than norms or particular political or economic systems. Personhood is the criterion by which all such laws or norms or systems are assessed.

The most serious problem arose for both Barth and John Paul when they differentiated forms of personhood along gendered lines and, perhaps subconsciously, attributed to women a lesser form of humanity (at minimum) or a lack of full humanity (at maximum). Dehumanizing women in this way leads to theories of right relations between men and women that prove disempowering and unjust for women and, I suggest, dehumanizing for men. In order to promote justice for all persons, a Christian theory of justice must be built upon an anthropology in which all human persons are considered fully human, regardless of gender, class, culture, race, sexual orientation, etc.

3. *Cultivating Justice.* When it comes to cultivating justice in society, I argued that Barth's Christological anthropology proved superior because he defines humanity as co-humanity rather than individual substance. In doing so, he changed the incentives for treating others with the dignity they deserve because the affirmation of one's own humanity is wrapped up in treating the other as fully human. This anthropology helps to overcome the either-or of choosing between one's own rights and the rights of the other. I am firmly convinced that theories of justice will benefit from starting with our co-humanity rather than starting with individual substance. One question that is left to be explored more fully is how this starting point in co-humanity might also be used to resist ongoing and repeated acts of injustice by one party.

As a person who left the purely academic life in order to make meager attempts at promoting social justice in the "real world," I have a great deal of respect and appreciation for these two men who proved mentors and partners in dialogue in shaping my own approach to social justice. I also wrestled through disappointment as I came to the realization that their theories dehumanized and marginalized half of the people in our world: women. Like all of us, these men were shaped by the eras in which they lived and worked for justice. Yet their thought continues to offer us robust anthropologies and rich theories that may act as a springboard into new ways of envisioning and cultivating societies that are just for all.

Select Bibliography

1. Primary Sources: Karol Wojtyla/John Paul II

Wojtyla, Karol. *The Acting Person.* Dordrecht: Reidel, 1979.
———. *The Collected Plays and Writings on Theater.* Berkeley: University of California Press, 1987.
———. *Faith According to St. John of the Cross.* San Francisco: Ignatius, 1981.
———. *Love and Responsibility.* San Francisco: Ignatius, 1993.
———. *Max Scheler.* Rome: Logos, 1980.
———. *Person and Community: Selected Essays.* New York: Lang, 1993.
———. *The Place Within: The Poetry of Pope John Paul II.* New York: Random House, 1994.
———. *Sign of Contradiction.* Translated by Mary Smith. Middlegreen, Slough, UK: St. Paul, 1979.
———. *Sources of Renewal: The Implementation of Vatican II.* San Francisco: Harper & Row, 1980.
———. *The Way to Christ: Spiritual Exercises.* Translated by Leslie Wearne. Cambridge: Harper & Row, 1984.
———. *The Word Made Flesh.* Translated by Leslie Wearne. San Francisco: Harper & Row, 1985.
John Paul II. "Basic Rights Do Not Depend On Positive Law." Address to International Union of Catholic Jurists. *L'Osservatore Romano* 50 (2000) 6.
———. *Crossing the Threshold of Hope.* New York: Knopf, 1994.
———. "Democracy Must Be Based On Moral Norms." Message to Pontifical Academy of Social Sciences on February 23, 2000. *L'Osservatore Romano* 10 (2000) 8.
———. "Development and Solidarity: Two Keys to Peace." Message of His Holiness Pope John Paul II for the Celebration of the World Day of Peace, 1 January 1987. Vatican City: Libreria Editrice Vaticana, 1987.
———. "Ecclesia in America." Apostolic Exhortation Given in Mexico City, January 22, 1999. http://www.vatican.va/holy_father/john_paul_ii/apost_exhortations/documents/hf_jp-ii_exh_22011999_ecclesia-in-america_en.html.
———. "Economy Must Respect Primacy of Person." Address to The Luigi Bocconi Business College, November 20, 1999. *L'Osservatore Romano* 3 (2000) 9.
———. "From the Justice of Each Comes Peace for All." Message of His Holiness Pope John Paul II for the Celebration of the World Day of Peace, January 1, 1998. Vatican City: Libreria Editrice Vaticana, 1998.
———. *Gift and Mystery.* New York: Doubleday, 1996.
———. *God, Father, and Creator: A Catechesis on the Creed.* Vol. 1. Boston: Pauline, 1996.

Select Bibliography

———. *Human Labour: Texts of John Paul II (October 1978–November 1979)*. Vatican City: Pontifical Commission on Justice and Peace, 1981.

———. "If You Want Peace, Reach Out to the Poor." Message of His Holiness Pope John Paul II for the Celebration of the World Day of Peace, January 1, 1993. Vatican City: Libreria Editrice Vaticana, 1993.

———. *Jesus, Son, and Saviour: A Catechesis on the Creed*. Vol. 2. Boston: Pauline, 1996.

———. "Letter of His Holiness Pope John Paul II to Mr. Benjamin Netanyahu." June 16, 1997. http://www.vatican.va/holy_father/john_paul_ii/letters/1997/documents/hf_jp-ii_let_19970616_netanyahu_en.html.

———. "Letter of His Holiness Pope John Paul II to Mr. Yasser Arafat." June 16, 1997. http://www.vatican.va/holy_father/john_paul_ii/letters/1997/documents/hf_jp-ii_let_1997061_arafat_en.html.

———. "Letter of Pope John Paul II to Women." June 29, 1995. http://www.vatican.va/holy_father/john_paul_ii/letters/documents/hf_jp-ii_let_29061995_women_en.html.

———. *Memory and Identity*. New York: Rizzoli, 2005.

———. "Message of the Holy Father to the Young People of Israel Palestine." September 2, 1999. http://www.vatican.va/holy_father/john_paul_ii/speeches/1999/september/documents/hf_jp-ii_mes_22091999_israel-palest_en.html.

———. "Protection of Human Rights is Indispensable." Address to the Conference of Presidents of European Union Parliaments on September 23, 2000. *L'Osservatore Romano* 40 (2000) 6.

———. *The Person, the Nation, and The State: Texts of John Paul II (October 1978–November 1979)*. Edited by William Murphy. Vatican City: Pontifical Commission on Justice and Peace, 1980.

———. "*Redemptoris Custos*: Of the Supreme Pontiff John Paul II on the Person and Mission of Saint Joseph." Speech given in Rome on August 15, 1989. http://www.vatican.va/holy_father/john_paul_ii/apost_exhortations/documents/hf_jp-ii_exh_15081989_redemptoris-custos_en.html.

———. *Reflections on* Humanae Vitae. Boston: St. Paul, 1984.

———. *The Social Agenda: A Collection of Magesterial Texts*. Edited by Robert A. Sirico and Maciej Zieba, OP. Citta Del Vaticano: Pontifical Council for Justice and Peace, Libreria Editrice Vaticana, 2000.

———. *The Social Teaching of John Paul II: The True Dimensions of Development Today, Texts of John Paul II (August 1979–February 1982)*. Vatican City: Tipografia Poliglotta Vaticana, 1982.

———. *The Spirit, Giver of Life and Love: A Catechesis on the Creed*. Vol. 3. Boston: Pauline, 1996.

———. *Spiritual Pilgrimage: Texts on Jews and Judaism 1979–1995*. Edited by Eugene J. Fisher and Leon Klenicki. New York: Crossroads, 1995.

———. *Ways of Peace: Papal Messages for the World Days of Peace, 1968–1986*. Vatican City: Pontifical Commission "Iustitia et Pax," 1986.

———. *The Whole Truth About Man*. Edited with Introduction by James Schall, SJ. Boston: Daughters of St. Paul, 1981.

Select Bibliography

2. Official Church Texts

Catechism of the Catholic Church. London: Catholic Truth Society, 1994.
Pope John Paul II. *Centesimus Annus.* http://www.vatican.va/holy_father/john_paul_ii/encyclicals/index.htm, 1991.
———. *Dives in Misericordia.* http://www.vatican.va/holy_father/john_paul_ii/encyclicals/index.htm, 1980.
———. *Dominum et Vivificantem.* http://www.vatican.va/holy_father/john_paul_ii/encyclicals/documents/hf_jp-ii_enc_18051986_dominum-et-vivificantem_en.html, 1986.
———. *Evangelium Vitae.* http://www.vatican.va/holy_father/john_paul_ii/encyclicals/index.htm, 1995.
———. *Fides et Ratio.* http://www.vatican.va/holy_father/john_paul_ii/encyclicals/index.htm, 1998.
———. *Laborem Exercens.* http://www.vatican.va/holy_father/john_paul_ii/encyclicals/index.htm, 1981.
———. *Redemptor Hominis.* http://www.vatican.va/holy_father/john_paul_ii/encyclicals/index.htm, 1979.
———. *Redemptoris Mater.* http://www.vatican.va/holy_father/john_paul_ii/encyclicals/index.htm, 1987.
———. *Redemptoris Missio.* http://www.vatican.va/holy_father/john_paul_ii/encyclicals/index.htm, 1990.
———. *Sollicitudo Rei Socialis.* http://www.vatican.va/holy_father/john_paul_ii/encyclicals/index.htm, 1987.
———. *Ut Unum Sint.* http://www.vatican.va/holy_father/john_paul_ii/encyclicals/index.htm, 1995.
———. *Veritatis Splendor.* http://www.vatican.va/holy_father/john_paul_ii/encyclicals/index.htm, 1993.
Pope Paul VI. *Humanae Vitae.* http://www.vatican.va/holy_father/paul_vi/encyclicals/documents/hf_p-vi_enc_25071968_humanae-vitae_en.html, 1968.
Second Vatican Council. *Dei Verbum.* London: Catholic Truth Society, 1966.
———. *Dignitatis Humanae.* London: Catholic Truth Society, 1966.
———. *Gaudium et Spes.* London: Catholic Truth Society, 1966.
———. *Lumen Gentium.* London: Catholic Truth Society, 1966.
———. *Nostra Aetate.* http://www.vatican.va/archive/hist_councils/ii_vatican_council/documents/vat-ii_decl_19651028_nostra-aetate_en.html, 1965.
———. *Unitatis Redintegratio.* http://www.vatican.va/archive/hist_councils/ii_vatican_council/documents/vat-ii_decree_19641121_unitatis-redintegratio_en.html.

3. Secondary Books: Karol Wojtyla/John Paul II

Amato, Joseph. *Mounier and Maritan.* Tuscaloosa: University of Alabama Press, 1975.
Aquinas, Thomas. *Contra Gentes.* Translated by Anton C. Pegis. London: University of Notre Dame Press, 1955.
———. *Summa Theologiae.* New York: McGraw-Hill, 1964–1981.

Select Bibliography

Barrett, Edward. *Persons and Liberal Democracy: The Ethical and Political Thought of Karol Wojtyla/Pope John Paul II.* Lanham, MD: Lexington, 2010.

Baum, Gregory, and Robert Ellsberg, eds. *The Logic of Solidarity: Commentaries on Pope John Paul II's Encyclical "On Social Concern."* Maryknoll, NY: Orbis, 1989.

Baum, Gregory, and John Coleman, eds. *Rerum Novarum. One Hundred Years of Catholic Social Teaching.* London: SCM, 1991.

Beabout, Gregory R. *Beyond Self-Interest: A Personalist Approach to Human Action.* Lanham, MD: Lexington, 2002.

———. *A Celebration of the Thought of John Paul II.* St. Louis: St. Louis University Press, 1998.

Beigel, Gerard. *Faith and Social Justice in the Teaching of Pope John Paul II.* New York: Lang, 1997.

Biffi, Franco. *The "Social Gospel" of Pope John Paul II: A Guide to the Encyclicals on Human Work and the Authentic Development of the Peoples.* Rome: Pontifical Lateran University, 1989.

Blazynski, George. *Pope John Paul II: A Man From Kraków.* London: Sphere, 1979.

Bransfield, J. *The Human Person: According to John Paul II.* Boston: Pauline, 2010.

Buttiglione, Rocco. *Karol Wojtyla: The Thought of the Man Who Became Pope John Paul II.* Grand Rapids: Eerdmans, 1997.

Conn, Joane Wolski, and Walter E. Conn, eds. *Catholic Feminist Theology.* Washington, DC: Georgetown University Press, 1992.

Craig, Mary. *Man from a Far Country: A Portrait of Pope John Paul II.* London: Hodder and Stoughton, 1979.

Curran, Charles E. *Directions in Catholic Social Ethics.* Notre Dame: University of Notre Dame Press, 1985.

———. *The Moral Theology of Pope John Paul II.* Washington, DC: Georgetown University Press, 2005.

Curran, Charles E., and Richard McCormick. *John Paul II and Moral Theology.* New York: Paulist, 1998.

Dalin, David, and Matthew Levering. *John Paul II and the Jewish People: A Jewish-Christian Dialogue.* Lanham, MD: Rowman & Littlefield, 2008.

Donahue-White, Patricia, et al. *Human Nature and the Discipline of Economics.* Oxford: Lexington, 2002.

Dulles, Avery. *The Splendor of Faith: The Theological Vision of Pope John Paul II.* New York: Crossroad, 1999.

Formicola, Jo Renee. *Pope John Paul II: Prophetic Politician.* Washington, DC: Georgetown University Press, 2002.

Gregg, Samuel. *Challenging the Modern World: Karol Wojtyla/Pope John Paul II and the Development of Catholic Social Teaching.* Lanham, MD: Lexington, 1999.

Hollenbach, David. *The Common Good and Christian Ethics.* Cambridge: Cambridge University Press, 2002.

Jeffreys, Derek. *Defending Human Dignity.* Grand Rapids: Brazos, 2004.

Kerr, Fergus. *After Aquinas.* Oxford: Blackwell, 2002.

Kijowski, Andrzej, and J. J. Szczepanski, with the collaboration of Krzysztof Zanussi. *From a Far Country: The Story of Karol Wojtyla of Poland.* Santa Monica: ERI/NEFF, 1981.

Kobler, John F. *Vatican II and Phenomenology.* Lancaster, PA: Nijhoff, 1985.

Select Bibliography

Lipien, Ted. *Wojtyla's Women: How They Shaped the Life of Pope John Paul II and Changed the Catholic Church.* Lanham, MD: NBN, 2008.

Lubac, Henri de. *Catholicism.* Translated by Lancelot Sheppard. London: Burns & Oates, 1950.

———. *Le Mystére du Surnaturel.* Paris: Aubier, 1965

Malinsky, Mieczyslaw. *Pope John Paul II: The Life of Karol Wojtyla.* New York: Seabury, 1979.

Mannion, Gerard. *The Vision of John Paul II: Assessing his Thought and Influence.* Collegeville, MN: Liturgical, 2008.

Mardas, Nancy, Agnes Curry, and George McLean. *Karol Wojtyla's Philosophical Legacy.* Washington DC: Council for Research in Values and Philosophy, 2008.

McClean, George, ed. *The Human Person,* ed. George McLean. Washington, DC: American Catholic Philosophical Association, 1979.

McDermott, John M., ed. *The Thought of Pope John Paul II: A Collection of Essays and Studies.* Rome: Editrice Pontificia Universitá Gregoriana, 1993.

McInerny, Ralph. *A First Glance at St. Thomas Aquinas.* Notre Dame: University of Notre Dame Press, 1990.

McNerny, John. *John Paul II: Poet and Philosopher.* New York: Burns and Oates, 2004.

Michener, James. *Poland.* New York: Fawcett Crest, 1983.

Moody, John. *Pope John Paul II.* New York: Park Lane, 1997.

Murphy, Francis X., and Norman Shaifer. *John Paul II: A Son from Poland.* South Hackensack, NJ: Shepherd, 1978.

Myers, Kenneth A., ed. *Aspiring to Freedom: Commentaries on* Sollicitudo Rei Socailis. Grand Rapids: Eerdmans, 1988.

Neuhaus, Richard John, ed. *The Preferential Option for the Poor.* Grand Rapids: Eerdmans, 1988.

Nichols, Aidan. *The Shape of Catholic Theology.* Edinburgh: T. & T. Clark, 1991.

O'Brien, Darcy. *The Hidden Pope: The Personal Journey of John Paul II and Jerzy Kluger.* New York: Daybreak, 1998.

O'Carroll, Michael. *Poland and John Paul II.* Dublin: Veritas, 1979.

Ong, Andre. *John Paul II's Philosophy of the Acting Person: A Personalistic Approach to Life.* Lewiston, NY: Mellen, 2008.

Oram, James. *The People's Pope: The Story of Karol Wojtyla of Poland.* San Francisco: Chronicle, 1979.

Perry, Tim S. *The Legacy of John Paul II: An Evangelical Assessment.* Downers Grove, IL: IVP Academic, 2007.

Reimers, Adrian. *The Truth about the Good: Moral Norms in the Thought of John Paul II.* Ave Maria, FL: Sanpientia, 2011.

Savage, Deborah. *The Subjective Dimension of Human Work and the Conversion of the Acting Person According to Karol Wojtyla/John Paul II and Bernard Lonergan.* New York: Lang, 2008.

Saward, John. *Christ is the Answer.* New York: Alba House, 1995.

Scheler, Max. *Selected Philosophical Essays.* Evanston, IL: Northwestern University Press, 1973.

Schall, James V. *The Church, the State, and Society in the Thought of John Paul II.* Chicago: Franciscan Herald, 1982.

Schmitz, Kenneth L. *At the Center of Human Drama.* Washington, DC: Catholic University Press, 1993.

Staude, John. *Max Scheler.* London: Collier-MacMillan, 1967.

Select Bibliography

Szulc, Tad. *Pope John Paul: The Biography*. New York: Scribner, 1995.
Tyburski, Zbiquniew. *The Encyclicals of John Paul II: Foundations of Catholic Faith and Morality*. Ave Maria, FL: Sapientia, 2011.
Walsh, Michael. *John Paul II: A Biography*. London: Fount, 1995.
Weigel, George. *Witness to Hope*. New York: HarperCollins, 1999.
———. *The End and the Beginning: Pope John Paul II, The Victory of Freedom, the Last Years, the Legacy*. New York: Doubleday, 2010.
Williams, George. *The Contours of Church and State in the Thought of John Paul II*. Waco, TX: Baylor University Press, 1983.
———. *The Mind of John Paul II: Origins of His Thought and Action*. New York: Seabury, 1981.
Williams, Oliver. *The Making of an Economic Vision: John Paul II's On Social Concern*. Lanham, MD: University Press of America, 1991.
Zdzinslaw, Józef Kijas. *Christ, Church and Mankind: The Spirit of Vatican II According to Pope John Paul II*. New York: Paulist, 2012.
Zieba, Maciej. *The Surprising Pope: Understanding the Thought of John Paul II*. Lanham, MD: Lexington, 2000.

4. Secondary Essays and Articles: Karol Wojtyla/John Paul II

Buttiglione, Rocco. "Toward an Adequate Anthropology." *Ethos* 2 (1996) 237–46.
———. "Wojtyla and the Council: Religious Liberty as the Heart of Vatican II." *Crisis* 11 (1993) 21–25.
Conley, John. "The Philosophical Foundations of the Thought of John Paul II." In *The Thought of John Paul II*, edited by John McDermott, 22–34. Rome: Editrice Pontificia Universita Gregoriana, 1993.
Finn, Daniel Rush. "John Paul II and the Moral Ecology of Markets." *Theological Studies* 59 (1998) 393–407.
Grondelski, John M. "Social Ethics in the Young Karol Wojtyla: A Study in Progress." *Faith and Reason* 22 (1996) 31–43.
Robert Harvanek. "The Philosophical Foundations of the Thought of John Paul II." In *The Thought of John Paul II*, edited by John McDermott, 1–22. Rome: Editrice Pontifica Universita Gregoriana, 1993.
Hebblethwaite, Peter. "John Paul II's Outlook: Church, Society, and Politics [thematic issue; bibliog]." *IDOC Bulletin* 11–12 (1982) 1–31.
———. "The Popes and Politics: Shifting Patterns in 'Catholic Social Doctrine.'" *IDOC Bulletin* 11–12 (1982) 15–28.
Hellman, John. "John Paul II and the Personalist Movement." *Cross Currents* (1980–1981) 409–19.
John Kavanaugh. "John Paul II and Philosophy." In *A Celebration of the Thought of John Paul II*, edited by Gregory Beabout, 17. St. Louis: St. Louis University Press, 1998.
Knasas, John F. X. "Fides et Ratio and the Twentieth Century Thomistic Revival." *Catholic Dossier* 6, no. 6 (2000), as translated into html by the Catholic Information Center on the Internet, http://www.catholic.net/rcc/Periodicals/Dossier/2000-12/article3.html.

Select Bibliography

Lescoe, Francis J. "Pope John Paul and Existential Personalism." In *Pastor of the Poles*, edited by Stanislaus A. Blejwas and Mieczyslaw B. Biskupski, 80–92. New Britain, CT: Polish Studies Program Monographs, 1982.

MacIntyre, Alisdair. "*Veritatis Splendor* and the Theology of Natural Law." In *Veritatis Splendor and the Renewal of Moral Theology*, edited by J. A. DiNoia and Romanus Cessario, 72–89. Princeton: Scepter, 1999.

McCool, Gerald. "The Theology of John Paul II." In *The Thought of John Paul II: A Collection of Essays and Studies*, edited by John McDermott, 29–54. Rome: Editrice Pontificia Universitá Gregoriana, 1993.

McInerny, Ralph. "Fides et Ratio." A paper presented at The Thomistic Seminar for the Jacques Maritain Centre, University of Notre Dame, 1999.

Plantinga, Alvin. "Philosophers respond to Pope John Paul II's Encyclical Letter, *Fides et Ratio*." *Christianity Today International/Books and Culture Magazine* 5, no. 4 (1999) 32.

Roos, Lothar. "The Message of Centesimus Annus." *Tripod* 65 (1991) 4–13.

Suro, Robert. "The Writing of an Encyclical." In *Aspiring to Freedom*, edited by Kenneth Myers, 159–69. Grand Rapids: Eerdmans, 1988.

Tymieniecka, Anna-Teresa. "The Origins of the Philosophy of John Paul the Second." In *The Human Person*, edited by George McLean, 16–27. Washington, DC: American Catholic Philosophical Association, 1979.

Waterman, A. M. C. "The Uses of Economics in Papal Encyclicals." In *Religion and Economics: Normative Social Theory*, 33–50. London: Kluwer Academic, 1999.

Williams, G. H. "John Paul II's Concepts of Church, State and Society." *Journal of Church and State* 24 (1982) 463–96.

———. "Karol Wojtyla and Marxism." In *Catholicism and Politics in Communist Societies*, edited by Sabrina P. Ramet, 356–81. Durham, NC: Duke University Press, 1990.

Wogamon, J. Phillip. "The Economic Encyclicals of John Paul II: Theological and Economic Perspectives." In *The Making of an Economic Vision*, edited by Oliver Williams and John Houck, 44–66. Lanham, MD: University Press of America, 1991.

5. Theses: Karol Wojtyla/John Paul II

Beigel, Gerard Paul. "The Person Revealed in Action: A Framework for Understanding How Social Justice is an Essential Part of the Gospel in the Teaching of Pope John Paul II." PhD thesis, Catholic University of America, 1994.

Kupczak, Jaroslaw. *The Human Person as an Efficient Cause in the Christian Anthropology of Karol Wojtyla*. STD diss., John Paul II Institute for Studies on Marriage and Family, 1996.

6. Primary Sources: Karl Barth

Barth, Karl. *Action in Waiting*. Including "Joy in the Lord" by Christoph Blumhardt. Rifton, NY: Plough, 1969.

———. *Against the Stream*. Translated by E. M. Delacour and Stanley Godman. London: SCM, 1954.

Select Bibliography

———. *Anselm*. New York: Meridian, 1962.
———. *The Christian Life*. Edinburgh: T. & T. Clark, 1981.
———. *The Church and the Political Problem of Our Day*. New York: Schribner's Sons, 1939.
———. *Church Dogmatics*. 14 vols. Edited by Geoffrey Bromiley and T. F. Torrance. Translated by G. T. Thomson et al. Edinburgh: T. & T. Clark, 1957–1969.
———. *Community, Church, and State*. Gloucester: MA: Smith, 1968.
———. *The Church and the War*. New York: Macmillan, 1944.
———. *Dogmatics in Outline*. Translated by G. T. Thompson. New York: Harper, 1959.
———. *Epistle to the Romans*. 2nd ed. London: Oxford University Press, 1933.
———. *Ethics*. Translated by G. W. Bromiley. Edinburgh: T. & T. Clark, 1981.
———. *Evangelical Theology*. Edinburgh: T. & T. Clark, 1963.
———. "Fate and Idea in Theology." In *The Way of Theology in Karl Barth: Essays and Comments*, edited by H. Martin Rumscheidt, 26–61. Allison Park, PA: Pickwick, 1986.
———. "First Letter to the French Protestants." In *A Letter to Great Britain from Switzerland*, 30–41. London: Sheldon, 1941.
———. *The German Church Conflict*. Richmond, VA: Knox, 1965.
———. *Gespräche: 1959–1962 Gesamtausgabe*. Zürich: Theologischer, 1995.
———. *The Göttigen Dogmatics: Instruction in the Christian Religion*. Vol. 1. Translated by Geoffrey Bromiley. Grand Rapids: Eerdmans, 1991.
———. *God Here and Now*. Translated by Paul M. van Buren. London: Routledge, 1964.
———. *The Holy Spirit and the Christian Life*. Translated by R. Birch Hoyle. Louisville: Westminster John Knox, 1993.
———. *How to Serve God in a Marxist Land*. New York: Association, 1959.
———. *The Humanity of God*. Richmond, VA: Knox, 1960.
———. *Karl Barth and Rudolf Bultmann: Letters 1922–1966*. Translated and edited by Geoffrey W. Bromiley. Edinburgh: T. & T. Clark, 1982.
———. *The Knowledge of God and the Service of God*. Gifford Lectures, 1937. London: Hodder and Stoughton, 1949.
———. *A Letter to Great Britain from Switzerland*. London: Sheldon, 1941.
———. "No!" Translated by Peter Fraenkel. In *Natural Theology: Comprising "Nature and Grace" by Emil Brunner and the Reply "No!" by Karl Barth*, 67–128. London: Centenary, 1946.
———. "Past and Future." In *The Beginnings of Dialectical Theology*, edited by J. Smart, 42–71. Richmond, VA: Knox, 1968.
———. *Protestant Theology in the Nineteenth Century: Its Background and History*. Translated by B. Cozens and J. Bowden. London: SCM, 1972.
———. *Revolutionary Theology in the Making: Barth-Thurneysen Correspondence, 1914–1925*. Translated by J. Smart. London: Epworth, 1964.
———. *Theology and the Church*. London: SCM, 1962.
———. *The Theology of John Calvin*. Translated by G. W. Bromiley. Grand Rapids: Eerdmans, 1995.
———. *The Word of God and the Word of Man*. Translated by D. Horton. London: Hodder and Stoughton, 1936.
Barth, Karl, and Heinrich Barth. *Zur Lehre vom heiligen Geist*. Vol. 1 of *Zwischen den Zeiten*. Munich: Kaiser, 1930.

7. Secondary Books: Karl Barth

Anderson, Ray. *On Being Human*. Pasadena, CA: Fuller Seminary Press, 1982.

———. *The Shape of Practical Theology: Empowering Ministry With Theological Praxis*. Downers Grove, IL: Intervarsity, 2001.

Balthasar, Hans Urs von. *The Theology of Karl Barth: Exposition and Interpretation*. Translated by E. Oakes. San Francisco: Ignatius, 1992.

Berkouwer, G. C. *The Triumph of Grace in the Theology of Karl Barth*. Translated by Harry R. Boer. London: Paternoster, 1956.

Beintker, Michael. *Die Dialektik in der "dialektischen Theologie" Karl Barths*. Munich: Kaiser, 1987.

Biggar, Nigel. *The Hastening That Waits: Karl Barth's Ethics*. Oxford: Clarendon, 1995.

Biggar, Nigel, ed. *Reckoning with Barth*. London: Mowbray, 1988.

Blumhardt, Christoph. *Thy Kingdom Come*. Edited by Vernard Eller. Grand Rapids: Eerdmans, 1980.

Bonhoeffer, D. *Ethics*. Edited by Eberhard Bethge. Translated by N. H. Smith. London: Fontana Library, 1964.

———. *Letters and Papers from Prison*. London: SCM, 1967.

———. *Sanctorum Communion*. Dietrich Bonhoeffer Works 1. Minneapolis: Fortress, 1998.

Bromiley, Geoffrey. *Introduction to the Theology of Karl Barth*. Grand Rapids: Eerdmans, 1979.

Brunner, Emil. *The Christian Doctrine of Creation and Redemption*. Vol. 2 of *Dogmatics*. Translated by Olive Wyon. Philadelphia: Westminster, 1952.

———. *The Divine Imperative*. London: Lutterworth, 1937.

———. "Nature and Grace." Translated by Peter Fraenkel. In *Natural Theology: Comprising "Nature and Grace" by Emil Brunner and the Reply "No!" by Karl Barth*, 1–66. London: Centenary, 1946.

Bullivant, Keith, ed. *Culture and Society in the Weimar Republic*. Manchester, UK: Manchester University Press, 1977.

Busch, Eberhard. *Karl Barth. His Life from Letters and Autobiographical Fragments*. London: SCM Press, 1976.

———. *Unter dem Bogen des einen Bundes: Karl Barth und die Juden 1933–1945*. Neukirchener: Neurkirchener, 1996.

Calvin, John. *Institutes of the Christian Religion*. Edited by John T. McNeill. Translated by Ford Lewis Battles. LCC 20–21. Philadelphia: Westminster, 1960.

Cullberg, John. *Das Problem der Ethic in der dialektischen Theologie*. Vol. 1, *Karl Barth*. Uppsala universitets årsskrift; 1938:4. Uppsala: Lundequist, 1938.

Chung, Paul. *Karl Barth: God's Word in Action*. Eugene, OR: Cascade, 2008.

Dahlke, Benjamin. *Karl Barth, Catholic Renewal, and Vatican II*. London: T. & T. Clark Clark, 2012.

Dorrien, Gary. *The Barthian Revolution in Modern Theology*. Louisville: Westminster John Knox, 1989.

Dyck, Arthur. *Rights and Responsibilities*. Washington, DC: Georgetown University Press, 2005.

Gay, P. *Weimar Culture: The Outsider as Insider*. Harmondsworth, UK: Penguin, 1974.

Gorringe, Timothy J. *Karl Barth: Against Hegemony*. Oxford: Oxford University Press, 1999.

Select Bibliography

Green, Clifford. *Karl Barth: Theologian of Freedom*. London: Collins, 1989.
Gunton, Colin. *Becoming and Being*, Oxford: Oxford University Press, 1978.
Gustafson, James M. *Ethics from a Theocentric Perspective*, Vol. 1. Chicago: University of Chicago Press, 1981.
Gustafson, James M. *Protestant and Roman Catholic Ethics*. Chicago: University of Chicago Press, 1978.
Harnack, Adolf von. *What Is Christianity?* Translated by Thomas Bailey Saunders. New York: HarperTorchbooks, 1957.
Harnack, Adolf von, and Wilhelm Herrman. *Essays in the Social Gospel*. Edited by G. M. Craik. Translated by Maurice Canney. London: Williams and Norgate, 1907.
Hart, Trevor. *Regarding Karl Barth*. Cumbria, UK: Paternoster, 1999.
Hauerwas, S. *Character and the Christian Life*. Notre Dame: University of Notre Dame Press, 1994.
———. *With the Grain of the Universe*. Grand Rapids: Brazos, 2001.
Heron, Alasdair. *A Century of Protestant Theology*. Cambridge: Lutterworth, 1980.
Hirsch, Emanuel. *Deutschlands Schicksal*. Göttingen, Vandenhoeck & Ruprecht, 1920.
Hood, Robert E. *Contemporary Political Orders and Christ: Karl Barth's Christology and Political Praxis*. Allison Park, PA: Pickwick, 1985.
Hunsinger, George. *How to Read Karl Barth. The Shape of his Theology*. Oxford: Oxford University Press, 1991.
———. *Karl Barth and Radical Politics*. Philadelphia: Westminster, 1976.
Joll, James. *Europe Since 1870*. London: Weidenfeld and Nicholson, 1973.
Joint Declaration on the Doctrine of Justification by Faith. Grand Rapids: Eerdmans, 2000.
Jüngel, Eberhard. *Barth-Studien*. Gutersloh: Gutersloher, 1982.
———. *Christ, Justice, and Peace: Toward a Theology of the State in Dialogue with the Barmen Declaration*. Translated by D. Bruce Hamill and Alan J. Torrance. Introductory Essay by Alan J. Torrance. Edinburgh: T. & T. Clark, 1992.
———. *God as the Mystery of the World*. Translated by Darrell Guder. Grand Rapids: Eerdmans, 1983.
———. *God's Being is in Becoming: The Trinitarian Being of God in the Theology of Karl Barth*. Edinburgh: T. & T. Clark, 2001.
———. *Karl Barth: A Theological Legacy*. Philadelphia: Westminster, 1986.
Kant, Immanuel. *Metaphysics of Morals*. Translated by Mary Gregor. Cambridge: Cambridge University Press, 1991.
Kettler, Christian D. *The Vicarious Humanity of Christ and the Reality of Salvation*. London: University Press of America, 1991.
Küng, Hans. *A Global Ethic for Politics and Economics*. Oxford: Oxford University Press, 1998.
———. *Global Responsibility*. London: SCM, 1981.
———. *Justification*. Philadephia: Wesminster, 1964.
Lane, Anthony N. S., *Justification by Faith in Catholic-Protestant Dialogue*. London: T. & T. Clark, 2002.
Lewis, John P. *Karl Barth in North America: The Influence of Karl Barth in the Making of a New North American Evangelicalism*. Eugene, OR: Wipf and Stock, 2009.
Lindsay, Mark. *Covenanted Solidarity*. New York: Lang, 2001.
Lovin, Robin W. *Christian Faith and Public Choices: The Social Ethics of Barth, Brunner, and Bonhoeffer*. Philadelphia: Fortress, 1984.

Select Bibliography

Marquardt, Friedrich-Wilhelm. *Verwegenheiten: Theologische Stucke aus Berlin*. Munich: Kaiser, 1981.

———. *Theologie and Socialismus: Das Beispiel Karl Barths*. Munich: Kaiser, 1972.

Matheny, Paul D. *Dogmatics and Ethics: The Theological Realism and Ethics of Karl Barth's Church Dogmatics*. New York: Lang, 1990.

Maury, Pierre. *Erwahlung und Glaube*. Zurich: EVZ, 1940.

———. *Predestination*. Translated by Edwin Hudson. London: SCM, 1960.

McCormack, Bruce L. *Karl Barth's Critically Realistic Dialectical Theology*. Oxford: Clarendon, 1995.

McCormack, Bruce L., and Clifford B. Anderson. *Karl Barth and American Evangelicalism*. Grand Rapids: Eerdmans, 2011.

McClean, Stuart. *Humanity in the Thought of Karl Barth*. Edinburgh: T. & T. Clark, 1981.

McKenny, Gerald. *The Analogy of Grace: Karl Barth's Moral Theology*. Oxford: Oxford University Press, 2010.

Migliore, Daniel L. *Commanding Grace: Studies in Karl Barth's Ethics*. Grand Rapids, Eerdmans, 2010.

Molnar, Paul D. *Divine Freedom and the Doctrine of the Immanent Trinity: In Dialogue with Karl Barth and Contemporary Theology*. Edinburgh: T. & T. Clark, 2002.

Mosley, Carys. *Nations and Nationalism in the Theology of Karl Barth*. Oxford: Oxford University Press, 2013.

Neder, Adam. *Participation in Christ: An Entry into Karl Barth's Church Dogmatics*. Louisville: Westminster John Knox, 2009.

Nimmo, Paul. *Being in Action*. London: T. & T. Clark, 2007.

Pachter, H. *Modern Germany: A Social, Cultural, and Political History*. Boulder, CO: Westview, 1978.

Parker, T. H. L. *The Doctrine of the Knowledge of God*. Edinburgh: Oliver and Boyd, 1952.

Pinson, Koppel S. *Modern Germany*. London: Collier-MacMillan, 1966.

Price, Daniel. *Karl Barth's Anthropology*. Grand Rapids: Eerdmans, 2002.

Reimer, A. James. *The Hirsch and Tillich Debate*. Lewiston, NY: Mellen, 1989.

Sartre, Jean Paul. *Being and Nothingness*. New York: Washington Square, 1966.

Schleiermacher, Freidrich. *A Brief Outline of the Study of Theology*. Lewiston, NY: Mellen, 1988.

Schwartz, Hans. *Theology in a Global Context*. Grand Rapids: Eerdmans, 2005.

Smart, J. *The Divided Mind of Modern Theology: Karl Barth and Rudolf Bultmann 1908–1933*. Philadelphia: Westminster, 1967.

Spencer, Archibald. *Clearing a Space for Human Action*. New York: Lang, 2003.

Spieckermann, Ingrid. *Gotteserkenntnis: Ein Beitrag zur Grundfrage der neuen Theologie Karl Barths*. Munich: Kaiser, 1985.

Strauss, Leo. *Natural Right and History*. Chicago: University of Chicago Press, 1953.

Stroble, Paul E. *The Social Ontology of Karl Barth*. San Francisco: Christian Universities Press, 1994.

Sykes, Stephen W. *Karl Barth: Centenary Essays*. Cambridge: Cambridge University Press, 1989.

Thielicke, Helmut. *Theologische Ethik*. Vol. 1. Tubigen: Mohr, 1951–1958.

Thompson, J. *Christ in Perspective: Christological Perspectives in the Theology of Karl Barth*. Edinburgh: St. Andrews, 1978.

Select Bibliography

Thurneysen, Eduard, ed. *Karl Barth—Eduard Thurneysen: Briefwechsel.* Vol. 2, 1921–1930. Zurich: TVZ, 1974.
Torrance, Alan. *Persons in Communion.* Edinburgh: T. & T. Clark, 1996.
Torrance, T. F. *Karl Barth: An Introduction to His Early Theology.* London: SCM, 1963.
———. *Karl Barth: Biblical and Evangelical Theologian.* Edinburgh: T. & T. Clark, 1990.
———. *The Mediation of Christ.* Grand Rapids: Eerdmans, 1983.
Villa-Vicencio, Charles, ed. *On Reading Karl Barth in South Africa.* Grand Rapids: Eerdmans, 1988.
Ward, Graham. *Barth, Derrida, and the Language of Theology.* Cambridge: Cambridge University Press, 1995.
Ward, W. R. *Theology, Sociology, and Politics: The German Protestant Social Conscience, 1890–1933.* Bern: Lang, 1979.
Webster, John. *Barth.* London: Continuum, 2000.
———. *Barth's Ethics of Reconciliation.* Cambridge: Cambridge University Press, 1995.
———. *Barth's Moral Theology: Human Action in Barth's Thought.* Edinburgh: T. & T. Clark, 1998.
Webster, John, ed. *The Cambridge Companion to Karl Barth.* Cambridge: Cambridge University Press, 2000.
West, Charles. *Communism and the Theologians.* Philadelphia: Westminster, 1958.
Willis, Robert E. *The Ethics of Karl Barth.* Leiden: Brill, 1971.
Winn, Christian T. Collins. *"Jesus is Victor!" The Significance of the Blumhardts for the Theology of Karl Barth.* Eugene, OR: Pickwick, 2009.
Zahn-Harnack, Agnes von. *Adolf von Harnack.* Berlin: de Gruyter, 1951.

8. Secondary Essays and Articles: Karl Barth

Anderson, Ray. "Barth and a New Direction for Natural Theology." In *Theology Beyond Christendom,* edited by John Thompson, 241–66. Allison Park, PA: Picwick, 1986.
———. "Isomorphic Indicators in Theological and Psychological Science." *Journal of Psychology and Theology* 17, no. 4 (1989) 373–81.
Baranowski, Shelley. "The Confessing Church and Antisemitism." In *Betrayal,* edited by Robert Ericksen and Susannah Heschel, 90–109. Minneapolis: Fortress, 1999.
Barth, Marcus. "Current Discussion on the Political Character of Karl Barth's Theology." In *Footnotes to a Theology: The Karl Barth Colloquium of 1972,* edited by Martin Rumschiedt, 77–94. Waterloo, OT: Canadian Corporation for Studies in Religion, 1974.
Brunner, Emil. "Nature and Grace." Translated by Peter Fraenkel. In *Natural Theology: Comprising "Nature and Grace" by Emil Brunner and the Reply "No!" by Karl Barth,* 17–64. London: Centenary, 1946.
Busch, Eberhard. "Church and Politics in Reformed Tradition." In *Church, Word, and Spirit,* edited by James Bradley et al., 163–81. Grand Rapids: Eerdmans, 1987.
———. "The Covenant of Grace Fulfilled in Christ as the Foundation of the Indissoluble Solidarity of the Church with Israel: Barth's Position on the Jews During the Hitler Era." *Scottish Journal of Theology* 52, no. 4 (1999) 476–503.
Deddo, Gary. "The Grammar of Barth's Theology of Personal Relations." *Scottish Journal of Theology* 47, no. 1 (1994) 183–222.

Select Bibliography

Ericksen, Robert. "Assessing the Heritage: German Protestant Theologians, Nazis, and the 'Jewish Question.'" In *Betrayal*, edited by Robert Ericksen and Susannah Heschel, 22–39. Minneapolis: Fortress, 1999.

Gogarten, Friedrich. "Das Problem einer theologischen Anthropologie." *Zwischen den Zeiten* 7 (1929) 493–511.

Gunton, Colin. "The Triune God and the Freedom of the Creature." In *Karl Barth: Centenary Essays*, edited by S. W. Sykes, 46–68. Cambridge: Cambridge University Press, 1989.

Hauerwas, Stanley. "On Honour: By Way of a Comparison of Barth and Trollope." In *Reckoning with Barth*, edited by Nigel Biggar, 145–69. London: Mowbray, 1988.

Hector, Kevin. "God's Triunity and Self-Determination: A Conversation with Karl Barth, Bruce McCormack, and Kevin Hector." *International Journal of Systematic Theology* 7, no. 3 (2005) 246–61.

Hood, Robert E. "Karl Barth's Christological Basis for State and Political Praxis." *Scottish Journal of Theology* 33, no. 3 (1980) 223–38.

Horden, William. "Barth as a Political Thinker." *Christian Century* 86 (1969) 411–13.

Hunsinger, George. "Barth and Liberation Theology." *Journal of Religion* 63 (1983) 247–63.

———. "Election and the Trinity." *Modern Theology* 24 (2008) 179–98.

———. "The Politics of the Nonviolent God: Reflections on Rene Girard and Karl Barth." *Scottish Journal of Theology* 51, no. 1 (1998) 61–86.

Kranzler, David. "The Swiss Press Campaign that Halted Deportations to Auschwitz and the Role of the Vatican, the Swiss and Hungarian Churches." In *Remembering the Future*, edited by Yehuda Bauer et al., 1:156–70. Oxford: Pergamom, 1989.

McCormack, Bruce. "Election and the Trinity." *Scottish Journal of Theology* 63 (2010) 203–23.

McKelway, Alexander. "Karl Barth and Politics." *Perspectives in Religious Studies* 15 (1988) 269–81.

Migliore, Daniel. "Sin and Self-Loss." In *Many Voices, One God*, edited by Walter Brueggeman and George W. Stroup, 139–54. Louisville: Westminster John Knox, 1998.

Molnar, Paul D. "The Trinity, Election and God's Ontological Freedom: A Response to Kevin W. Hector." *International Journal of Systematic Theology* 8, no. 3 (2006) 294–306.

Moltmann, Jürgen. "Christian Faith and Human Rights." *Christian Faith and Social Responsibility, Tugon* 2, no.1 (1991) 1–85.

———. "Christian Theology and Political Religion." In *Civil Religion and Political Theory*, edited by L. Rouner, 41–58. Notre Dame: University of Notre Dame Press, 1986.

———. "The Cross and Civil Religion." In *Religion and Political Society*, edited and translated by The Institute of Christian Thought, 11–47. London: Harper & Row, 1974.

———. "Political Theology." *Theology Today* 28 (1971) 6–23.

Osborn, Robert T. "A 'Personalistic' Appraisal of Barth's Political Ethics [reply to criticism by George Hunsinger]." *Studies in Religion* 12, no. 3 (1983) 313–24.

Ruether, Rosemary Radford. "Christian Tradition and Feminist Hermeneutics." In *Image of God and Gender Models in Judaeo-Christian Tradition*, edited by Kari Elisabeth Børresen, 258–81. Oslo: Solum, 1991.

Select Bibliography

Salomonsen, Joan. "Love of Same, Love of Other." *Studia Theologica* 57 (2003) 103–23.
Söhngen, Gottlieb. "Analogia Fidei: Die Einheit in der Glaubenswissenschft." *Catholica* 3, no. 4 (1934) 176–208.
———. "Analogia Fidei: Gottähnlichkeit allein aus Glauben?" *Catholica* 3, no. 3 (1934) 113–36.
Theimann, R. F. "The Significance of Karl Barth for Contemporary Theology." *Thomist* 50 (1986) 512–39.
Torrance, Alan. "Christian Experience and the Divine Revelation in the Theologies of Friedrich Schleiermacher and Karl Barth." In *Christian Experience in Theology and Life*, edited by I. Howard Marshall, 83–113. Edinburgh: Rutherford, 1988.
Torrance, James. "Interpreting the Word by the Light of Christ or the Light of Nature? Calvin, Calvinism, and Barth." In *Calviniana*, edited by R. Schnucker, 255–67. Kirksville, MO: Sixteen Century Journal, 1988.
Wall, Donald. "Karl Barth and National Socialism." *Fides et Historia* 15, no. 2 (1983) 80–90.
Webster, John. "'Assured and Patient and Cheerful Expectation': Barth on Christian Hope as the Church's Task." in *Toronto Journal of Theology* 10 (1994) 35–52.
Werpehowski, William. "Justification and Justice in the Theology of Karl Barth." *Thomist* 50 (1986) 623–42.

9. Theses: Karl Barth

Aboagye-Mensah, R. K. "Socio-Political Thinking of Karl Barth:Trinitarian and Incarnational Christology as the Ground for his Social Action and its Impications for Us Today." PhD diss., University of Aberdeen, 1984
James, William. "An Analysis of Karl Barth's Theological Anthropology as a Basis for an Ethic of Social Justice and Human Rights." PhD diss., University of Aberdeen, 1995.
Johnson, Keith. "*Analogia Entis:* A Reconsideration of the Debate between Karl Barth and Roman Catholicism, 1914–1964." PhD diss., Princeton Theological Seminary, 2008.
Sanders, Robert J. "Political Responsibility for Economic Life in the Mature Theology of Karl Barth." PhD diss., Graduate Theological Union, 1986.

10. Other Sources

BBC. "Liberation Theology." Last Updated September 17, 2009. http://www.bbc.co.uk/religion/religions/christianity/beliefs/liberationtheology.shtml.
Brown, Chris. "Universal Human Rights: A Critique" in *Human Rights in Global Politics*, edited by Timothy Dunne and Nicholas Wheeler, 106–10. Cambridge: Cambridge University Press, 1991.
Colson, Charles, and Richard Neuhaus, eds. *Evangelicals and Catholics Together.* London: Hodder & Stoughton, 1996.
Cromartie, Michael. *A Preserving Grace*, in *A Preserving Grace: Protestants, Catholics, and Natural Law.* Grand Rapids: Eerdmans, 1997.

Select Bibliography

Daniel Westberg, "The Reformed Tradition and Natural Law." In *A Preserving Grace: Protestants, Catholics, and Natural Law*, edited by Michael Cromartie, 114–18. Grand Rapids: Eerdmans, 1997.

Dieter, Theodor, and Reinhard Hütter, eds. *Ecumenical Ventures in Ethics*. Cambridge: Eerdmans, 1998.

Farley, Melissa, et al. "Comparing Sex Buyers with Men who Don't Buy Sex." Paper presented at Psychologists for Social Responsibility Annual Meeting, July 15, 2011, Boston, MA. http://www.demandabolition.org/wp-content/uploads/2011/07/ComparingSexBuyersReport.pdf. Accessed July 17, 2014.

Friedman, John. *Empowerment: The Politics of Alternative Development*. Cambridge, MA: Blackwell, 1992.

MacIntyre, Alistar. *After Virtue: A Study of Moral Theology*. London: Duckworth, 1981.

———. *Whose Justice? Which Rationality?* Notre Dame: University of Notre Dame Press, 1988.

McCormack, Bruce, and Thomas Joseph White. *Thomas Aquinas and Karl Barth: An Unofficial Catholic-Protestant Dialogue*. Grand Rapids: Eerdmans, 2013.

Myers, Bryant. *Walking with the Poor*. Maryknoll, NY: Orbis, 1999.

Smith, Stephanie Mar. "Justification of Human Rights and the Implications for HIV Prevention." *Theology Today* 66, no. 1 (2009) 45–59

Tutu, Desmond. *No Future Without Forgiveness*. New York: Doubleday, 2000.

www.ingramcontent.com/pod-product-compliance
Lightning Source LLC
Chambersburg PA
CBHW051639230426
43669CB00013B/2372